A Guide to Software Configuration Management

For a listing of recent titles in the *Artech House Computing Library,* turn to the back of this book.

A Guide to Software Configuration Management

Alexis Leon

Artech House
Boston • London

Library of Congress Cataloging-in-Publication Data
Leon, Alexis.
    A guide to software configuration management / Alexis Leon.
    p.   cm. — (Artech House computing library)
    Includes bibliographical references and index.
    ISBN 1-58053-072-9 (alk. paper)
    1. Software configuration management.   I. Title.   II. Series.
QA76.76.C69 L46   2000
005.1—dc21   00-021719
                                                 CIP

British Library Cataloguing in Publication Data
Leon, Alexis
    A guide to software configuration management. — (Artech
    House computing library)
    1. Software configuration management   2. Computer software —
    Development
    I. Title
    005.1

    ISBN   1-58053-072-9

Cover design by Igor Valdman

© 2000 ARTECH HOUSE, INC.
685 Canton Street
Norwood, MA 02062

International Standard Book Number: 1-58053-072-9
Library of Congress Catalog Card Number: 00-021719

10 9 8 7 6 5 4 3 2 1

To my father, Leon Alexander, and my mother, Santhamma Leon,
for their love, encouragement, and support

Contents

Preface

Software configuration management (SCM) is the discipline whose objective is to identify the configuration of software at discrete points in time and the systematic control of changes to the identified configuration for the purpose of maintaining software integrity, traceability, and accountability throughout the software life cycle.

To accomplish this objective, four SCM functions are used: identification, control, status accounting, and audits. These functions should be performed by people who have been trained in their use and have the necessary expertise. Practicing configuration management in a software project has many benefits, including increased development productivity, better control over the project, better project management, reduction in errors and bugs, faster problem identification and bug fixes, and improved customer goodwill. But a single SCM solution is not suited for all projects; in fact, each project is different and although the core SCM objectives and functions remain the same, the SCM system has to be tailored for each project.

In order to maintain software integrity, traceability, and accountability in today's highly complex and sophisticated software development environments, a good SCM system is a must. The software development environment is changing. Now a single product can be developed by more than one company. Even within the same company, different subsystems of the same product/system can be developed by teams that are geographically wide apart, possibly even on different continents. So managing these projects without any scientific tools will invite trouble that could result in costly product recalls or project failures. Software configuration management is the ideal solution for managing the chaos and confusion in today's complex software development projects, because its primary objective is to bring control to the development process.

This book is about the practice of the SCM discipline. The book starts with the basics—the definition of SCM, its objectives, and functions—and explains SCM as it should be practiced in the software development process. The different phases in the software development life cycle are explained and how the SCM plays a role in each phase is discussed in detail. The different phases of the SCM implementation life cycle are also discussed.

Another important aspect of this book is that it does not rely on any specific tool for explaining the SCM concepts and techniques. In fact, one of the main objectives of this book is to give the reader detailed information about SCM, the mechanics of SCM, and SCM implementation. The book gives information on how to select the right SCM tool for an organization/project and how to implement the tool so that the organization can reap the full benefits of SCM.

How to use this book

The chapters in this book are organized in such a way that the concepts of software configuration management are developed from the ground up. Ideally it should be read from start to finish. But such a reading plan will not suit many busy readers, and therefore I have tried to write individual chapters in such a way that they can be read on their own. If you come across a term that is not described in the chapter, the glossary can be used to look it up and then you can continue reading. Readers who are not familiar with software configuration management or who are novices in this profession should read the book from the beginning to get the most use out of it.

Appendixes A, C, and D contain many World Wide Web references. It is quite possible that some of these URLs will change; that is the nature of the web. So I have created a companion web site for the book at *http://www.lnl.net/books/scm*, where all the links mentioned in the book are kept and regularly updated. I will also be adding links to the new SCM-related sites.

Who should read this book?

This book is written for software project managers who must plan for SCM for their project, for SCM practitioners who will implement SCM, and for software developers and acquirers who will be affected by it. The style and approach of the book is intended to be practical rather than theoretical. It is written in an easy-to-understand and jargon-free style, so that it will become an invaluable tool for understanding the discipline of software configuration management and a useful guide for planning and implementing SCM in a software development project.

Acknowledgments

I am deeply grateful to all of the people who helped me take this book from an idea to a printed reality.

I would like to express my gratitude to my reviewer Susan Dart for her comprehensive and thorough review of the manuscript. Her comments and suggestions have played a vital role in improving the organization, content, technical accuracy, and readability of the book.

I am grateful to my brother Mathews Leon for his suggestions, reviews, and comments and for helping me with the illustrations for the book.

Thanks are also due my father Leon Alexander and my mother Santhamma Leon for their love and support.

I would like to acknowledge the efforts of Viki Williams, Susanna Taggart, Michael Webb, and Ruth Young of Artech House for making the writing of this book a painless and pleasurable process. Thanks also to the competent editorial staff, designers, and production team at Artech House for their valuable contribution in making this project a success.

A lot of people have made valuable contributions to the discipline of software configuration management. These people, through their research, writing, preaching, and practice, have made the software community realize the importance and benefits of software configuration management. I salute those magnificent men and women for their efforts.

Finally, I would like to thank all of the readers of this book and wish them all the very best in their configuration management efforts.

Alexis Leon

CHAPTER

1

Contents

Overview of software configuration management

Introduction

In today's world in which software projects are becoming more and more complex—in size, sophistication, and technologies used—the need for configuration management is more pronounced than ever. Now most software products cater to millions of users, they support different national languages, and come in different sizes and shapes—desktop, standard, professional, enterprise, and so on. For example, operating systems, word processors, and even enterprise resource planning (ERP) packages support multiple languages (and in the case of ERP systems, multiple currencies!). Almost all application software products (such as word processors, ERP packages, and even SCM tools) support more than one hardware and/or software platform. For example, we

1

have ERP systems that run on mainframes and client/server systems; different versions of web browsers for the PC and Mac; database management systems that run on MVS, UNIX, Windows NT, Linux, and so on. The competition and the advancements in technology are driving the software vendors to include additional functionality and new features in their products—just to stay in business.

In addition, users of software systems have matured and the bugs and defects in a system are detected and publicized faster than ever—thanks to the Internet. In today's software development environment, where the communication facilities are advanced, the news that a software product is bad and has a bug can spread very fast. This is evident from the newsgroup postings and the news alerts that one gets so often nowadays. So if the company has to save face and prevent its market share from dropping, it has to provide the fixes and patches very quickly. The time that a company gets to do damage control—that is, find the cause of the bug, identify the problem area and fix the bug, ensure that the bug-fixing has not created additional bugs, do regression testing, and get the bug-fixed version of the software to the customer—is much less compared to the early days. Companies must react very quickly in order to keep their reputations intact.

Thus, today's software development environment is very complex and the reaction or response times are very short. To survive in this brutally competitive world, organizations need some sort of a mechanism to keep things under control or total chaos and confusion will result that could lead to product/project failures and put the company out of business.

Software configuration management (SCM) is a method of bringing control to the software development process. As Babich [1] has stated, "... On any team project, a certain degree of confusion is inevitable. The goal is to minimize the confusion so that more work can get done. The art of coordinating software development to minimize this particular type of confusion is called configuration management. Configuration management is the art of identifying, organizing and controlling modifications to the software being built by a programming team. The goal is to maximize productivity by minimizing mistakes."

This chapter is intended as an introduction to the discipline of software configuration management.

A brief history of SCM

Configuration management has its origins in the manufacturing industry, more specifically in the U.S. defense industry. When the products that were developed were small and the product sophistication level lower, the activities of product development and design change during the entire product life cycle could be managed by a single person or a group of close-knit people. But when the complexity of the products began to increase—as embodied by products such as fighter planes, tanks, guns, and so on—it was impossible for a single person or group to maintain control over the design and production and, more importantly, the design changes. Moreover, the development of these products spanned many years and was handled by more than one person, so when control was transferred from one person to another the associated information was lost, because no formal methods existed for documenting the design and the changes made to it.

So in 1962, the American Air Force responded to the control and communication problems in the design of its jet aircraft by authoring and publishing a standard for configuration management, AFSCM 375-1. This was the first standard on configuration management [2]. This standard was followed by many standards mainly from the U.S. military and the Department of Defense (the MIL and DoD standards).

As computers became popular, the importance of and focus on the software development industry began to increase. More and more people began to use computers and software products. Software systems made life easier by automating many tasks that had been done manually until then. As people got used to the convenience of the automated systems, they began to demand more and more features. The software development organizations were left with no choice as more and more players entered the market with newer and better products. Thus the computer programs became more and more complex in size (they are bigger than the earlier systems), sophistication (they are more complex and are used for mission-critical applications), and technologies used (today's applications use the latest technologies such as workflow automation, groupware, Internet, e-commerce, and so on). Also the size and the nature of the development teams have changed. Now development teams consist of thousands of people, from different cultural and social backgrounds, and the various subsystems of a system could easily be developed by different companies from around the world.

As computer programs became more and more complex and difficult to manage and as computer project teams became larger and more distributed, the problems that plagued the production engineers—such as inability of a single person to control and manage the development process, difficulty in managing change, communications breakdowns, and difficulty in transferring the knowledge when transferring responsibility—began to appear in the software development processes also. The U.S. Department of Defense and several international organizations, including IEEE, ANSI, and ISO, all started to address the problem of configuration management in the software development process and all came out with their own standards. Among these the most widely used standards are the ANSI/IEEE[1] standards. More about the different standards is given in Appendix B. Now SCM is accepted as a discipline and is practiced by most software organizations, if not all. The awareness about the need and importance of SCM is also increasing. Hundreds of tools and packages are available that help automate the SCM process and make the practice of SCM easier.

SCM: Concepts and definitions

Proper application of software configuration management is a key component in the development of quality software. Changes to the software under development are usually a significant cause of changes to a project's schedule and budget; unmanaged change is the largest single cause of failure to deliver systems on time and within budget.

Bersoff, Henderson, and Siegel [3] have defined SCM as the discipline of identifying the configuration of a system at discrete points in time for purposes of systematically controlling changes to this configuration and

---

1. ANSI/IEEE has the most comprehensive set of standards on software configuration management among the international standards. It is used worldwide, whereas MIL standards are used by the United States and NATO countries and other standards such as ISO 9000-3 do not cover the software configuration management discipline very comprehensively. The use of standards by other organizations like EIA, AIA, NSIA, AEA, EPRI, ECMI, FAA, INPO, ESA, and NIRMA are generally limited to its members.

maintaining the integrity and traceability of this configuration throughout the system life cycle.

The IEEE [4] defines configuration management as a discipline applying technical and administrative direction and surveillance to identify and document the functional and physical characteristics of a configuration item, control changes to those characteristics, record and report change processing and implementation status, and verify compliance with specified requirements.

What does this definition mean? First, SCM is a *discipline*—a discipline applying technical and administrative direction and surveillance. The term *discipline* refers to a system of rules, so the practice of SCM cannot be done at the whims and fancies of individuals—it has to follow a set of rules. These rules are to be specified in a document called the *SCM plan* (discussed later in this chapter). The rules should be applied in a technical and administrative framework and monitoring (surveillance) should be constant so as to ensure that the rules are followed. This means that SCM needs an organizational setup for carrying out the technical and administrative monitoring. SCM requires one group of people to carry out different SCM functions, and another group to monitor that the SCM activities are performed according to the rules. The size and organizational structure of this group—the SCM organization or SCM team—will vary with the size and complexity of the projects.

Second, the SCM function should identify the *configuration items* and document their functional and physical characteristics. IEEE [4] defines a configuration item as an aggregation of hardware, software, or both that is designated for configuration management and treated as a single entity in the configuration management process. So the SCM discipline must *identify* the components (documentation, programs, functions, component libraries, data, and so on) of a software system. Then it should *document* the components' functional characteristics, such as what they are supposed to do, performance criteria, and features as well as the physical characteristics such as size, number of lines, number of modules, functions, and libraries.

Once the configuration items are identified and their characteristics documented, the SCM system should control the changes to those characteristics. This means that once the SCM system is in place, any change to a configuration item should take place in a controlled way. Control does not mean prevention. It means that the SCM system should institute

procedures that will enable people to request a change or an enhancement to a configuration item. Well-defined methods should be in place
for evaluating these requests, studying the impact of each request
on other configuration items, and then carrying out the changes if
deemed appropriate. In other words, the SCM system should ensure
that no changes are made to the configuration items without proper
authorization.

Third, the SCM system should *record* the change management process
and *report* it to all those who are involved. This necessitates the documentation of the change management process. The status of the change
requests should be tracked and recorded from the point of origin until
completion. Processes such as change requisition, evaluation, impact
analysis, decisions as to whether to make the change or not, and so on
should be documented and reported to all people involved.

Last, there should be some mechanism to *verify* that the system that is
being developed and delivered is the one that is specified in the requirements definition and other related documents. In other words, the SCM
system should ensure that what is developed and delivered is exactly
what was required and specified. For this there should be some sort of an
auditing or verification mechanism.

So, translated into plain English, SCM requires the components of a
software system to be identified and their characteristics (both functional
and physical) documented. Once this is done, then any changes to these
items should only be made through proper channels. This means that
somebody without proper authorization cannot make changes to an
item. The entire process of change management should be documented
and reported to all those who are involved. A mechanism should exist for
checking and verifying that the system is being developed in accordance
with the specifications.

According to Ben-Menachem [5], SCM is a process used for more efficiently developing and maintaining software, which is accomplished by
improving accountability, reproducibility, traceability, and coordination.
All the processes of SCM—the identification of configuration items,
documentation of characteristics, controlling change, and so on—work
toward the purpose of ensuring integrity, accountability, visibility,
reproducibility, project coordination, traceability, and formal control of
system/project evolution.

The SCM plan

According to Davis [6], effective SCM is not just having a tool that records who made what change to the code or documentation and when. It is also the thoughtful creation of naming conventions, policies, and procedures to ensure that all relevant parties are involved in changes to the software. SCM is not just a set of standard practices that applies uniformly to all projects. SCM must be tailored to each project's characteristics—size of the project, volatility, development process, extent of customer involvement, and so on. The best place to record how SCM should be performed for each project is in the SCM plan.

The SCM plan documents what SCM activities are to be done, how they are to be done, who is responsible for doing specific activities, when they are to happen, and what resources are required. SCM planning information is divided into six classes:

1. Introduction;

2. SCM management;

3. SCM activities;

4. SCM schedules;

5. SCM resources; and

6. SCM plan maintenance.

The introduction provides a simplified overview of the SCM activities so that those approving, those performing, and those interacting with SCM can obtain a clear understanding of the plan. The introduction must include four topics—purpose of the plan, scope, definition of key terms, and references.

SCM management describes the allocation of responsibilities and authorities for SCM activities to organizations and individuals within the project structure.

SCM activities identify all functions and tasks required for managing the configuration of the software system as specified in the scope of the SCM plan. Both technical and managerial SCM activities must be identified.

SCM schedules establish the sequence and coordination for the identified SCM activities and for all events affecting implementation of the SCM plan.

SCM resources identify the software tools, techniques, equipment, personnel, and training necessary for the implementation of the specified SCM activities.

The SCM plan can undergo change. For example, one might find that the meetings of the CCB should be weekly instead of monthly due to the large number of change requests. This is something that was not foreseen during the development of the SCM plan. So the plan has to be changed to reflect the change in procedure—that the CCB meetings will be weekly instead of monthly. The SCM plan has a section—SCM plan maintenance—that identifies the activities and responsibilities necessary to ensure continued SCM planning during the life cycle of the project.

SCM functions

IEEE [7] divides the SCM functions into the following four activities: (1) configuration identification, (2) configuration control, (3) status accounting, and (4) audits and reviews.

Configuration identification is an element of configuration management, consisting of selecting the configuration items for a system and recording their functional and physical characteristics in technical documentation.

Configuration control is the element of configuration management consisting of the evaluation, coordination, approval or disapproval, and implementation of changes to configuration items.

Status accounting consists of the recording and reporting of information needed to manage a configuration efficiently. This information includes a listing of the approved configuration identification, the status of proposed changes to the configuration, and the implementation status of approved changes.

Auditing is carried out to ensure that the SCM system is functioning correctly and to ensure that the configuration has been tested to demonstrate that it meets its functional requirements and that it contains all deliverable entities. A functional configuration audit (FCA) authenticates that the software performs in accordance with the requirements and as stated in the documentation. A physical configuration audit (PCA) authenticates that the components to be delivered actually exist and that they contain all of the required items, such as the proper versions of source and object code, documentation, installation instructions, and so on.

The auditing can be done by anybody, such as the team leader, members of the SCM team, or anybody who has been designated for that purpose. The frequency and timing also can vary. It all depends on how the SCM system is defined. Usually major baselines/releases will be audited. Items supplied by subcontractors will be audited. These details—who, what, when, and why—of auditing should be decided during the SCM system design and should be documented in the SCM plan.

We will look at these four SCM functions in more detail in later chapters.

Importance of SCM

Poor configuration management or lack of it often causes the most frustrating software problems. Some examples of these problems are missing source code, changed component libraries, inability to determine what happened to a particular program or data, inability to track why, when, and who made a change, and difficulty in finding out why programs that were working suddenly stop working. The problems are frustrating because they are very difficult to fix, and they often occur at the worst possible times [8]. For example, a difficult bug that was fixed suddenly reappears, a program that was working mysteriously stops working, a developed and tested feature is missing, the updated version of the requirements document is not found, the source code and the executable program are different versions, and so on.

Software configuration management helps reduce these problems by coordinating the work and effort of many different people working on a common project. SCM plays an important role in the software development process—analysis, design, development, testing, and maintenance—by ensuring (through configuration audits) that what was designed (as specified in the characteristics document) is what is built.

The key role of software configuration management is to control change activity so that problems (communications breakdown, shared data, simultaneous updates, multiple maintenance, and so on) can be avoided. SCM is not easy; one has to do a lot of work to keep an SCM system in good shape. But the effort is worth it. Only when problems begin to crop up do users realize the importance of SCM, but by then it is too late and getting a project back on track can be a very tedious task without SCM.

But for an SCM system to work, the people who are involved must be convinced of the importance and benefits of SCM. If SCM is done for the sake of doing it, then SCM will fail to deliver on its promises. If SCM is done just to get some certification and not in its true spirit, then it will definitely fail. If SCM is treated as a management tool or a contractual obligation, it can easily become a bureaucratic roadblock that impedes the work [8].

Conclusion

SCM systems if designed properly, implemented judiciously, and used efficiently will raise the productivity and profits of companies dramatically. For this to happen, the people should be educated on the potential benefits of SCM, what it is capable of, and how it can help improve developmental productivity.

Many myths surround SCM. Many people consider it to be a bureaucratic process and additional work. These concerns were true to some extent in the case of manual SCM systems, but today's SCM tools automate most of the SCM functions and make the practice of SCM easier and painless.

References

[1]   Babich, W. A., *Software Configuration Management: Coordination for Team Productivity*, Boston, MA: Addison-Wesley, 1986.

[2]   Berlack, H. R., *Software Configuration Management*, New York: John Wiley & Sons, 1992.

[3]   Bersoff, E. H., V. D. Henderson, and S. G. Siegel, *Software Configuration Management, An Investment in Product Integrity*, Englewood Cliffs, NJ: Prentice-Hall, 1980.

[4]   *IEEE Standard Glossary of Software Engineering Terminology* (IEEE Std-610-1990),
        IEEE Standards Collection (Software Engineering), Piscataway, NJ: IEEE, 1997.

[5]   Ben-Menachem, M., *Software Configuration Guidebook*, London: McGraw-Hill
        International, 1994.

[6]   Davis, A. M., *201 Principles of Software Development*, New York: McGraw-Hill,
        1995.

[7]   *IEEE Standard for Software Configuration Management Plans* (IEEE Std-828-1990),
        IEEE Standards Collection (Software Engineering), Piscataway, NJ: IEEE, 1997.

[8]   Humphrey, W. S., *Managing the Software Process*, New York: Addison-Wesley,
        1989.

Contents

The software development process

Introduction

The software development process is that set of actions required for efficiently transforming the user's need into an effective software solution. *Efficiency* means doing things in the right way and *effectiveness* is doing the right things. So for the software development process to succeed, one not only has to do the right things, but also do them in the right way.

Humphrey [1] defines the software development process as the set of tools, methods, and practices that we use to produce a software product. The software development process defines the activities required for building the software systems and incorporating the methods and practices to be adopted. It also includes the activities essential for planning the project, tracking its progress, and managing the complexities of building the software. Scientific software development—also known as software engineering—uses scientific and management

13

techniques and productivity improvement tools for developing the software.

There is no universally accepted definition for software engineering. According to Jones [2] software engineering is a methodology that uses a set of recognized criteria (functionality, reliability, timeliness, and so on) and has its foundations in computer science, mathematics, engineering, management, and so on. The practice of software engineering is a discipline, with a defined process for software development and maintenance. Software engineering aims at developing a full product that goes well beyond a small program and uses a set of tools and techniques for improving the productivity and quality of work.

So software engineering is not just programming; it is not development of a small program; it is the process of developing a software system or product. It demands management skills and communication ability. It requires analysis and design skills. It means following standards and procedures and working as a team.

Software engineering is not an art. A software engineer is constrained by user requirements, team decisions, and management instructions, and the software product is the fruit of the entire team's effort rather than the creation of an individual. Also the scope of software engineering extends far beyond the development of the software product. It involves marketing, maintenance, and after-sales support. Just because the product you have developed is the best does not mean it is going to succeed. Discipline, teamwork, marketing, money management, planning, and many other nontechnical skills play a vital role in the success of a software product or system. Thus the objective of software engineering is not limited to the development of a high-quality product, but includes the tasks of successfully marketing and maintaining the product.

Software development life cycle models

Every software product has a lifetime—it starts its life as a response to a user's need or as a new product concept and ends up being obsolete. The life span of software systems varies from product to product. During its lifetime, the software goes through various phases. IEEE [3] defines the software life cycle as the period of time that starts when a software product is conceived and ends when the product is no longer available for use.

The software life cycle typically includes a requirements phase, design phase, implementation phase, testing phase, installation and checkout phase, operation and maintenance phase, and, sometimes, a retirement phase.

Many theories and models have been advanced concerning how the software goes through these phases (and whether it goes through all the phases). A software development process model describes how and in what order these stages are put together to trace the entire life history of the product [2]. There are many life cycle models, the most prominent of which are the waterfall model [4], spiral model [5], throwaway prototype model, incremental model [6–8], operational model [9], component assembly model [10], and cleanroom software engineering [11]. We briefly introduce each of these models next.

Waterfall model

In the waterfall model [4], the software moves through each phase in its life cycle in an orderly fashion. Each successive phase happens only after the completion of the previous phase. So the design phase starts only after the completion of the analysis phase, and the coding phase starts only after the completion of the design phase, and so on. The waterfall model is shown in Figure 2.1.

The waterfall model was enthusiastically accepted by software project management teams because it offered a means of making the development process more visible. Because of the cascade from one phase to another, there is a definite beginning and end to each phase of the development cycle, and it is easier to plan and schedule the activities and allocate the resources.

The waterfall model was put into use but it soon became very clear that it was suited only for some classes of software systems. Although management found it easier for planning and reporting, the realities of software development did not accord with the activities identified in the model. The software development process, and the activities involved in it, is a complex and variable process that cannot readily be represented using such a simple model.

Spiral model

This "risk-based" or spiral model by Boehm [5] advocates developing software systems through ongoing refinement and enhancement of

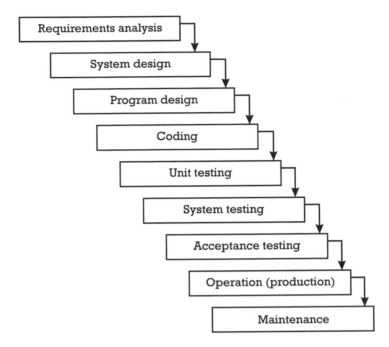

Figure 2.1   The waterfall model.

high-level system specifications into source code components. The key characteristic of the spiral model is an assessment of management risk items at regular stages in the project and initiation of actions to counteract these risks. Before each cycle, a risk analysis is initiated and at the end of the cycle, a review procedure assesses whether to move on to the next cycle of the spiral. There is no real beginning or end in the spiral model; just constant refinement based on ever-increasing knowledge. You do not "freeze" requirements because they come from imperfect knowledge. Things are not built according to some master plan, but piece by piece, organically. Modular development, gradual transformation of prototypes into the production system, phased implementation, and the awareness that the system is never really "finished" are attributes of this model.

Throwaway prototype model

The throwaway prototype model was developed to counter problems such as lack of clear understanding of the user requirements. If the user and the developers get to see a model—prototype—of what they are designing, then it will help them to better understand the product. It will give the users a better idea about the product that is being developed so that they can tell whether the system that is being developed is what they want.

A prototype is a partially developed product that enables the customers and developers to examine the various aspects of the proposed system and decide if it is suitable or appropriate for the final product. Often the higher level elements, like the user interface, are built and tested in a prototype so that the users understand what the new system will be like and the designers get a better idea about how the users interact with the system. Thus the prototype is used to refine the requirements analysis and design phases as shown in Figure 2.2, so that the final product that is being developed will better approximate the users' needs.

Incremental development model

The incremental development model [6–8] advocates developing systems by first providing essential operating functions, then providing system users with improved and more capable versions of a system at regular

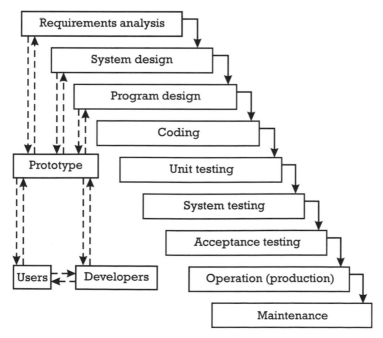

Figure 2.2   The throwaway prototype model.

intervals. This model refers to the process of developing to completion only a part of the requirements at a time. By selectively developing part of the requirements, designing, coding, and testing software that meets the required functions, the software product is built incrementally until the final product is completed.

For example, if one is developing a word processing system, the first system will just have a rudimentary text editor, then features such as the ability to change a font, make the text bold or italic, and so on are incorporated. In the next stage, more complex features such as inclusion of graphics, spell-checking, and so on, are introduced. This process continues until the system meets all of the users' needs.

Operational model

The operational model [9] concentrates on the accurate and technical specification of the software system from an algorithmic view rather than an implementation view. Unlike the conventional models where the specifications are transformed into design and code, the operational model requires the specifications themselves to be executable. With this model, the specifications require the major effort. When the specifications are deemed to be accurate and correct, they are transformed into code that is specific to a particular environment using tools (such as CASE tools).

The advantage of this model is that once the specification is captured, then developing the system for different environments is easy. The disadvantage is the difficulty of capturing the specifications accurately.

Component assembly model

In the component assembly model [10], the software system is developed using existing components that are used wherever possible. The components can be from a component library or be part of existing systems. The parts or various components are fitted together so that the final product is mainly made up of the components. The component assembly model leads to software reuse and reduction in software development time.

Cleanroom software engineering

The cleanroom software approach [11] is different from the traditional software development models. This concept depends on the following:

application of statistical quality control techniques, a structured architecture, a specification language based on a mathematical approach for specifying the functional requirements, elimination of unit or module testing, and emphasis on usage testing or functional testing.

This method uses mathematical and statistical techniques to specify correctly and precisely the functional and performance requirements. Then a structured architecture and design methodology is used to build the various functional components that are integrated without unit testing. The testing that is conducted is usage testing where the performance of the components under actual usage or operational conditions are tested.

Software development life cycle phases

We have seen a brief description of some of the popular software life cycle models. But the purpose of this chapter is not to explore these life cycle models further. Software goes through certain phases before, during, and after the development process. We will look at those phases and examine each phase in detail. The when, why, and how of these phases are taken care of by the life cycle models. The various phases or steps in the software development life cycle (SDLC) are:

▶ Project start-up;

▶ Requirements analysis;

▶ Systems analysis;

▶ Systems design (high-level and low-level design);

▶ Development/coding and unit testing;

▶ System/integration testing;

▶ Acceptance testing;

▶ Project wind-up; and

▶ Maintenance.

All of these phases will not be present in all projects. Also, all of the activities described in each phase will not be present in many projects.

Depending on the size, nature, and complexity of the project, many of the activities and even some phases might not be present. Also, in many projects the activities might be performed in an informal manner. For example, small projects will not have a very detailed requirements definition document (RDD) or systems analysis document (SAD). Also, in many projects the alpha and/or beta testing phases could be absent.

The phases described next are for a fairly large project; but depending on the nature of the project and organizational policies some of these phases might get clustered together, omitted, or practiced under a different name. Keeping this in mind, let's look at the different phases of software development in a little more detail.

Project start-up

The start-up phase is sort of a curtain raiser for the project. The project team is formed and the project leader identified. The project is organized—modules identified, key members enlisted, and the people who will carry out the support functions such as internal quality assurance, configuration management, and so on are identified. The senior members of the project team sit down together and prepare the project plan so as to ensure completion of the project within the cost, time, and resource constraints based on the details available.

The main tasks in this phase are as follows:

▶ Studying the project proposal and contract document (if it is a contracted work), estimation work papers, and other documents available;

▶ Obtaining clarification on matters such as scope, contractual obligations, and client participation in the project, if required;

▶ Defining the operational process for the project;

▶ Deciding on the format and standards for documenting the project plan;

▶ Documenting the project plan per the chosen structure and format; and

▶ Designing the SCM system and preparing the SCM plan.

It is during this last phase that the project team leader and other members, such as representatives from the QA team, SCM manager, and so on, sit together and design the SCM system and SCM procedures to be used in the project. The SCM manager is the person responsible for performing the SCM functions in the project. Sometimes the project leader will serve as the SCM manager or in other cases a person will be designated for that post. If the company has a standard SCM plan, then that plan is tailored for the project. The proposed SCM system is documented in the SCM plan.

This phase also sets up the hardware and software environment for the next phase covering the hardware, system software, standards, and guidelines. The main tasks performed in this phase are as follows:

▶ Ensure that the environment defined in the project plan is still valid for the next phase and, if not, change it.

▶ For each resource that is defined as a part of the environment, check its availability. It is during this time that requests are raised to the respective support groups for supplying or arranging the required resources.

▶ Ensure that the required hardware and software are in place.

▶ Test the environment, if required.

▶ Obtain the working space, machines, and other infrastructure requirements for the team members.

▶ Add new procedures or modify current procedures to be followed by the team.

Most organizations will have their own software development standards and guidelines, and if the work is done for a particular client, the project will have to follow the standards of that company. In cases where project standards are not available, they must be developed and finalized during this phase. The standards for various phases include the following:

▶ Documentation standard for requirements definition document (RDD);

▶ Documentation standard for systems analysis document (SAD);

> Guidelines for various analysis techniques such as data modeling and process modeling;

> Documentation standard for HLD document;

> Database and file design standards;

> Documentation standard for test plans and test specifications;

> Documentation standard for user documents;

> Documentation standard for LLD document;

> Documentation standard for unit test plans and specifications;

> Programming standards;

> Documentation standard for defect logs;

> System test plan standards;

> Test data preparation standards; and

> Testing standards.

The output of this phase is the project plan, SCM plan, and the standards for the next phases. This phase is usually done by a high-level team comprised of the project leader, management representatives, SCM manager, support team representatives, and so on.

Requirements analysis

During this phase, user requirements are captured and documented and a detailed plan for the phase is prepared. The high-level activities for this phase are expanded so that each activity spans not more than one or two person-weeks. The dependencies between the various activities of this module are identified and the activities are scheduled. Plans for housekeeping activities like backup/recovery and security are formulated. The resources required are estimated and the team members are allocated tasks.

One of the main tasks of this phase is understanding the current system (manual or computerized). This is not applicable for a new product development project where the task is understanding the functions the software is supposed to perform. The task should be undertaken with a view to examining its adequacy and identifying problem areas. The main tasks that are performed in this phase are understanding the current system by discussing it with the users and studying the documentationavailable. The main areas that are studied are organization objectives, activities, procedures, rules and standards, files and interfaces, and so on.

Every existing system, whether manual or computerized, will have some problems or inadequacies. That is why it is being redesigned. Even if the system is functioning smoothly, there might be areas that could be improved. These existing problems, possibilities, and constraints are identified. The existing system, problems, and constraints are documented for future reference and the findings are discussed with the client or user.

The next step in this phase is the definition of the user requirements. The main activities performed in this phase are diagnosing existing problems, and defining the user requirements. To do this, the context of the problems has to be understood, the scope of the problems has to be assessed, and the user requirements, application requirements, and information requirements have to be determined.

Once the user requirements have been defined, the next step in this phase is to prepare the RDD. Once the initial draft of the RDD is created, it is given to all the parties of the software project—users, clients, project team, and the support functions. After incorporating suggestions from all quarters, the final RDD is prepared.

The output of this phase is the documentation of the existing system and the RDD. The requirements analysis and the preparation of the RDD are usually done by systems analysts in collaboration with users. The RDD is usually put under configuration control. So once the final RDD is prepared, it is reviewed, approved, and a baseline is established. Normally, the first baseline consists of an approved RDD, and is known as the *functional baseline*. By establishing a baseline, the functional and other requirements described in the RDD become the explicit point of departure for software development, against which changes can be proposed, evaluated, implemented, and controlled. The functional baseline usually is the first established baseline in the SCM process.

Systems analysis

In the systems analysis phase, the proposed system is defined after analyzing various alternatives. These are the main tasks performed in this phase:

▶ Study the approved RDD.

▶ Generate alternatives (solutions or designs) for the proposed system. To do this, one must access prior knowledge, customize candidate solutions, partition the system, and prototype the system if necessary.

▶ Evaluate alternatives. Perform impact or cost/benefit analyses for tangible costs (one-time and recurring costs, such as cost of the tools used in the project) and for intangible costs (procedural and personnel-related costs such as costs of training employees on tools to be used in the project).

▶ Select an alternative.

▶ Determine system requirements with respect to reliability, performance, security, backup/restore, error recovery, and other quality factors.

▶ Discuss the proposed system with the client.

In some cases the project management may decide to develop a prototype of the system to demonstrate the understanding of the user requirements and the functionality that will be provided in the proposed system. Prototyping is required if a lack of clear understanding of the user requirements is considered a major risk in the project. The major activities in prototyping are as follows:

▶ Determine the objectives of the prototype. A prototype can be built to demonstrate an understanding of the existing system, functionality of the proposed system, data to be maintained, functions to be provided, data entry screens to be provided, inquiries and reports to be provided, and external interfaces to be provided.

▶ Decide on the type of prototype, that is, whether it should be evolutionary or throwaway.

▶ Decide on the software and hardware platforms and the tools to be used for developing the prototype. Then set up the environment.

▶ Build a prototype to meet the chosen objectives.

▶ Demonstrate the prototype to the client/users and obtain feedback.

▶ Incorporate suggestions for improvement.

Once the prototype is developed and the feedback is obtained, the next step is to prepare the systems analysis document, where the proposed system's functionality is documented. While preparing the SAD, a usability plan is also prepared. The usability plan is prepared when the system that is being built uses commercial off-the-shelf (COTS) packages for performing some tasks in the system. The usability plan will compare the available packages and help to identify the one that is best suited for the system in terms of cost effectiveness, amount of customization, method of integration of the selected package into the software system, and so on. This plan is needed only if the system uses off-the-shelf packages.

During this phase the project plan, SCM plan, and the RDD are refined and updated based on the project progress and changes in the scope of the project. The output of the systems analysis phase is the prototype (if developed), the SAD, the usability plan, the updated project plan, and the RDD.

In addition, the SCM system is implemented in the project and the items that are to be brought under SCM control such as the project plan, SCM plan, standards used in the project, the RDD, SAD, and so on are identified and baselines are established. A baseline is a specification or product that has been formally reviewed and agreed on and thereafter serves as the basis for further development. So the listed documents are reviewed and then given a baseline. Once the baselines for the items has been established, changes to those items can only be carried out using the change management procedures. More about baselines is given in Chapter 5.

High-level design

In this phase the system design objectives are defined. The following steps are carried out in order to properly design the system:

▶ Study the SAD and ensure that requirements are understood so that the high-level design documents can be properly written.

▶ Understand the features and capabilities of the hardware and software environments in which the proposed system is to be implemented.

▶ Study standards and guidelines prepared for the HLD phase.

  ▶ Establish design objectives, constraints, and guidelines with respect
    to usability, user interface, performance (response time, memory,
    throughput), reliability, design directives, storage, and so on.

Sometimes a prototype is developed to demonstrate the user interface
design, screens, navigation, and other features of the system. Developing
a prototype in the HLD phase is required if the developers want to demonstrate to the user the design features of the system such as system architecture, user interfaces, and system functionality. Sometimes a prototype
is developed during the systems analysis phase to demonstrate an understanding of the user requirements and the functionality that will be
provided in the proposed system. If such a prototype exists, then this
prototype is refined during the HLD phase to demonstrate the user interface design, screens, navigation, and other features of the system.

It is in this phase that the system components such as modules, programs, functions, and routines are identified. The system components are
identified hierarchically to the level required. The inputs and outputs of
the system are defined. These include menus, screens, navigation, levels
of help and help screens, reports, error messages, the user interface, and
so on. The programs for each component are identified and classified. The
programs can be classified as on-line/batch, reports, transactions, drivers,
functions, libraries, and so on. The performance requirements for each
component are established and the components that can be reused are
identified. The following items are produced as a part of this exercise:

  ▶ System components list;

  ▶ User interface design;

  ▶ Programs and the interface definition between programs;

  ▶ Screens and report definitions;

  ▶ Screen navigation details; and

  ▶ Help screens and messages.

The next step in this phase is to define the system architecture. The
system architecture is established in terms of security, data access, communication, restart/recovery, audit, and user interface. The system architecture deals with issues such as whether the proposed system will be a
client/server system, mainframe system, or geographically distributed

system; what technology should be used; how the communications network should be set up; and so on. The program dependencies and interfaces are identified and the system architecture for each class of programs is finalized and documented.

Another task in this phase is the creation of a first-cut database and finalization of the database/file design. The database/file design is derived from data model or data store identified during analysis. This should include content, access, and organization of the database/files. The contents of each of the tables/files in the database and the access path are defined. The necessary normalization of the database tables is performed to ensure processing efficiency. This step produces the database design document.

The final task in this phase is preparation of the HLD document. The HLD document is prepared as per documentation standards for HLD. The documents that have been prepared thus far, such as the design objectives document, the system architecture document, the database design document, and so on, are used as the input for the HLD document. The system test plan is a part of the HLD document. So while the HLD is compiled the system test plan (STP) and system test specification (STS) are also prepared, and they then form part of the HLD document. The preparation of the initial draft of user documents such as user manual, capabilities manual, and tutorials are started during this phase.

So this phase produces the following documents: high-level design (HLD) document, system test plan (STP) and system test specification (STS), and the initial draft of the user documents. All of the documents produced in this phase are reviewed and baselines are established. If changes are required for any of the items, which were baselined in the earlier phases, then the change procedures are initiated and the changes are effected.

Low-level design

In this phase the copy libraries, common routines, and program skeletons to be used are finalized. The HLD is analyzed to understand the system architecture, components, programs, and their interfaces. The standards prepared for the LLD phase are studied. The component libraries to be used for each of the programs in the system are identified, as are the common routines and the input and output for these common routines. If program skeletons or templates are to be used for various types of programs, then the scope and contents of such skeletons and templates are decided. The specifications for the component libraries, common routines, and skeletons are written.

The major task in this phase is to write the specification for each program in the system. Writing program specifications is essential for projects involving developments in procedural languages. For each program and reusable routine identified in the system, the program logic is determined; the structure chart is prepared (if necessary); the inputs, outputs, error messages, and help messages are finalized; and the program specification is prepared. As part of the program specification, the unit test specification (UTS) and unit test plan (UTP) are prepared.

The last step of this phase is the preparation of the LLD document consisting of program specifications for all programs, component libraries, skeletons, and templates of the system. All documents, specifications, program templates, and so on produced during this phase are usually subject to configuration control.

At the end of this phase the project plan is updated, the RDD, SAD, HLD, STP, STS, and the user documents are refined based on the changes and additional information obtained during this phase. These changes are made following the change control procedures because these items are under configuration management and hence unauthorized changes are not allowed.

The baseline that is established at the end of the design phase is usually called the *allocated baseline*. The allocated baseline contains the initial approved specifications that form the basis for the software development and testing. The allocated baseline represents the logical progression from the functional baseline and represents the link between the design process and the development process.

Coding and unit testing

During this phase the programs, copy libraries, functions, and other program elements are coded (or generated) and tested (unit testing). The main people involved in this phase are the developers/programmers, the analysts, the QA team, and the testers. Among all of the life cycle phases, this is the phase that involves the largest number of people. The SCM team is up and running and will be involved in activities like change management and control, repository management, defect tracking, change request evaluation, impact analysis, and so on. These are the major activities during this phase:

 ▶ Study LLD document, test cases, and data.

 ▶ Include additional test cases if needed.

 ▶ Code the programs per the program specifications.

 ▶ If the evolutionary prototyping approach is followed, the prototype should be refined to yield the final code.

 ▶ Finalize all error and help messages.

 ▶ Conduct unit testing in accordance with the UTS.

 ▶ Record the test results.

 ▶ Log the following unit test errors: errors external to the program (where the error cannot be fixed in the program being tested), errors in LLD and test specifications, errors caused due to the standards adopted, and errors in the reused code

 ▶ Diagnose and fix the errors.

 ▶ Update defect logs.

 ▶ Initiate corrective action, as applicable. This might involve revisiting the earlier phases of SDLC.

 ▶ Consolidate test results and findings and record appropriately.

The output of this phase is the unit-tested programs all of which—the source code, the test results, the associated documentation, the change/problem reports, and so on—will be under configuration management.

System testing

This is the phase in the software development life cycle where the system testing or integration testing is carried out. The system test is done using the STP, STS, and system test data. Many companies do alpha and/or beta testing also. Alpha testing is done when the system or product has a lot of new previously untested features. Because a lot of the functionality is untested, the development team might be uncomfortable proceeding with the final testing and release of the product until they get a feedback from a limited number of users/customers. So the developers use the alpha testing primarily to evaluate the success or failure (or acceptance) of the new features incorporated into the system.

Beta testing is required when the development team decides that some level of customer evaluation is needed prior to the final release of the product. In the case of beta testing, the developers are no longer look-ing for user inputs on functionality or features. The product has all the functionality incorporated in it, so the development team will be looking for the beta testers to uncover bugs and faults in the system. Unlike alpha testing the beta testing is done on a much larger scale; that is, the number of people who will be doing the beta testing will be much higher than that for alpha testing. Companies usually distribute the beta releases free of cost to the people who have enrolled in the beta testing program and in many cases the beta versions will be available for download from the company's web site. New products will have the alpha testing followed by the beta testing. In the case of new versions of existing products, however, either alpha or beta testing is done.

The tasks in this phase are as follows:

- ▶ Carry out system test according to the STP and STS. For alpha and beta testing, there will be no test plans. In the case of alpha testing, the testers will be evaluating the acceptability of the new features or functionality; in the case of beta testing, the testers will be trying to find bugs or problems in the product.

- ▶ Record the test results.

- ▶ Log the test errors.

- ▶ Diagnose and fix errors.

- ▶ Update defect logs.

- ▶ Initiate corrective action as applicable. This might involve revisiting earlier phases of SDLC.

- ▶ Perform regression testing.

- ▶ Consolidate and report test results and findings.

The major players involved in this stage are the QA team, the testers, the development team (for bug/problem fixing), and the actual users of the system. If alpha and/or beta testing is used, then the number of people who will be testing the system will increase dramatically. In this phase the SCM team will have their hands full because they are the ones who coordinate the change requests/problem reports and see to it that the changes are made according to the procedures and that all people concerned are aware of the changes.

Once the project is successfully tested the functional and physical configuration audits are performed to ensure that the final product is complete and satisfies the specifications. A baseline is established at this stage. This is called the *product baseline*. The product baseline represents the technical and support documentation established after successful completion of the functional configuration audit and physical configuration audit.

Acceptance testing

Acceptance testing is the formal testing that is conducted (usually by the user, client, or an authorized entity) to determine whether or not a system satisfies its acceptance criteria and to enable the customer to determine whether or not to accept the system. This phase is carried out only if the system is developed for a particular client/customer. In this phase the project team prepares for the acceptance test by ensuring the availability and completeness of all work items needed for the acceptance test and populating the acceptance test data. The project team will assist the client/customer in acceptance testing, recording the errors found and fixing them. These are the main tasks in this phase:

- ▶ Provide support to the client in conducting acceptance test. Ensure that documentation-related tests are also completed.
- ▶ Record acceptance test results.
- ▶ Log acceptance test errors.
- ▶ Diagnose and fix errors.
- ▶ Update the defect logs.
- ▶ Revisit earlier phases of SDLC, as required, in order to fix errors.
- ▶ Perform regression testing.
- ▶ Prepare a report summarizing the test results. Highlight any disagreements.

Project wind-up

In this phase the project wind-up activities are completed. All the resources acquired for the project are released. Here are the main activities:

▸ Carry out project-end appraisals.

▸ Release project team members and hardware and software resources.

▸ Return client-supplied products, if any.

▸ Ensure availability of project documentation copies in library.

Project maintenance

Once the system has been developed and tested, it is released to the users. From this point onward, the maintenance phase starts. Once people start using the system, many errors that escaped the testing will be found. The users might ask for new features and enhancements. It is the responsibility of the maintenance team to attend to these requests and to fix the bugs that are found.

If the project has not followed any standards and has not been documented, then the job of maintaining the system can turn into one of most difficult assignments that software professionals can have. A very good example of this is seen in the Y2K projects, for which people have to fix the problems in programs that are more than 20 to 30 years old, programs that have no documentation and that were developed without any programming standards or naming conventions.

It is during the project maintenance stage that the full impact and usefulness of the software configuration management process can be felt. If the project was developed following a good SCM system, then all the documentation, defect and defect prevention details, help desks, and so on will be available. All the programs, technical documents, user documents, and so on will be readily available. There will not be any chaos and confusion. Everybody will know exactly where to look for any item—programs, libraries, documents, change histories, and so on. Also, since the re-creation of any particular component or version could be done with very high accuracy, the change management and problem solving processes become much easier than without an SCM system. The job of the maintenance team and the technical support team could be made a lot easier if the project had a good SCM system.

Conclusion

We have seen the various phases involved in the software development process. All of these phases may not be present in all the projects and as already mentioned the order in which the various steps are executed will vary.

Most of the times, some degree of overlap will occur between the various phases. The software life cycle model that is adopted will determine these things. We have seen the various outputs of each phase and the role of SCM in the project life cycle. We also saw how and when the different SCM activities are performed in a project. These aspects are summarized in the Figure 2.3.

References

[1]   Humphrey, W. S., *Managing the Software Process*, New York: Addison-Wesley, 1989.

[2]   Jones, G. W., *Software Engineering*, New York: John Wiley & Sons, 1990.

[3]   *IEEE Standard Glossary of Software Engineering Terminology* (IEEE Std-610-1990), *IEEE Standards Collection (Software Engineering)*, Piscataway, NJ: IEEE, 1997.

[4]   Royce, W., "Managing the Development of Large Software Systems: Concepts and Techniques", *Proc. IEEE WESCON*, 1970.

[5]   Boehm, B. W., "A Spiral Model for Software Development and Enhancement," *IEEE Computer*, Vol. 21, No. 5, 1988, pp. 61–72.

[6]   McDermid, J. A., and P. Rook, "Software Development Process Models," in *Software Engineer's Reference Book*, J. A. McDermid, Ed., Boca Raton, FL: CRC Press, 1994, pp. 15.26–15.28.

[7]   Brooks, F. P., "No Silver Bullet: Essence and Accidents of Software Engineering," *IEEE Computer*, Vol. 20, No. 4, 1987, pp. 10–19.

[8]   Mill, H. D., "Top-Down Programming in Large Systems," in *Debugging Techniques in Large Systems*, R. Rustin, Ed., Englewood Cliffs, NJ: Prentice-Hall, 1971.

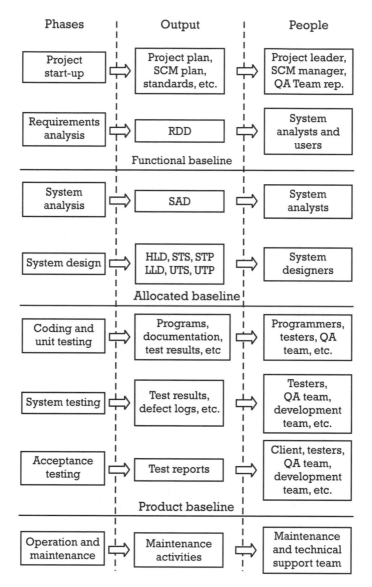

Figure 2.3 Life cycle phases and their relationship with SCM.

[9]   Zave, P., "The Operational Versus Conventional Approach to Software
      Development," *Commun. ACM*, Vol. 27, No. 2, 1992, pp. 104–118.

[10] Nierstrasz, "Component-Oriented Software Development," *Commun. ACM*,
      Vol. 35, No. 9, 1992, pp. 160–165.

[11] Dyer, M., *The Cleanroom Approach to Quality Software Development*, New York:
      John Wiley & Sons, 1992.

Contents

Pitfalls in
the software
development process

Introduction

The software development process is very different from other production or manufacturing processes. According to Jones [1], software products are intangible, because there is no need for physical mechanisms, structures, or processes. The software engineers do not use most of the concepts familiar to traditional engineering and their work is mostly independent of natural science. Also software products are much more complex and sophisticated, thus requiring special care in conceptualizing, managing, organizing, and testing. Software products are manufactured by a simple copying process, so almost all of the production effort is dedicated to design and development.

Because the software development process is different from regular industrial practice, normal rules of production or manufacturing do not apply here. For example, Brook's law [2] states that "Adding manpower to a late software project makes it later." It might sound strange, but it is true. If you calculate the time required to train the new people, the added communication channels because of the new people, and other related complexities, the project in question (the already late project) could be finished earlier if more people were not inducted. This is not true in a construction project where additional manpower can speed up the project.

So now that we have established that the software development process is different from the other manufacturing or production processes, we need to look at some of the problems that plague many a software project and can result in time and cost overruns if corrective actions are not taken. The most frequent among these are the communications breakdown problem, shared data problem, multiple maintenance problem, and simultaneous update problem. In this chapter we look at each of these problems in greater detail, because an understanding of these is crucial for realizing the importance of the configuration management function.

Communications breakdown problem

The era when a single person developed a software product is long gone. Today's software projects consist of teams with hundreds of members in different modules. The modules or subsystems of a project might be located in different continents and might very well include developers with different social, cultural, and educational backgrounds.

In a single-person project, communications breakdowns never occur. According to Rawlings [3], "When only one person is working on a project, that one person has a rather singular communication path with no need for interpretative cognition. The person has only him or herself to communicate with and, hopefully understands his or her own thought processes. When two people are working on the same project, there are now two communicators and two listeners with four potential communication paths. Not only is there a dramatic increase in the number of communication paths, there is also the problem of interpretative cognition, which now comes into play."

As more and more people are added to the project team, the total number of communication paths increases dramatically as shown in

Figure 3.1. And as the number of communication paths increases, the potential for communication errors also increases.

Interpretative cognition is a part of the process that occurs when two or more people communicate with one another. It is a measure of how much of a person's communication is understood by the other person or persons. You must have encountered situations in daily life when you

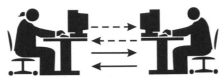

2 communicators and 2 listeners (4 communication paths)

3 communicators and 3 listeners (12 communication paths)

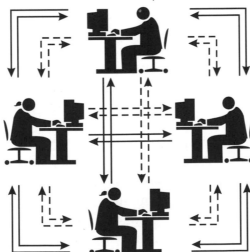

4 communicators and 4 listeners (24 communication paths)

Figure 3.1 Increase in number of communication paths with increasing team size.

said something and the listener understood something else, resulting in misunderstanding and confusion. In such cases we say that the interpretative cognition did not work. When a person wants to communicate some idea, he or she must describe it using words, pictures, drawings, gestures, and so on. The person who is listening to this communication should see and hear the communication directed at him or her and should reconstruct the idea in his or her mind. If the two ideas are the same then we say that the communication has been successful.

The complexity of this process increases as the idea that is communicated becomes more complex or if the people who are involved are not familiar with one another's mannerisms and communication methods. Failing to understand a gesture or body language can convey the wrong meaning to the listener.

So in the case of large software projects, where complex and sophisticated systems are being developed, the ideas that are to be communicated are complex. Also the project team as we have mentioned may be working in different parts of the world, thus the chance to communicate face to face will be rare. Because of the different cultural and ethnic backgrounds, the gestures, the phrases, and colloquial usages will not be understood by all team members. So the lack of proper communication between team members or a communications breakdown can result in the failure of the project.

How do you control the communications and keep everyone informed about the tasks and activities that affect them? How will a project leader make sure that all team members are communicating with each other and that all people are aware of what is happening? How will he or she ensure that the effort is not duplicated and the work of one person is not destroyed by another?

In the case of small projects, where the number of people involved is limited to two or three, effective communication is easier to establish. If the team members have been working together for quite some time and are familiar with each others' communication patterns and work methods, then the chances of a communications breakdown and associated problems can be minimized, but not completely eliminated. Even in projects involving two or three people, efforts can be duplicated, one can overwrite the code the other person has just fixed, and so on.

If in a small project, the problems just mentioned can happen, then think about a project having, say, five modules and 100 members. It will be total chaos if some sort of control mechanism is not in place and that control mechanism is configuration management.

Shared data problem

The shared data problem is a very common source of trouble in any environment where two or more programmers or programs share a common resource. It can be a function that is shared by two programmers. It can be a component library that is common to two programs. It can be a housekeeping program or an error-handling subroutine that is being used by all the programs in the project. The trouble arises when one developer makes a change to any of the common or shared resources, without telling others.

Consider two programmers, A and B, sharing a function (Figure 3.2). To improve functionality, programmer A makes some changes to the function. Programmer B is not aware of the change. But next time B tries to execute his program it may "abend" or it may not function correctly depending on what changes A has made. B is completely in the dark about the change made by A to the function. He is amazed by the fact that the program that was working fine up to that point is suddenly not working. He can spend hours in debugging, but if he is not very lucky he will never find the cause, as he has no reason to doubt the function, which is the real culprit. This type of situation occurs very commonly in almost all projects where more than one person is involved and in some cases in single-person projects also.

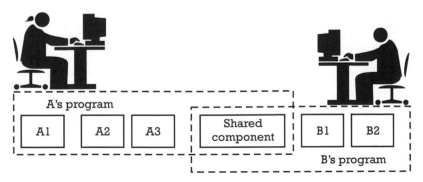

Figure 3.2 Shared data problem.

The software developers found a way to solve this problem: by creating separate and independent work spaces where each programmer has her own copy of the resources she needs (Figure 3.3). In this situation, even if one programmer modifies the code of a shared resource, others are not affected because they are using separate copies of the same resource.

But the solution given has one major drawback. It creates multiple copies of the same function or program throughout the project, which in most cases will not be identical. So a lot of space is wasted. But the real trouble is that this creates another problem—the multiple maintenance problem.

Multiple maintenance problem

This is a variation of the shared data problem. It occurs when there are multiple copies of the shared components in the system. The main problem created by having multiple copies is keeping track of them (Figure 3.4). How many copies of the function exist in the project? Which program uses which copy? How many copies are still in the original state? What changes were made? To which copies were those changes made? In the ideal situation all the copies across the system should be identical; but rarely is the situation ideal.

Suppose programmer A finds a bug and makes the necessary corrections to a function. It is her duty to inform all the people who are using a copy of the function in question that she has made the change; otherwise while she will be using the "bug-fixed" version of the function, everyone

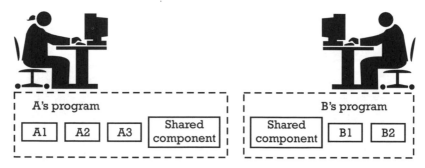

Figure 3.3   Shared data problem solved by using independent work spaces.

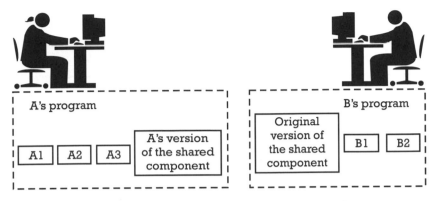

Figure 3.4 Multiple versions of the same component in use.

else will be using the one with the bug. When the time comes to integrate all of the common functions, the multiple copies will create problems for the programmers depending on which version of the function is actually used. So, if the new version—the one that is fixed—is used, then all the programs that have used the old version will be in trouble.

As with any problem, programmers found a way to solve the multiple maintenance problem too. They created centralized libraries (Figure 3.5).

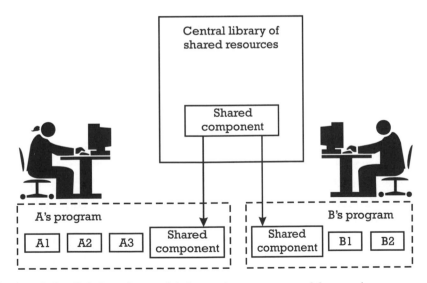

Figure 3.5 Solving the multiple maintenance problem using a central library.

The shared components were kept in a central location. The different pro-grammers took the required resources from the central library. If a bug was discovered in a function, then the copy in the library was updated, so that it was available to all. These centralized libraries could be considered the predecessors of today's repositories.

There was a problem, however, with these shared libraries. There was no control over the changes made to a shared resource (program, func-tion, specification, and so on) in the central library of shared components. Anybody could make a modification. There was also no formal mecha-nism for informing all users that a particular module or function had been changed. And there was no proper authority to decide whether a particu-lar change was necessary or not. This lack of proper control mechanism led to another problem—the simultaneous update problem.

Simultaneous update problem

Consider this situation. Programmer A has found a bug and has fixed it. She copies the bug-fixed version to the central library, thus overwriting the existing copy. According to the procedure we saw in the previous section, this is how it should be done. That is, the changes are incor-porated to the copy in the central library where all the shared resources were kept.

But what if programmer B also finds the same bug. He is not aware of the fact that A has found the bug and is fixing it or has already fixed it. He also fixes the bug and then copies the function to the library, thus overwriting the copy that was created by programmer A. So the work that was done by programmer A to fix the bug is lost.

This creates a lot of problems (Figure 3.6). One, a lot of time and resources are wasted because two people, working in isolation, corrected the same mistake. Two, different people will have different opinions about how to fix the same problem. Who will decide which one is the best and which one is to be used?

Now consider another variation (which is much more serious) of this problem. Programmer A finds a bug and fixes it. During the same time, programmer B finds a different bug and fixes it. But depending on which programmer updates the library copy last, the other programmer's work

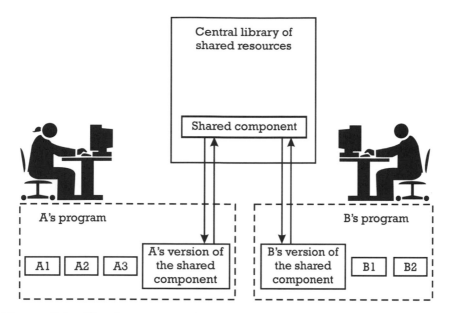

Figure 3.6 Simultaneous update problem.

is lost. But both bug fixes are necessary and need to be incorporated into the function. This means that the uncontrolled and unmanaged functioning of these central libraries where the shared resources are kept is not going to solve the problem. Or in other words, just by creating a repository of shared components and leaving it unmanaged and uncontrolled so that anybody can make changes to the items in the repository is not going to solve the problem.

Conclusion

We have seen the four major problems that create trouble in the software development process and can drive programmers and developers crazy. Is there a solution to these problems? A good change management and control system can solve these problems and can bring discipline into the development process and improve the development productivity. A lot of time that would otherwise be spent on debugging and reworking can be saved.

References

[1]   Jones, G. W., *Software Engineering*, New York: John Wiley & Sons, 1990.

[2]   Brooks, F. P., *The Mythical Man-Month*, New York: Addison Wesley Longman, 1995.

[3]   Rawlings, J. H., *SCM for Network Development Environments*, New York: McGraw-Hill, 1994.

Contents

Need and importance of software configuration management

Introduction

In Chapter 1 we saw what SCM is; in Chapter 2 we got a brief introduction to the software development process and how the various SCM activities fit into the development process. In Chapter 3 we discussed some of the most common problems that plague the software development process. In this chapter we look at why SCM is important and why it should be implemented in all software projects irrespective of the size (small, medium, large, or very large), complexity (simple or complex), and the stage (conceptual, design, development, testing, or maintenance) of the project.

Here are just some of the reasons for implementing software configuration management: (1) increased complexity of the software systems, (2) increased demand for software, and (3) the changing nature of software and need for change management. Some of the benefits of SCM are as follows:

- ❯ Improved software development productivity;
- ❯ Lower software maintenance costs;
- ❯ Better quality assurance;
- ❯ Reduction of defects/bugs;
- ❯ Faster problem identification and bug fixes;
- ❯ Process-dependent development rather than person-dependent development; and
- ❯ Assurance that the correct system was built.

Increased complexity and demand

Information technology is revolutionizing the way in which we live and work. It is changing all aspects of our lives and lifestyles. The digital revolution has given humankind the ability to treat information with mathematical precision, to transmit it at very high accuracy, and to manipulate it at will. These capabilities are bringing into being a whole world within and around the physical world.

The amount of calculational power that is available to humankind is increasing. Computers and communications are becoming integral parts of our lives. The driving force behind these advancements is the computer software. Computer software is becoming more and more complex and the amount of software that is being developed each year is increasing at an exponential rate. Also, the software is being used to control a range of activities from mission-critical applications such as controlling the operations of satellites and intercontinental ballistic missiles, managing the functioning of banks and hospitals, handling the airline and railway reservation systems, and so on, to performing mundane tasks like operating a door locking system or for desktop publishing.

Musa [1] estimates that the demand for software systems increases by 900% each decade. Boehm and Papaccio [2] predict that the expenditure on software development increases by 200% each decade, whereas the productivity of software professionals increases by only 35%. So the gap between supply and demand is very large. Software companies, nonsoftware organizations, and governmental agencies are producing hundreds of new applications and modifying thousands of existing ones every year. All of them are finding it difficult to develop high-quality software that they need on time and within budget.

Another aspect of the software that has changed is the complexity. According to Jones [3], in the early days of software development, computer programs were typically less than 1000 machine instructions in size, required only one programmer to write, seldom took more than a month to complete, and the entire development costs were often less than $5000. Today, however, some of the large systems exceed 25 million source code statements, usually require thousands of programmers, can take more than 5 years to complete, and have development costs in the range of $500 million.

In the early days of software development, all of the parts or modules of a software system were developed in the same place. But the different components of today's complex software systems are not even built by the same organization. Many software systems are built jointly by different organizations working in different parts of the world. They may communicate via Internet, e-mail, or videoconferencing technologies. So in this distributed development environment where face-to-face communication is rare, managing and coordinating the development process is a difficult task.

This increasing demand for new software, the need to modify or maintain the existing software, the increasing complexity of the software development process, and the critical nature of the applications in which software is being used dictate that software development cannot be accomplished in the same way it was during the early days. As Jones [4] has stated, "Software has become the central component in many complex activities. For this reason, the challenge of producing it requires specialized and powerful techniques. It is not possible to rely on luck, guesswork and innate talent for dependable results." We need scientific methods and techniques for developing software.

Changing nature of software and need for change management

Software systems are subject to constant changes—during design, during development, and even after development. The pioneering work in this area has been done by Lehman and Belady [5] and is detailed as a set of laws called *Lehman's laws*. According to Lehman's law of continuing change, any large software system that is being used will undergo continual change because the system's use will suggest additional functionality. It will change until it becomes more cost effective to rewrite it from scratch [6]. This means that the software will be subject to constant changes other than the bug fixes and defects that are already in the software and which will be detected during and after its development.

This is not all; the software system that is perfectly developed and that has met all requirements and passed all audits and reviews will also change. According to Lehman [7], even if a system were built in complete conformance to the requirements, the system would still evolve because the system is introduced into the real world and the environment into which the system is introduced is subject to change. So in order to adapt to the changes in the environment in which the system works it has to change. Or, in other words, no matter how perfectly you built the system, it will have to be changed to meet the changes in the environment.

So it is clear that the only constant thing about software is change. If the changes are not managed, then it will lead to chaos and confusion. So a mechanism for managing the change and controlling it is required.

Improved software development productivity

In Chapter 3 we looked at the various problems—communications breakdown problem, shared data problem, multiple maintenance problem, and simultaneous update problem—that reduce the productivity of software professionals and result in wasted effort, duplicated effort, and a host of other complications.

If software development were carried out in an environment where these problems did not occur, then productivity would naturally increase, because problems and mistakes would be reduced. For example, if the communication channels are well defined and functioning smoothly, if changes are made in a controlled fashion, if all team members are aware of how to handle change (i.e., each member of the team knows what to do when they have to change something), then a lot of time and effort can be saved. This means an improvement in development productivity.

Lower maintenance costs

When dealing with software costs, most people address only the short-term or visible costs like the costs associated with design, development, and testing. But long-term costs are associated with system operation and maintenance that often constitute a large percentage (as high as 75%) of the total life cycle cost for a given system. Blanchard [8] called this the *iceberg effect,* in which the initial costs are the visible part of the iceberg—the tip of the iceberg—and the operational and maintenance costs (which amounts to more than 75% of the total life cycle costs) are the submerged part of the iceberg.

So the maintenance costs constitute a significant amount of a software system's total life cycle costs. Software maintenance is usually classified as follows:

▸ *Corrective maintenance:* Correct the mistakes that escaped the testing phase and are found during actual usage.

▸ *Adaptive maintenance:* Change the software to perform in a new environment or with some new interfaces.

▸ *Perfective maintenance:* Modifying the software to include new functionality or additional features.

According to Lientz and Swanson [9], the perfective maintenance costs account for 65% of costs; 18% are adaptive; and 17% are corrective.

There are many reasons for the high maintenance costs irrespective of which class they fall into. The most important among these is the absence of a proper method for handling these maintenance issues. Almost all maintenance issues involve changing something, making modifications to the existing code, or adding new code to the existing system. The people who are supposed to do these activities should have a good understanding of what they have to do, how they have to do it, where they have to make the change or modifications, and what the impact of the change will be on other programs.

If the software was developed in a systematic manner, if the documentation is perfect, the changes made to the programs are recorded, and the program dependencies are defined, then the task of the maintenance team is easy. So from the design stage onward, proper mechanisms,

which ensure that the design and development are done in a systematic
and controlled fashion, need to be in place. These control mechanisms
will play a vital role in reducing the maintenance costs.

Better quality assurance

One of the main objectives of a quality assurance (QA) system is to prevent defects from occurring. In the old days where the concept of quality
control (QC) was prevalent, the idea was to find the defects once they
had occurred. If we take the manufacturing industry as an example,
the QC team was interested in finding defects before the parts were
shipped. So the QC team concentrated on the final inspection with the
objective that not even a single defective part got past the final inspection stage.

   With the advent of the QA philosophy, the focus changed from the
final inspection to the assembly line. The idea was to *prevent* the defects
from occurring rather than reject defective parts during final inspection.
QA teams thus worked to identify the causes of the defects, why they
were occurring, where they were occurring, when they were occurring,
and how they were occurring.

   This is true in the case of software development also. In the early days,
the major thrust was given to finding the errors or bugs and fixing them
before the product or system was delivered to the customer. So the focus
was on finding the errors and fixing them. Nobody really cared about the
causes of these defects and how they originated and so on. As long as they
were found and fixed, life was good.

   But the QC philosophy had a problem; it was costly. A lot of time and
effort could be saved if the defects were detected early. But more important was that in the QC approach, because nobody was looking into the
causes of the defects, they remained undetected and reappeared in
the next project. For example, suppose a defect was occurring because the
programmer was not good at the CASE tool that she was using to generate
the code. So every time she generated new code, the same mistakes were
repeated. But a causal analysis would have revealed this problem and the
programmer could be trained on the tool so that the problem will not
occur again. But to do a causal analysis, one needs to have data. So there

has to be a formal mechanism for problem reporting or defect logging and tracking.

Reduction of defects/bugs

Once you have a defect logging and tracking system in place, once the QA teams start looking into the causes of the problems and correcting them, once the checks and audits are made to ensure that the project standards and guidelines are followed, then the number of bugs and problems will be reduced. In most cases the problems occur because the documentation is not in sync with the development, the RDD and SDD are not updated to reflect the latest changes, and different people are using different versions of the same program or function. In many projects, there are no formal mechanisms to find out which code belongs where and what changes were made and why and when, and so on. If the development process has a system that takes care of these types of issues, then the software development and maintenance processes will be easier.

Faster problem identification and bug fixes

In the usual system of testing, bugs are found and fixed. But if there is a mechanism for logging the bug/problem reports, categorizing them, analyzing the causes, and recording how the problem was solved, then much time can be saved the next time a similar bug/problem occurs. A lot of time and effort can be saved by not having to reinvent the wheel each and every time a bug/problem that has occurred in the past reappears.

Also, by recording the bugs, their causes, and the corrective actions, a knowledge base will be created that will grow with time and will be an invaluable resource for future tasks. When a problem is reported, the knowledge base can be searched for similar problems and if one exists, the solution for the previous bug will help resolve the current problem faster. The knowledge base as I have mentioned earlier will grow in size and value as time goes on and as new problems and solutions are added to it. This also means that even when people who are working on a project leave, they leave behind the knowledge that they have gained for others to use.

Process-dependent development rather than person-dependent development

In early days, when software projects were simple and small, the design and details of a project were often handled by a single individual. Even though projects have become larger and more complex, the dependency on the individual still exists. For example, in many projects, if you remove a few key people, the projects will come to a standstill, basically because the other members of the team do not have the whole picture of the project. There is no way they can have the whole picture because no documentation exists and, even if it does exist, it is often understood only by the people who wrote it. In many cases these documents have not been updated and are not in sync with the system that is being developed.

This kind of dependency on people is very dangerous. What happens if a key person leaves the company or is not able to work anymore? In such cases, the entire process of design and development has to start all over again, because nobody knows what to do with the current system. It is for this reason that the software engineering pioneers have always said that the software development has to be process dependent, not people dependent.

Boehm [10] has said that talented people are the most important element in any software organization and it is crucial to get the best people available. According to him, the better and more experienced they are, the better the chance of producing first-class results. But the problem with these geniuses is that their capability to work as a team, in most cases, will not be in the same class as their talent.

Software development has become too complex and software systems so huge that it is not possible for one individual to complete a project regardless of how talented she is. To develop software systems successfully, even the best and most talented professionals need a structured and disciplined environment, which is conducive for teamwork and cooperative development. According to Humphrey [11], "Software organizations that do not establish these disciplines condemn their people to endless hours of repetitively solving technically trivial problems. There may be challenging work to do, but their time is consumed by mountains of uncontrolled detail. Unless these details are rigorously managed, the best people cannot be productive. First-class people are essential, but they need the support of an orderly process to do first-class work."

Assurance that the correct system has been built

Software development, as we have seen, starts with the requirements analysis. We have also seen that during the software development life cycle, the requirements will undergo many changes. So how do we make sure that the system that is being delivered to the customer is what the customer initially wanted and contains all the changes that were suggested during the development period? In other words, how does the client or the customer know that what he is getting is what he asked for?

There should be some sort of process for documenting the initial requirements and the changes made to them. There should also be some mechanism for checking or auditing the software system or product that is being delivered to the customer and certify that the product satisfies the requirements. In other words, there should be a facility to conduct audits (or reviews) to ensure that what is developed and delivered is complete in all respects and is exactly what was specified.

Conclusion

We have seen that software systems are becoming more and more complex and sophisticated and are being used increasingly in mission-critical applications. We have also seen the changing nature of software and software development. We also saw that unless there is a system to manage and control change, it can lead to chaos and confusion that can result in low quality, lower productivity, and even the scrapping of a project. We saw why quality assurance is important and how it can help to reduce bugs and maintenance costs. We also saw that we need a process-dependent system to be successful in the long run.

Software configuration management is an ideal solution for the issues discussed and an excellent foundation from which other process improvement methodologies can be launched. SCM provides a mechanism for managing, documenting, controlling, and auditing change. So in today's complex software development environment, SCM is a must for all projects irrespective of their nature, size, and complexity and it is better to have the SCM functions in place as early as possible. According to Davis [12], the SCM procedures should be designed and approved and recorded in a document—the SCM plan. This document should be written early in a project (as we have seen in Chapter 2, as early as the project start-up phase), typically getting approved around the same time that the software requirements specifications are approved.

References

[1]   Musa, J. D., "Software Engineering: The Future of a Profession," *IEEE Software*, Vol. 22, No. 1, 1985, pp. 55–62.

[2]   Boehm, B. W., and P. N. Papaccio, "Understanding and Controlling Software Costs," *IEEE Trans. Software Engineering*, Vol. 14, No. 10, 1988, pp. 1462–1477.

[3]   Jones, C. T., *Estimating Software Costs*, New York: McGraw-Hill, 1998.

[4]   Jones, G. W., *Software Engineering*, New York: John Wiley & Sons, 1990.

[5]   Lehman, M. M., and L. Belady, *Program Evolution: Processes of Software Change*, London: Academic Press, 1985.

[6]   Lehman, M. M., and L. Belady, "A Model of Large Program Development," *IBM Syst. J.*, Vol. 15. No. 3, 1976, pp. 225–252.

[7]   Lehman, M. M., "Software Engineering, the Software Process and Their Support," *Software Engineering J.*, Vol. 6, No. 5, 1991, pp. 243–258.

[8]   Blanchard, B. S., *System Engineering Management*, New York: John Wiley & Sons, 1991.

[9]   Lientz, B. P., and E. B. Swanson, *Software Maintenance Management*, Reading, MA: Addison-Wesley, 1980.

[10] Bohem, B. W., *Software Engineering Economics*, Englewood Cliffs, NJ: Prentice-Hall, 1981.

[11] Humphrey, W. S., *Managing the Software Process*, New York: Addison-Wesley, 1989.

[12] Davis, A. M., *201 Principles of Software Development*, New York: McGraw-Hill, 1995.

Contents

SCM: Basic concepts

Introduction

Software configuration management is the set of activities that is performed throughout the project life cycle—from requirements analysis to maintenance. SCM is important because software is subject to constant change. Software systems undergo changes when designed, when built, and even after being built. Uncontrolled and unmanaged change can create confusion and lead to communications breakdown problems, shared data problems, multiple maintenance problems, simultaneous update problems, and so on. So change has to be controlled and managed.

A software development project produces the following items:

▸ Programs (source code, object code, executable programs, component libraries, functions, subroutines, and so on);

▸ Documentation (requirements definition, systems analysis, systems design, high-level design, low-level design, test specifications, test plans, installation manuals, release notes, user manuals, and so on); and

▶ Data (test data and project data).

These items are collectively called a *software configuration*. IEEE [1] defines a software configuration as the functional and physical characteristics of the software as set forth in technical documentation or achieved in a product.

The SCM system[1] identifies these items (the software items) and records their properties and relationships. This task would be very easy if the items and the systems were not subject to change. But unfortunately that is not the case.

Changes can occur at any time. Bersoff's [2] first law of system engineering states that no matter where you are in the system life cycle, the system will change and the desire to change it will persist throughout the life cycle. So we have to deal with change and SCM does that. But that is not the only thing that SCM does; it also—through audits and reviews—ensures that the items that are being released satisfy the requirements that were set forth in the requirements and design documents.

So we can define SCM as the set of activities whose main purposes are to identify the configuration items (the items that are supposed to change or that will undergo change); find the properties, characteristics, and interdependencies of these items and record them; monitor these items; manage the changes made to these items; document and report the change process; and ensure that the items delivered are complete and satisfy all requirements.

Overview of SCM

To identify, control, and manage change, one must first identify which items in the project will be subject to change. So we must first identify the items that we plan to control and manage. These items are called, in the SCM terminology, *configuration items.* IEEE [1] defines configuration items as an aggregation of hardware, software, or both that is designated

---

1. The SCM system refers to the tools, plans, and procedures as implemented in the project. It is the collection of all activities and personnel and other resources that perform SCM.

for configuration management and treated as a single entity in the configuration management process. It can be a program, a group of programs, a component library, a function, a subroutine, project documentation, user manual, test plan, test data, project data, and so on. The SCM system is supposed to record the functional and physical properties (like the features, what it is supposed to do, what performance criteria it is supposed to achieve, the size, lines of code, and so on) of these configuration items. Some examples of configuration items in a project follow:

- Project plan;
- SCM plan;
- Requirements definition document (RDD);
- Analysis, design, coding, testing, and auditing standards;
- System analysis document (SAD);
- System design document (SDD);
- Prototypes;
- High-level design (HLD) document;
- Low-level design (LLD) document;
- System test specifications;
- System test plan;
- Program source code;
- Object code and executable;
- Unit test specifications;
- Unit test plans;
- Database design documents;
- Test data;
- Project data; and
- User manuals.

This list is by no means exhaustive. It varies from project to project. The designers of the SCM system for a particular project decide which items should be configuration items. The characteristics of each configuration item and their interdependencies with one another are recorded. Usually this information is recorded in what is called a *configuration management database* or the repositories in the case of SCM tools. We will learn more about the configuration management database later in this chapter.

Once the configuration items are identified and their characteristics recorded, the next steps in software configuration management, as we saw in Chapter 1, are configuration control, status accounting, and configuration audits. We look briefly at these activities later in this chapter. But before we proceed, we should familiarize ourselves with some of the SCM terminology and concepts that we will be using in this book: baselines, deltas, versions, variants, branches, builds, releases, and so on.

Baselines

Baselines play a very important role in managing change. During the software development process, the configuration items are developed. For example, design documents are created, programs are coded and tested, user manuals are prepared, etc. When a configuration item is complete it is handed over to the configuration management team for safekeeping. The configuration management team will check whether the item that is given to them is complete (or contains all the necessary components) per the SCM plan and assigns a baseline to it. Baseline is an SCM concept that helps to control change. IEEE [1] defines baseline as a specification or product that has been formally reviewed and agreed on, which thereafter serves as the basis for further development and which can be changed only through formal change control procedures. So once a baseline is established for a configuration item, then that item can be changed only through a formal change management process. Pressman [3] compares the process of change management using baselines to a room with two doors: the IN and OUT doors. According to him, when an item has passed through the IN door—to the controlled environment—the baseline is established to the item. Then the only way to make changes to the item is get it out through the OUT door—using formal change management methods.

The baseline is the foundation for configuration management. The definition of SCM contains the concept of identifying the configuration—the functional and physical characteristics—of each configuration item at discrete points in time during the life cycle process. The configuration of software at a discrete point in time is known as a *baseline*. Thus, a baseline is the documentation and software that make up a configuration item at a given point in its life cycle. Each baseline serves as a point of departure or reference for the next development stage. Usually, baselines are established after each life cycle phase at the completion of the formal review that ends the phase. Thus we have the functional baseline, allocated baseline, product baseline, and so on, as we saw in Chapter 2. Thus a baseline provides the official standard or point of reference on which subsequent work is based and to which only authorized changes are made. After an initial baseline is established, every subsequent change made to the items is done using the configuration control process or, in other words, using formal change management procedures. Whenever an item is changed, all the processes involved in making the change—change initiation to change requests[2] to change disposition and implementation—are recorded. Then the item that is being changed is reviewed and saved as a new version of the item. For all of these change management processes the baseline—the snapshot of the item and its properties at a particular point in time—serves as a reference point.

Baselines should be established at an early point in the project. But bringing all items under configuration control too early will impose unnecessary procedures and will slow the programmer's work. This is because before a software configuration item becomes a baseline, changes may be made to it quickly and informally. For example, consider a programmer developing a program. After he has completed coding, while doing the unit testing, the programmer stumbles on a better algorithm to accomplish some task in the program. Because the program has not been baselined, the programmer can make the necessary change to the program, recompile it, and continue with the testing. But if the same situation occurs after the program has been baselined, then the programmer will have to make a change request and follow the change management procedures to make the change.

---

2. A change request or CR is a request to make a change or modification. A change request form (paper or electronic) is used to initiate a change. It contains the details of the change such as the name of the change originator, item to be changed, details of changes, and so on.

So when should a configuration item be baselined? There are no hard and fast rules on this issue. It depends on the nature of the project and how the SCM system designers (the people who designed the SCM system) think. Establishing baselines involves a trade-off between imposing unnecessary procedures (thus reducing productivity) and letting things go uncontrolled (which will result in project failure). So these two factors should be kept in mind when deciding when to baseline. As long as the programmers can work on individual modules with little interaction, a code baseline is not needed. As soon as integration begins, formal control is essential.

So prior to a configuration item becoming a baseline, only informal change control[3] is applied. The developer of the item can make whatever changes justified by project and technical requirements, as long as these changes do not conflict with the system requirements.[4] But once the object has undergone formal technical review and has been approved, a baseline is created. Once the configuration item becomes a baseline, project level change control or formal change control is implemented.

Check-in and check-out

We have seen that once a configuration item is baselined it is kept in a controlled library or repository. This process of reviewing, approving, and moving an item into the controlled environment is called *check-in*.

Once an item is checked in, it becomes a controlled item and all change management procedures apply to it. It cannot be taken out and modified whenever a programmer feels like doing so, even if he, or she, is the author or developer of the item.

For making changes to an item that is in the controlled library, the change management process, which is discussed in detail in Chapter 8,

---

3. Informal change control is applicable when the developers can make changes to their programs without following the SCM procedures. This is possible when the item has not been checked in and is not under SCM control.

4. The developer can find out whether the changes that she makes to her program conflict with the system requirements by going through the system design specifications and high-level design documents. For example, in a program, whether the developer first calculates the tax and then subtracts it from the earnings or whether she multiplies the earnings by $(1 - \text{tax}/100)$ does not conflict with the system requirements. This is a decision that the programmer makes according to her idea about which is the best algorithm.

must be followed. That is, a change request has to be submitted, it has to be approved, and so on. Once the change request is approved, the configuration manager will copy the item from the controlled library so that modifications can be made. This process is called *check-out.* Thus to make a change to a baselined item, it has to be checked out of the controlled library. Then after the changes are made, it is again tested, reviewed, and if approved is again checked in to the controlled environment and a new baseline is created for the item. The check-out/check-in process is shown in Figure 5.1. Today's SCM tools have made this whole process of check-in and check-out an easy task. Many tools allow the programmers to work on the configuration items without physically checking out the items. Also today's SCM tools allow more than one person to simultaneously work on the same configuration item (concurrent development). These facilities provided by the modern SCM tools are discussed later in this chapter.

Versions and variants

During the software development life cycle, the configuration items evolve until they reach a state where they meet the specifications. This is

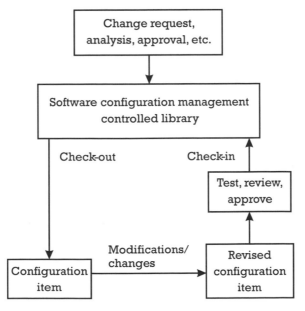

Figure 5.1 Check-in and check-out.

when the items are reviewed, approved, baselined, and moved into the controlled environment. But we have seen that the story does not end there. The item will undergo further changes (due to various reasons such as defects and enhancements) and to make those changes, the change control procedures must be followed. The items have to be checked out, the changes implemented, tested, reviewed, approved, and again base-lined. This change process produces a new version or revision of the item.

A *version* is an initial release or re-release of a configuration item. It is an instance of the system that differs in some way from the other instances. New versions of the system may have additional functionality or different functionality. Their performance characteristics may be different or they may be the result of fixing a bug that was found by the developer, tester, user, or customer.

Some versions can be functionally equivalent but may be designed for different hardware and/or software environments. In such cases they are called *variants*. For example, two different instances of the same item, say, one for Windows and the other for OS/2, can be called variants rather than different versions. Unlike a version, one variant of an item is in no sense an improvement on another variant.

As we have seen, the items once moved into the controlled environment can be changed only by using SCM change control methods. Each such change produces a revision or version. So each change to a controlled item produces a new version and except for the first, each version has a predecessor and except for the most recent, each version has a successor. The different versions of an item represent its history. It explains how an item got transformed or evolved from its initial form or stage to its current form. Usually a new version of an item is created by checking out the most recent copy and making changes to it.

Parallel development and branching

So far we have seen that an item is checked out, changes are made and then tested, reviewed, approved, and checked in. So the versions will form a linear line as shown in Figure 5.2.

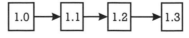

Figure 5.2   Version numbers.

But in real life this linear development might not always be possible. In such cases we use what is called a *branch*. Branches (Figure 5.3) are deviations from the main development line for an item. They are a convenient mechanism for allowing two or more people to work on the same item at the same time—parallel, concurrent development—perhaps for different goals. A common scenario is having one person working to add new features to the product, while a second is doing bug fixes on prior versions.

The version numbers of branches can be a little confusing, so they warrant a quick discussion. Version numbers on the main development line have only two parts: a major and minor number. Branches have four parts to their numbering scheme. The first two parts represent the point at which the branch splits off the main line. The third number indicates which of the many possible branches it is. For example, in Figure 5.3, we have only one branch originating from 1.3. As such, its numbering starts at 1.3.1.0, and proceeds from there. If a second branch is later formed from 1.3, then its numbering will begin with 1.3.2.0, as shown in Figure 5.4.

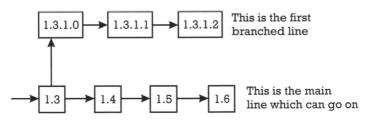

Figure 5.3   Branching for parallel development.

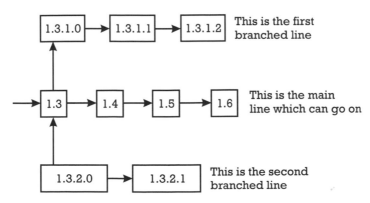

Figure 5.4   Multiple branches.

Branches can also extend from existing branches. For example, a branch can be formed from 1.3.1.1. This branch will have a six-part numbering scheme starting with 1.3.1.1.1.0 as shown in Figure 5.5. The first four parts represent the point at which the branch split off from the parent branch. The fifth number indicates which of the many possible branches it is. For example, in Figure 5.5 we have only one branch originating from 1.3.1.1. As such, its numbering starts at 1.3.1.1.1.0 and proceeds from there. If a second branch is later formed from 1.3.1.1, then its numbering will begin with 1.3.1.1.2.0.

Branches are often used as a temporary means of allowing parallel and concurrent development on a single file. Sooner or later, the edits made to the branched line must be incorporated into the main evolutionary line for the file. When doing this, the changes made by the different persons have to be merged. If the changes are made at different parts of the item, then the merge is an easy task. But if two people have changed the same lines of an item, then a decision has to be reached about how the merge is to take place. The person who does the merging should decide which one to keep and which one to discard. The SCM tools have automatic merging facilities that allow interactive merging, in which the tool will compare the changed portions of the two changed files to the original file (usually called the ancestor) and the user can choose which change to accept. In the author's opinion, however, it is always better to do an interactive or manual merge, because human judgment is better that the judgment afforded by algorithm used by the system.

After the merge occurs, the branches have outlived their utility and no longer need to evolve separately.

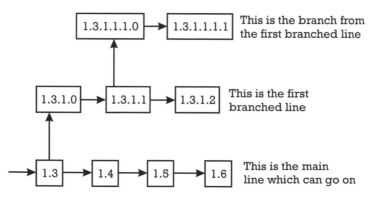

Figure 5.5   Branch from an existing branch.

Naming versions

We have seen that all configuration items have to be named and that the name has two parts: a number part, which changes with each version, and the name of the item (including the project, type, and other details). The names should be descriptive. For example, in a large project with many modules and subsystems, a simple name for a configuration item is not a good idea. In such cases the name should have elements of the project, subsystem, module, and other components in it so that it can be easily identified with a project or subsystem. The number part of the name should be designed in such a way as to determine its relative position in the version hierarchy. For example we have seen that the first version will be identified as 1.0, subsequent revisions 1.1, 1.2, 2.0, 2.1, and so on. A branch from version 1.1 will be identified as 1.1.1.0 and its subsequent versions 1.1.1.1 and so on. A second branch will be identified as 1.1.2.0 and so on.

Source and derived items

An item that is created from another item or set of items is called a *derived item*. The items from which a derived item is created are called *source items*. For example, an executable program is a derived item—an item that is derived from the source code using a compiler. In the case of derived items, the details like the list of source items used to derive the item, the tool or tools used to derive the item, the environment in which the derivation was done, and so on are important and should be documented. This is important from the point of view of reproducibility and repeatability. For example, if you want to derive the particular version of a derived item, you will need all the above information to do so. Also if a problem is detected with a version of the derived item, then the following questions need to be answered to solve the problem:

▸ Which versions of which source elements were used to build the item?

▸ Which tools were used for the process?

▸ What environment variables and parameters were used to build the item?

These are the first questions that will have to be answered if a problem occurs, and a good SCM system should be able to provide the answers to these questions. The derived item is fully described by:

▶ The name and version of each of the source elements from which the item was built;

▶ The tool or tools used for building the item; and

▶ The options and parameters (like compile and link-edit options) given to the tools while building the item.

System building

System building is the process of combining "source" components of a system into components, which execute on a particular target configuration. The system or parts of it have to be rebuilt after every change in the "source." The following factors must be considered:

▶ Have all components that make up the system been included in the build instructions (dependencies resolved, include paths set, and so on) and do they have the proper version?

▶ Are all required ancillary files (data, documentation) available on the target machine?

▶ Are the required tools (e.g., the compiler or linker) available, and do they have the right version?

The system is built using a command file which specifies the components of the system (both source and derived), their versions, their location in the controlled environment, the system building tools (like a compiler, linker, and so on) and their versions, the options and environmental parameters that were set, and so on. In the IBM mainframe this file is usually a JCL file, in UNIX it is a shell script, in modern integrated development environments such as Visual C++ and Visual Basic it is a make file or project file. These command files are also configuration items and are necessary for reproduction of the particular configuration.

The build management facility of many SCM tools automates the process of constructing the software system and ensures that the systems are built completely and accurately at any time. These configuration builders save time, shorten build cycles, and eliminate build errors by providing repeatable, automated builds of the software development projects. In most cases the system building tools work with the version management tools and extract the correct versions of development objects from libraries. This simplifies the system building process and eliminates errors when building complex versions on multiple operating systems.

Releases

A release consists of more than just the executable code. It includes installation files, data files, setup programs, and electronic and paper documentation. A system release is the set of items that is given to the customers. Each system release includes new functionality or features or some fixes for the faults found by customers, developers, or testers. Usually, there are more revisions of a system than system releases. Revisions or versions, as mentioned before, are created for internal use and may never be released to customers. For example, a revision may be created for testing.

When a release is produced (using the system building process), as we have seen, it is important to record the environment in which it was produced: the operating system, versions of the components used, other parameters such as compile and link-edit options, and so on. This is important from the SCM point of view, because at a later stage, it might become necessary to reproduce the exact configuration that was released. For example, consider a bug that is discovered after the system is released. The easiest way to find the source of the problem is to find out what components were changed. The problem could be either due to a bug in one of the changed components or due to some environmental variables being changed (like some compiler or linker options). So if we have a record of the components and the environment details used for the release, then it is easy to track the source of the defect. One merely needs to compare the details of the current release with the previous release and see what has been changed. So it is imperative that a proper mechanism to record the details of each and every release be instituted.

A release to a client—a system release—should contain identifiers indicating the release or version number and should also include a release note containing the following information:

- Installation requirements, such as required operating system, memory, processor specifications, and so on;

- How to install the system and how to test the system to ensure that the installation was successful;

- How to upgrade from an earlier version of the system;

- The key or serial number of the product, if such a number is required for installation;

- A list of known faults and limitations of the particular version of the system and a list of the faults that were fixed in the current release;

- New features introduced in the release; and

- Instructions for contacting the supplier of the system for technical support or if problems arise.

Today, most of the above-mentioned activities including the registration of the product are done by the installation programs, so release notes are not as important as they once were.

Deltas

In an ideal situation, all changes made to the configuration items should be recorded and all of the different versions of the items should be kept. This is because, in a software system not all users will be using the latest version. So, even though the system may be in version 6.0, some users will still be using version 1.0 or 2.1. So configuration management systems should be able to produce the details of the latest as well as past versions and should be able to reproduce the components of every version. For example, years after a system is released, a request for a component in the first version can come up. Even if the system is currently in its seventh or eighth version, companies cannot ignore a client who still uses the initial version.

Ideally, copies of all versions should be in a repository. But this is not practical, because of the amount of disk space required. Instead, we create what is known as a *delta*. When a new version is created, the difference between the new and the previous version is called delta. So instead of storing full copies of all versions, one version and the deltas are stored, so that at any point in time the required version can be derived by applying the relevant deltas to the base version. The concept of deltas is shown in Figure 5.6.

Deltas are smaller than the source code of a system version, so the amount of disk space required for version management is greatly reduced. The two types of delta storage are *forward deltas* and *reverse deltas,* as shown in Figure 5.7.

The principle of forward delta storage is that the system maintains a complete copy of the original file. After this, whenever a new version is checked in, the two versions are compared and a delta report is produced. Then this delta report is stored instead of storing the full copy of the new version. Whenever the new version is required, the delta is applied to the original to get the new version.

In the case of reverse delta storage, only the most recent version of the module is kept in the complete form. Whenever a new version is checked in, it is compared to the previous version and the delta is created. Then the previous version is deleted and the new version is stored.

The problem with forward delta storage is that as more revisions are added, more computation is required to obtain the latest revision. So the greater the number of revisions, the longer the retrieval time will be. This is because in the case of the forward delta, the change manager must always start with the original version and then apply the deltas one at a time to create the latest version. In the case of the reverse delta option, no

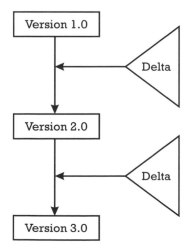

Figure 5.6 Use of deltas.

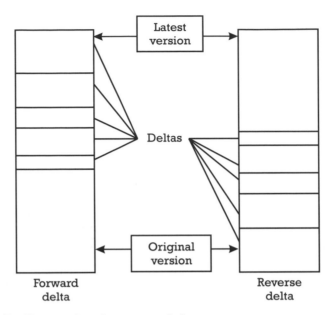

Figure 5.7   Forward and reverse deltas.

computation is required to get the latest version, because it is stored in its full form.

The decision to go for forward delta storage or reverse delta storage depends on the nature of the project. If the latest versions are more frequently required, then it is always better to use the reverse delta. In the real world more than 75% of archive accesses are for the latest version and this explains the popularity of reverse delta storage among the change management tools.

Configuration management database

We have seen that the properties, characteristics, and interdependencies of the configuration items should be recorded in a database—the configuration management database. The configuration management database is used to record all relevant information related to configurations. The principal functions of such a database are to assist in assessing the impact of system changes and to provide information about the SCM process. The configuration management database, in addition to the details about the configuration items, contains information about change requests (which are also configuration items), their status, and information regarding the review and audit processes.

The contents and structure of the configuration management database should be defined during the SCM system design stage and should be documented in the SCM plan. In modern CASE environments, the configuration database is part of the system and the details of the items are automatically recorded. In the case of manual SCM systems, the details have to be entered manually into the system. Precautions should be taken to prevent items being entered into the SCM system without their details being recorded in the configuration database. If a configuration item is added without an entry in the database, then the integrity of the data in the database and the usefulness of the database are lost.

A configuration management database should be able to provide answers to queries such as these:

- What is the current configuration? What is its status?

- Which person has taken delivery of a particular version of the system?

- What hardware and operating system configuration are required to run a given system version?

- How many versions of a system have been created and what were their creation dates?

- What changes have been made to the software, documentation, and other items in the project, who made them, when were they made?

- Were the changes approved by somebody or just informally done?

- What versions of a system might be affected if a particular component is changed?

- How many change requests are pending on a particular item?

- How many reported faults exist in a particular version?

- Can I recreate the original from the changed version or the changed version from the original?

- Can I find out what happened to a specific item at some point in time, such as what changes were made to it and so on?

▶ Does the change that I make affect anybody else or are anyone else's changes affecting my program?

With the increasing popularity of SCM tools, the necessity for a configuration database is decreasing. The SCM tools have their own repositories where they can store SCM-related information. The advantage of these systems is that SCM information is captured automatically as and when each activity is performed. So there is no need to enter details manually when a change request is initiated, when an item is released, when a change is made, and so on. This feature saves considerable time and effort and reduces the chance of creating errors that can occur when manual data entry is used. Also, with the facility to automatically capture the SCM information, such as when the activities happen, the SCM tool user has the ability to capture comprehensive SCM information without any additional effort.

Configuration control, status accounting, and configuration audits

We have seen that configuration identification is the process of defining each baseline to be established during the software life cycle and describing the software configuration items and their documentation that make up each baseline. First, the software must be grouped into configuration items. Once the configuration items and their components have been selected, some way of designating the items must be developed. This is done by the development of a numbering and naming scheme that correlates the code and data items with their associated documentation. Finally, each configuration item must be described by the documentation in terms of its functional, performance, and physical characteristics.

Configuration control is the process of evaluating, coordinating, and deciding on the disposition of proposed changes to the configuration items, and also includes implementing approved changes to baselined software and associated documentation. The change control process ensures that changes which have been initiated are classified and evaluated, approved or disapproved, and that those approved are implemented, documented, and verified.

Configuration status accounting is the process used to trace changes to the software. It ensures that status is recorded, monitored, and reported on both pending and completed actions affecting software baselines.

Configuration auditing is the process of verifying that a deliverable software baseline contains all of the items required for that delivery, and that these items have themselves been verified to determine that they satisfy requirements.

We will examine these activities in greater detail in Chapters 8, 9, 10, and 11.

SCM: The different scenarios

SCM can be practiced in a variety of situations. Projects where SCM is practiced can vary from small, single-person projects to very large and complex projects involving hundreds of people. Even though the SCM concepts are the same irrespective of the size of the project, the way in which SCM is practiced, the procedures followed, the degree of control and presence of formal procedures, use of SCM tools, level of automation, and so on are not the same. They will vary from project to project.

Also the development environment is changing. Now we have integrated development environments (IDEs) and CASE environments. These are quite different from the earlier project environments. Today a software system can be cross-platform (the software system can span more than one hardware/software platform) and can involve more than one development environment. The use of CASE tools for application development is now commonplace. We now have distributed development environments with development happening in different parts of the world. In this section we will see how configuration management is practiced in these situations.

SCM and project size

The size and number of people involved in a project can definitely have an impact on how SCM is practiced in a project. There can be single-person projects, a single person managing more than one project, projects involving more than one person, projects involving thousands of people, and so on. In the case of a single person doing a project, SCM is not an absolute must, because issues such as communications breakdowns, shared data problems, and simultaneous update problems are not encountered. But even in this kind of a project practicing SCM is useful because due to human characteristics such as carelessness, oversight, and forgetfulness the work that is already done can get overwritten, the same problem might be solved more than once, and so on.

Also the person who is doing the project will not be around forever. So when a new person takes charge of the project, she has to have the information available to her. So if there is no documentation and no records, and the only record of what happened to the project is in the other person's head, then it will be difficult for the new person to manage the project. Questions such as why was this change made, what items were changed, and if this module is changed which items will be affected will not have answers. To get those answers, the new person will have to go through all of the programs and if she is lucky she will be able to find the answers.

So even in the case of small projects where only one person is involved, practicing SCM is a good idea. Here there is no need to use an SCM tool and formal change management procedures with CCB meetings and so on. An informal SCM system, where every change, the reasons for change, the item dependencies, information about versions and releases, and so on are documented would be more than enough. If the organization has an SCM tool and if all the developers have been trained on the tool, then even small projects can benefit from using an SCM tool.

In the case of larger projects involving many people, SCM must be practiced. In the earlier chapters, we saw why practicing SCM is important. It is always advantageous (because it will improve development productivity and reduce errors) to automate the various SCM functions using SCM tools. In today's brutally competitive world, where everyone is fighting for survival—and market share—SCM can be used as a strategic weapon that will give the organization an edge over the others who are not using SCM or using it less effectively.

SCM in integrated development environments

An integrated development environment (IDE) is a programming environment integrated into an application. So an IDE is a set of programs that runs from a single user interface. Some of the most popular IDEs include Visual C++, PowerBuilder, and Visual Basic.

The advantage of using an IDE is that you can design, develop, test, debug, and run the applications without leaving the development environment. So when using an IDE, it is quite natural to assume that even for SCM functions one does not have to leave the development environment. Many of the today's SCM tools integrate seamlessly with the integrated environments, so that they become part of the environment. Therefore, when carrying out SCM functions, the developer does not have to leave the development environment. Some examples of tools are Continuos CM integrating with Visual C++, PVCS integrating with PowerBuilder, and Visual SourceSafe integrating with Microsoft's IDEs. Thus these tools make the configuration management process in an IDE more intuitive and painless.

SCM in distributed environments

As we saw earlier, today's development environment is often a distributed one. Different teams working from different locations develop a software product or system. This is an ideal situation for SCM because lack of control can lead to chaos and result in project failures. With the advancements in telecommunications and networking technologies, distributed computing is becoming easier and easier.

Today, project teams that are thousands of miles apart can work as if they share the same office. The SCM tools have evolved to incorporate these technologies. Today's SCM tools are capable of supporting distributed development, parallel and concurrent development, and so on. The capabilities and features of the modern SCM tools are so advanced that users do not have to bother about the complexities involved. They can work as if they are working in the same office and the system will manage issues such as networking, communication, security, and concurrency management.

SCM and CASE tools

CASE tools provide automated methods for designing and documenting traditional structured programming techniques. The ultimate goal of CASE is to provide a language for describing the overall system that is sufficient to generate all the necessary programs. Thus a CASE tool is a software package that is used for developing an information system. It is used in all phases of software development: analysis, design, programming, testing, and so on. For example, data dictionaries and programming tools aid in the analysis and design phase while application generators help speed the programming phase. Automated testing tools and test data generators help in the testing phase.

Most CASE tools store project information in their repositories, and they use this information for code generation, test plan creation, test data generation, and so on. Because a CASE tool uses the information from its repository to generate the application code, the information stored in a CASE tool's repository is very detailed. For example, many CASE tools use the entity-relation (ER) models as a starting point for analysis. So their repositories will contain details about the various entities, their attributes, and so on. These repositories also contain information about the interdependencies of the various objects, programs, and so on because this type of information is required for application generation and testing.

We have seen that SCM systems also use the same information (maybe not to the detail as that of CASE tools) to function. So a CASE tool's repository contains the information that is needed for an SCM system. Many CASE tools have rudimentary SCM functions built into them. For example, CASE tools can manage changes, keep an audit trail of modifications to the changes to an item, and so on.

CASE tools do not, however, have the full functionality of an SCM tool, but they do provide the inputs that are required by the SCM system. Thus if the CASE tools and SCM systems can be integrated, so that the SCM systems draw the information from the CASE tools and then perform the SCM functions, much time and effort that would otherwise be spent on information gathering can be saved. The ideal solution to this scenario is that of a CASE tool that is so tightly integrated with an SCM tool that they share the same repository, and hence users could perform all SCM functions without leaving the CASE environment.

Conclusion

In this chapter we studied the various configuration management concepts and learned SCM terminology. We learned about SCM functions and how they relate to one another. We gained an understanding of the fundamental concepts of SCM such as versions, variants, branching, merging, deltas, system building, and releases.

We also examined the different scenarios in which SCM is implemented. SCM can be implemented in many diverse environments. However, irrespective of the environment in which it is implemented, the SCM fundamentals and the concepts will be the same. Factors such as methodology, tools, and automation vary with the environment in which the SCM is implemented.

In today's business environment, where competition is fierce and one has to constantly improve and innovate to stay ahead of the competition, SCM can give an organization a strategic advantage over its competitors. As mentioned before, an organization that uses SCM definitely has an edge over others who do not use SCM or use it inefficiently or ineffectively.

References

[1]   *IEEE Standard Glossary of Software Engineering Terminology* (IEEE Std-610-1990), *IEEE Standards Collection (Software Engineering)*, Piscataway, NJ: IEEE, 1997.

[2]   Bersoff, E. H., V. D. Henderson, and S. G. Siegel, *Software Configuration Management, An Investment in Product Integrity*, Englewood Cliffs, NJ: Prentice-Hall, 1980.

[3]   Pressman, R. S., *Software Engineering: A Practitioner's Approach*, New York: McGraw-Hill, 1997.

Selected bibliography

Babich, W. A., *Software Configuration Management: Coordination for Team Productivity*, Boston, MA: Addison Wesley, 1986.

Ben-Menachem, M., *Software Configuration Guidebook*, London: McGraw-Hill International, 1994.

Berlack, H. R., *Software Configuration Management*, New York: John Wiley & Sons, 1992.

Conradi, R. (Ed.), *Software Configuration Management: ICSE'97 SCM-7 Workshop Proc.*, Berlin: Springer-Verlag, 1997.

IEEE Standards Collection, Software Engineering, New York: IEEE, 1997.

Magnusson, B. (Ed.), *System Configuration Management: ECOOP'98 SCM-8 Symp. Proc.*, Berlin: Springer-Verlag, 1998.

Pressman, R. S., *Software Engineering: A Practitioner's Approach*, New York: McGraw-Hill, 1997.

Sommerville, I., *Software Engineering*, Reading, MA: Addison-Wesley, 1996.

Whitgift, D., *Methods and Tools for Software Configuration Management*, Chichester, England: John Wiley & Sons, 1991.

Contents

The different phases of software configuration management

Introduction

We have seen that SCM is a set of activities that must be performed throughout the life cycle of the software system. Even though SCM activities can be initiated at any stage during a project's life cycle, it is better to have the SCM system in place from the beginning.

Company management should be convinced about the need for and importance of having an SCM system, preferably during the early stages of the project. Also the people who will be using the system—the developers, the project leaders, the QA team members, company management, and so on—should be made aware of the benefits of good configuration management. The benefits of SCM as discussed in Chapter 4 could be used for this purpose. SCM systems are capable of delivering dramatic productivity improvements, cost reductions, error/defect reductions, and so on. It can improve customer goodwill, because the company will be able to provide customers with better quality products and better technical support. Also if the myths about SCM—such as SCM is nothing more than just additional documentation, SCM is additional work, and so on—could be dispelled, then company management and potential users of the system might be convinced about the need for an SCM system. Also, today's SCM tools are so sophisticated and advanced that they make the whole process of performing SCM functions easy.

There is a misconception that SCM is only for big companies and large projects. In the author's opinion, SCM should be implemented in all software projects—irrespective of the size of the project and organization—for the very reason that change is inevitable in all projects, and unmanaged and uncontrolled change is trouble all the way. It is the author's experience that companies that use the scientific methods of software development from the very beginning—that are, even when they are small—have a workforce and work culture that is more willing and able to learn new technologies and adapt to changes and implement new procedures. The programmers and managers of these companies have gotten used to standard software engineering practices and procedures, and the work cultures of these companies evolve around these practices. New employees joining the company will also follow the procedures and methods, because peer pressure will be high.

The advantage of this scenario is that the methodologies and procedures will produce dramatic results in such companies because people are doing things because they believe in them, not because they have to do it. For example, consider SCM. Everyone knows that SCM is not easy; it is difficult to keep a good SCM system (a system that is efficient and effective) up and running. But the effort is worth it.

If an SCM system is to become a success, however, and deliver the promised results, the people who are involved have to be convinced of its worth. Just doing SCM for the sake of getting some certification will not produce the results that it is capable of. So it is better to have the SCM system in place during the early stages of a project rather than wait for the maintenance phase to commence!

Different phases of SCM implementation

Like any project, SCM implementation goes through different phases. There are no clear separating lines between these phases and in many cases one phase will start before the previous one is completed. But a logical order is followed. The logical order is the order in which the phases are listed. As mentioned, some overlap occurs between the phases, but the third phase cannot start before the second phase and so on.

Note that all of the phases discussed in this chapter may not be applicable in all cases. For example, in a small project where a single person is responsible for SCM, there will not be an SCM team and SCM team training; or if the organization has already identified an SCM tool, then the preselection screening and tool evaluation phases (part of SCM system design) are not required.

The different phases of the SCM implementation are listed here and also illustrated in Figure 6.1:

▶ SCM system design;

▶ SCM plan preparation;

▶ SCM team organization;

▶ SCM infrastructure setup;

▶ SCM team training;

▶ Project team training;

▶ Configuration identification;

▶ Configuration control;

▶ Configuration status accounting; and

▶ Configuration audits.

The initial phases—from SCM system design up to SCM infrastructure setup—are performed by the SCM system design team with the help and support of company management. SCM team training is done jointly by the SCM design team and SCM experts (outside consultants or in-house experts). If SCM tools are used, then the training on those tools is given by the tool vendor's representatives or in-house tool experts.

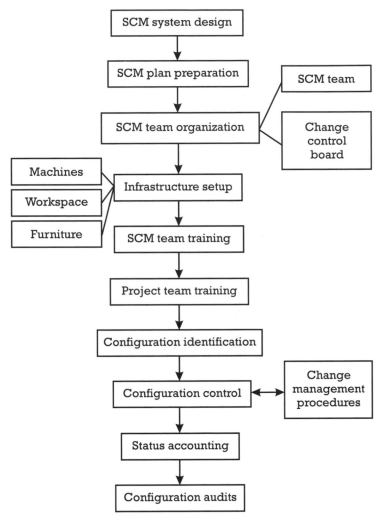

Figure 6.1   Different phases of SCM implementation.

The project team members are trained by the SCM team members, the design team members, the tool vendor's representatives, and the SCM experts. Here the role of the SCM experts and the SCM system design team members is to develop a loyalty among the employees for SCM. Because these people will be quite senior in the organizational hierarchy and have the necessary stature, they can convince people better than the SCM team members. So these top-level people should give their support, pledge their allegiance, and give an overview of SCM and its benefits to the employees. Training on the details and the day-to-day operational formalities can be handled by the SCM team members. The support and encouragement of top management and the full cooperation of all people involved are essential factors in the successful implementation and smooth functioning of any SCM system.

A question that naturally arises is that of how can SCM team members and project team members be trained on the SCM system before the system is implemented. That is, how can somebody be trained on something that does not exist? Actually the system exists, but it has yet to be implemented. The SCM system is designed, procedures are documented and defined in the SCM plan, and the tools that are going to be used are selected, purchased, and put in place. The SCM team and project team training takes place so that people can use the systems properly. So the main objective of the training is to establish the best practices and to convince users about the need for, importance of, and benefits of the SCM system—the one they are going to use.

Although the SCM implementation phases may seem very linear and distinct from each other, in reality, throughout an actual implementation, the phases are quite fluid. In addition, the phases are repeated. For example, even the SCM plan can undergo changes. So if it is felt that the current system needs changes, the changes are incorporated into the SCM plan, and if that change necessitates training then that is done. Everyone involved in the SCM process is informed about the changes made to the SCM plan. The change management procedures are repeated many times—every time a change request is initiated. Status accounting, the function that records the happenings and reports the information, is a routine task. SCM audits and reviews are also done quite often depending on the criteria specified in the SCM plan.

We now look at each phase in some detail.

SCM system design

Once project management or company management decides to support SCM, the SCM system must be designed. If the company already practices SCM and already has guidelines, then the job is easy. The job of the designers is to tailor the company guidelines to suit the needs of the particular project.

Here one important thing to remember is that no two projects are the same. So even if the guidelines are taken from similar projects, it is necessary to customize them to suit the needs of the current project. The standards and guidelines must be customized depending on the nature of the project. The guidelines will be generic and will have to be customized to suit the project. Some portions might need to be modified, some project-specific things might need to be added, and unwanted portions might need to be deleted. For example, if the guidelines talk about subcontractor control and the current project does not have any sub-contracted items, then that can be deleted.

The SCM system design team should include the project manager, the person who is going to be the SCM team leader, and key personnel from the project team, QA department, and so on. It is not a good idea to have too many people on the design team; it will only result in lowering the productivity of the team. The responsibilities of the SCM design team include (but are not limited to) development of the SCM system, customizing the SCM system (if guidelines already exists), preparation of the SCM plan, maintenance of the SCM plan, selection of the SCM team, and constitution of the change control board.

If the company does not have any guidelines for the development of an SCM system, then SCM standards can be used, as discussed in Appendix B. The design team defines the scope of the SCM system, what activities it will perform, how they will be performed, which activities will be automated, what tools will be used, what method will be used for version numbering, and how release management will be accomplished, among others.

The SCM system design team also determines whether to use tools, whether to make them or buy them, and so on. If the decision is made to buy tools, then the team will evaluate the tools available in the market and select the tools that are best suited to the needs of the company.

The team also decides the composition of the SCM team. Team size varies depending on the nature and size of the project. Large projects will have a full-fledged team with many people, whereas a small project may have a team comprised of a single person or a person working part-time. The design team also determines the constitution of the change control board (CCB) and defines guidelines for its functioning.

Once all issues regarding the SCM system have been finalized, the details are documented. This document is called the SCM plan.

SCM plan preparation

As we have seen, the SCM system design team decides on the particulars of the SCM system that is to be used. Once the system details are finalized, the decisions and procedures have to be documented. This document is called the SCM plan. The idea behind the SCM plan is to ensure that all members of the SCM team and the project team are aware of the procedures and the duties and responsibilities that each one is supposed to carry out. It will also tell them what resources are to be used and how they are to be used. It acts as a guideline in the resolution of conflicts. According to the IEEE [1], the SCM plan should contain the following sections: Introduction, Management, Activities, Schedules, Resources, and Plan Maintenance. We were introduced to SCM plans in Chapter 1 and we will look at them again in more detail in Chapter 11.

The SCM design team will prepare the plan and distribute it among the members. This document forms the basis for SCM training. The plan also contains a section that lists the procedures required to keep it up to date. So the plan is constantly reviewed and any required changes are made to it. The SCM plan is also an item that is placed under configuration control, which happens once the plan is finalized, reviewed, and approved. It usually forms part of the functional baseline because the SCM plan is usually created during or before the requirements phase. So once a baseline is established for the SCM plan, all changes to the plan will have to be made in accordance with the change management procedures.

SCM team organization

As we have seen, the SCM team size can vary from a single person to a full-fledged team depending on the size and nature of the project. The SCM system design team selects the members of the SCM team and will allocate responsibilities to each member.

The constitution of the CCB and its workings are also finalized. The CCB usually consists of the SCM team leader and one or two key team members in addition to the project team leader, QA representative, marketing team representative, and in some cases the client representatives.

SCM infrastructure setup

While the SCM team is formed and their responsibilities assigned, the infrastructure facilities that will help the team function properly must also be arranged. The SCM is not a one-week or one-month affair. It is a continuous function that will be there for the entire life cycle of the project. So the SCM team needs permanent facilities, not some makeshift arrangements. (Although, again, this will ultimately depend on the size of the team.) Ideally the SCM team should have a separate office that is close to the project with which it is associated. This type of a setup is required for manual SCM systems in fairly large projects.

Today with most companies using SCM tools and as more and more SCM functions are automated, the concept and practice of having a separate SCM team are no longer in vogue. SCM tools give a lot of power and capabilities to the development team. These tools automatically perform most SCM functions so the need for a full-fledged SCM team does not arise even in fairly large projects. One or two people will be responsible for monitoring the SCM system to ensure that it is working properly.

SCM team training

The members of the SCM team may be veterans with many SCM projects under their belts or they may be fresh faces that do not have any idea about what SCM is. The idea behind SCM team training is to familiarize the team members with the discipline of SCM and train them regarding how it is going to be practiced in a particular project.

The team members are trained on how to carry out their duties and responsibilities in the most efficient and effective manner and told what they are supposed to do and what they are not supposed to do. If SCM tools are being used in the project, then the team members are given training on the tools also. They are also briefed about their access privileges and rights. Because the configuration management process is a job that involves a lot of tact and diplomacy, in the author's opinion the training should also have a module on effective communication.

As mentioned in the previous section, the increasing popularity of SCM tools and the level of automation that is being achieved by these tools have reduced the role of the SCM team. In a manual SCM system, where all SCM functions used to be carried out manually, full-fledged SCM teams were required. But today, with the high degree of automation and more and more capabilities and responsibilities being given to the development team members, the number of tasks that need to be performed by SCM team members has been reduced considerably.

Project team training

The success of an SCM system depends on the participation and cooperation of the project team members and on the understanding and dedication of the SCM team. So training of the project team members about the fundamentals of SCM, its concepts, advantages, and benefits, is necessary. Also, project team members should be briefed about how they are to participate in the SCM functions and carry out the SCM activities. If the project uses automated tools for change management, problem reporting and tracking, and so on, then the project team members should be trained in how to use those tools.

Both the SCM team training and the project team training are continuous activities and provisions should be made to keep it that way. Training never ends; it is an ongoing process. This is because new people will join both the teams and existing members will leave. So the new members need to be trained, possibly by an outgoing member or some other person designated by the project management.

The training of both of these teams is based on the foundation detailed in the SCM plan. The SCM plan contains the details of how SCM is to be practiced for the particular project, and all training activities should be based on that.

There has been a brief overview of the next four phases in Chapters 1 and 6, but the same material is repeated again for the sake of completeness. These four activities, or phases, form the core of the SCM activities and are discussed in detail in Chapters 7 through 10.

Configuration identification

Configuration identification is an element of configuration management that consists of selecting the configuration items for a system and recording their functional and physical characteristics in technical documentation.

Configuration control

Configuration control is the element of configuration management consisting of the evaluation, coordination, approval or disapproval, and implementation of changes to configuration items.

Configuration status accounting

Status accounting consists of the recording and reporting of information needed to manage a configuration efficiently. This information includes a listing of the approved configuration identification, the status of proposed changes to the configuration, and the implementation status of approved changes.

Configuration audits

Auditing is carried out to ensure that the SCM system is functioning correctly and that the configuration has been tested to demonstrate that it meets its functional requirements and contains all deliverable entities. A functional configuration audit authenticates that the software performs in accordance with the requirements and as stated in the documentation. A physical configuration audit authenticates that the components to be delivered actually exist and that they contain all of the required items, such as the proper versions of source and object code, documentation, and installation instructions.

Conclusion

SCM implementation needs to change the way people have been doing things, and lots of procedures are introduced for the functioning of SCM. Resistance to SCM implementation is natural, because it is human nature to resist change. Making people accept SCM and implementing it is difficult because of the myths surrounding SCM, such as SCM causing additional work and more documentation.

Most people are not aware of the potential benefits of SCM. For the SCM system to succeed and deliver those benefits, the organization has to design a good system, install procedures, and train the SCM team and project team. Once these tasks are done, there is a natural tendency to feel satisfied or complacent—complacency about what has been achieved— by the implementation team.

One important factor that should be kept in mind is that the postimplementation phase is very critical. SCM functions are continuous and should be performed throughout the life cycle of the project. To reap the full benefits of the SCM system, the system should get project-wide/company-wide acceptance. To get project-wide acceptance for the SCM system, every member of the project should be made aware of the need, importance, and benefits of SCM.

Just as courtships and honeymoons are different from marriages, living with an SCM system is different from installing it. Implementing a good SCM system is not an easy job, but it is how the projects mesh with SCM system that determines the value that is received from it. It is how the SCM system is used in the project that makes the difference. Even a well-designed system can be a failure if the people using it are not cooperative.

Reference

[1]   *IEEE Standard for Software Configuration Management Plans* (IEEE Std-828-1990), *IEEE Standards Collection (Software Engineering)*, Piscataway, NJ: IEEE, 1997.

Configuration identification

Introduction

Configuration identification is the basis for subsequent control of the software configuration. The configuration identification process involves the selection, designation, and description of the software configuration items. *Selection* involves the grouping of software into configuration items that are subject to configuration management. *Designation* is the development of a numbering and/or naming scheme that correlates the software components and their associated documentation. *Description* is the documentation of functional, performance, and physical characteristics for each of the software components.

IEEE [1] defines configuration identification as an element of configuration management, consisting of selecting the configuration items for a system and recording their functional and physical characteristics in technical documentation. In other words, configuration identification is the process whereby a system is separated into uniquely identifiable components for the purpose of SCM. This is the first major SCM function that has to be carried out in a project (the design of the SCM system and the preparation of the SCM plan are done before configuration identification begins).

The software under control is usually divided into configuration items also known as computer software configuration items (CSCIs). *Configuration item* (CI) is the term used for each of the logically related components that make up some discrete element of software. For example, if a system contains several programs, each program and its related documentation and data might be designated a configuration item. Determining what characteristics must be captured so that the properties and requirements of the product are correctly reflected is an important decision. The configuration identification process should capture all characteristics of the software to be controlled: its content, the content of documents that describe it, the different versions as the contents are changed, data needed for operation of the software, and any other essential elements or characteristics that make the software what it is.

To accomplish configuration identification, the following steps are performed:

1. Select configuration items.

2. Select configuration documentation to be used to define configuration baselines for each CI.

3. Establish a release/version management system for configuration documentation.

4. Define and document interfaces to and between CIs.

5. Enter each item of configuration documentation and computer software source code into a controlled environment.

6. Establish the functional and allocated baselines.

7. Assign identifiers to CIs and their associated configuration documentation, including version numbers where appropriate.

8. Ensure that the marking or labeling of items and documentation with their applicable identifiers enable correlation between the

CI, and other associated data. The documents that capture the functional and physical characteristics of the CI and the corresponding documentation will become part of the CI. The naming of those items should be consistent with that of the CI for easy association. For example, if the name of the documentation for a program PGM_XYZ is DOC_XYZ it will help in better correlation.

9. Ensure that applicable identifiers are embedded in the software and on its storage media. For example, the source code of the program named PGM_XYZ can contain the name PGM_XYZ. (Consider a COBOL program named PGM_XYZ; here the program name can be embedded in the source code as PROGRAM ID in the IDENTIFICATION DIVISION.)

Impact of configuration item selection

Poor CI selection can adversely affect costs and scheduling and can become an unnecessary administrative and technical burden during and after software development. The number of CIs in a system is a design decision—a decision made by the people who design the SCM system. They are the people who decide which items should be brought under configuration control.

This process should be done carefully, because the selection of CIs needs to be correct: You should not select more nor less than what is necessary. But with the introduction of SCM tools, this issue—what items should be made into configuration items—is not very important. Modern tools can efficiently and effortlessly handle any number of CIs without any problems. So the problems and issues of CI selection are mainly applicable only to systems where the configuration management functions are performed manually.

Effects of selecting too many configuration items

Selection of too many CIs may result in hampered visibility and management rather than providing improved control. Instances of such difficulties can include the following:

▶ Increased administrative burden in preparing, processing, and reporting of changes, which tends to be proportional to the number of CIs.

▶ Increased development time and cost as well as potential creation of an inefficient design. When there are too many CIs, the documentation and other procedures increase and take valuable time that could be devoted to design and development. So too many CIs will result in increased development time. And once the concentration is shifted from design and development to maintaining the SCM records, the chances of creating an inefficient design arise.

▶ Potential increase in management effort, difficulties maintaining coordination, and unnecessary generation of requirements, design, test, and system specifications for each selected CI.

Effects of selecting too few configuration items

Too few CIs can result in costly logistics and maintenance difficulties, such as these:

▶ Loss of visibility down to the required level to effect maintenance or modification. For example, if CIs are chosen only at the module level, then maintaining a function in that module will be quite difficult, because finding the subroutine will be difficult as there will not be any records in that name. Because the CIs are defined only at the module level, only the modules will be visible.

▶ Difficulty in effectively managing the changes (for example, managing changes to individual items, which are part of a CI). If there are too few CIs, say, only at the module level, then check-in/check-out and change implementation will be difficult because check-out happens at the CI level and a lot of unwanted items will also need to be checked out, tested, verified, and checked back in.

Once again, readers are reminded of the fact that in projects using modern SCM tools the number of configuration items does not have a major impact because the tools can scale up or down to meet the requirements without any degradation in performance.

Baselines

As the CIs go through their development process, more and more components are developed until the final CIs are available for use. Generally, the life cycle process will first result in a set of requirements, then a design, then code for individual elements of the CI, and then integrated code with test cases and user manuals. The definition of SCM contains the concept of identifying the configuration of each CI at discrete points in time during the life cycle process, and then managing changes to those identified configurations.

The configuration of software at a discrete point in time is known as a *baseline*. Thus, a baseline is the documentation and software that make up a CI at a given point in its life cycle. It includes the user documentation (if any), the specifications document (or the document that contains the functional and physical characteristics), and software (if any) that make up the CI at a given point. Each baseline serves as a point of departure or reference for the next development stage. Baselines are usually established after each life cycle phase at the completion of the formal review that ends the phase. Thus we have the functional baseline, allocated baseline, product baseline, and so on. We saw an overview of this in Chapter 2, which was summarized in Figure 2.3.

Each baseline is subject to configuration control and must be formally updated (using the change management procedures) to reflect approved changes to the CI as it goes through the next development stage. At the end of a life cycle phase, the previous baseline and all approved changes to it become the new baseline for the next development stage. The term *baseline management* is often used to describe this control process.

Normally, the first baseline consists of an approved software requirements document and is known as the *functional baseline*. The functional baseline is the initial approved technical documentation for a configuration item [1]. Through the process of establishing a baseline, the functional and other requirements described in the requirements document become the explicit point of departure for software development, against which changes can be proposed, evaluated, implemented, and controlled. The functional baseline is usually the first established baseline in the SCM process. When the functional baseline is established at the conclusion of the requirements analysis phase of a project, the formal change control process commences. The functional baseline is also the basis against which the software is authenticated.

The *allocated baseline* is the initial approved specifications governing the development of configuration items that are part of a higher level configuration item [2]. The allocated baseline represents the next logical progression from the functional baseline and represents the link between the design process and the development process. The functional baseline describes the functions that the system should have. Then the software system is designed by allocating the various functions to various components or subsystems.

Based on the RDD (part of the functional baseline), the different functions of the software product are determined and during the design process these various functions—user interface, database operations, error handling, input data validation—are allocated to the various subsystems and components. This allocation of the different functionality happens during the design phase, and at the end of the design phase the allocated baseline is established where the components of the system would have their functionality assigned to them. So at the allocation baseline stage, the functionality defined in the functional baseline is allocated to CIs.

The *product baseline* represents the technical and support documentation established after successful completion of the functional configuration audit and physical configuration audit. The product baseline [3] is the initial approved technical documentation (including source code, object code, and other deliverables) defining a configuration item during the production, operation, maintenance, and logistic support of its life cycle.

According to Ben-Menachem [2], the process of establishing baselines describes the construction of the aggregates (the software system) from the components (the CIs). So the baselines also define how the aggregates must be constructed, what tools should be used, which parts are connected and which are not, what the nature of these interconnections is, and so on. As mentioned before, once the item is tied into a baseline, changes can be made only through the formal change management process. Thus baselines define the state of a system at a given point in time and the proper recording of this information is absolutely critical for the success of any project.

Configuration item selection

A software system is generally split into a number of CIs that are independently developed and tested, and then finally put together at the software system integration level. Each CI essentially becomes an independent entity as far as the SCM system is concerned, and the SCM functions are carried out on each CI. The division of the software into CIs may be contractually specified or may be done during the requirements analysis or preliminary design phase. As a general rule, a CI is established for a separable piece of the software system that can be designed, implemented, and tested independently. Some examples of items that are to be identified include project plan, requirements specifications, design documents, test plans and test data, program source codes, data, object code, executables, EPROMS, Media, make files, tools, user documentation, quality manual, and SCM plan.

Checklist for selection of configuration items

When a software project or system is broken down into components (the structural decomposition), we can create a sort of tree structure. The decomposition can be, say, project–modules–submodules–programs–functions–link libraries–icons and other small minor components and so on. Decomposition to this detail is neither necessary nor advisable because it will create many problems in managing the CIs and will create too many specifications and documentation. But if we reduce the number of CIs by limiting the system decomposition to, say, the second level (module level), it will result in poor visibility of the overall design and development requirements.

The number of CIs is determined by the system granularity desired by the SCM system's designers. The granularity decides the level of decomposition of the software system. There are no hard and fast rules here. It varies from project to project and is a decision that has to be made by the SCM system development team. But as mentioned before with the focus on SCM tools, this is no longer an important issue.

We have seen that there are no hard and fast rules when choosing CIs, but the following questions can be used as a guide when doing so:

1. Is the item critical/high risk and/or a safety item?

2. Would the item's failure or malfunction adversely affect security, human safety, or the accomplishment of a mission, or have significant financial implications?

3. Is the item individual and can it be designed, developed, and tested as a stand-alone unit?

4. Is the item newly developed? For example, a system or subsystem might be developed to add certain requested enhancements.

5. Does the item incorporate new technologies?

6. Is the item highly complex or does it have stringent performance requirements? For instance, does the item have complicated algorithms or does it need to meet the stringent performance requirement such as having a small footprint?

7. Does the item encapsulate interfaces with other software items that currently exist or are provided by other organizations?

8. Is the item installed on a different computer platform from other parts of the system?

9. Does it interface with other CIs whose configuration is controlled by other entities, for example, a system that interfaces with an off-the-shelf package?

10. Is it likely to be subject to modification or upgrading during its service life? Is the item subject to modification at a rate that is much higher than that of the other items? For example, consider an interface that reads data from some external source. Every time the external source changes (assuming that data formats will be subject to frequent changes) the item has to be modified.

11. Is it likely that the item will be reused?

12. Is there a requirement to know the exact configuration and status of changes made to an item during its service life? This refers to the criticality of the item. Some items in a system are critical or more important than others. So project management will necessarily be more interested in those types of items.

If the majority of these questions can be answered "no," the item should probably not be a CI. If the majority of questions can be answered "yes," the item should probably be a CI. But there are no hard and fast rules and no magic formulas to help in CI selection. *The bottom line is that selection of CIs is a management decision based on experience and good judgment.*

Designation: Naming of configuration items

Each software component must be uniquely identified. According to IEEE [3], the identification methods could include naming conventions and version numbers and letters. The identification system or the naming convention should facilitate the storage, retrieval, tracking, reproduction, and distribution of the CIs. A good naming system will make it possible to understand the relationship between the CIs from their names.

A good naming system uses numbers or alphabets to represent the position of the CI in the hierarchy. For example, an item labeled 1.4 is definitely created after an item with the label 1.2 and before one with the label 1.6. Note that the number is only a part of the name—the time-related part that changes when the item undergoes revisions. The other part of the name, which defines the item, is usually derived from the project or system and the type of the item and the item name. It can be a simple name such as "PGMPAY" indicating that it is the payroll calculation program named PGMPAY or it can be a composite name like "PRJ_MOD_PGM_SRC_PGMPAY" indicating the project, module, CI type, and name. The decision on the complexity and detail of the names will depend on the size and complexity of the project.

One important thing to remember is that the naming system should be developed in such a way that the derived names do not produce duplicates, because this can create chaos and confusion. For large and complex projects that have thousands of CIs the naming system is usually quite detailed to facilitate easy identification and tracking. As we have seen, the name part of the identification system will remain constant over time for each item, whereas the number part will undergo changes.

Configuration item description

Software components are described in specifications (i.e., software requirements specifications, software architectural design specifications, software detailed design specifications, interface control documents, and software product specifications). The description of the component becomes more detailed as the design and development proceeds through the life cycle. The description forms the basis for configuration control and configuration status accounting. The description is also the basis for the configuration audits and reviews, which ensure that the software is complete and verified. The documents or portions of documents that describe each CI must be identified and made part of the CI.

Acquisition of configuration items

The last activity of the configuration identification function is the acquisition of the CIs for configuration control. This means that the controlled items, both intermediate and final outputs (source code, executable, user documentation, design documents, databases, test plans, test cases, test data, project plan, SCM plan, etc.), and the elements of the environment (such as compilers, operating systems, and tools) should be acquired and stored in a controlled environment (controlled software libraries) so that they can be retrieved and reproduced when required. IEEE [3] specifies that for each such library the format, location, documentation requirements, receiving and inspection requirements, and access control procedures must be specified. Once the CIs are acquired and placed in the controlled library, the configuration control procedures will apply to them.

Conclusion

Configuration identification is the process of selecting the configuration items for a system and recording their functional and physical characteristics in technical documentation. We have seen why it is important to select the configuration items, how to select them, and how to establish baselines. Configuration identification is one of the important phases of

SCM because it decides the level of granularity or detail to which SCM will be performed in a project.

References

[1]   *IEEE Standard Glossary of Software Engineering Terminology* (IEEE Std-610-1990), *IEEE Standards Collection (Software Engineering)*, Piscataway, NJ: IEEE, 1997.

[2]   Ben-Menachem, M., *Software Configuration Guidebook*, London: McGraw-Hill International, 1994.

[3]   *IEEE Standard for Software Configuration Management Plans* (IEEE Std-828-1998), Piscataway, NJ: IEEE, 1998.

Selected bibliography

Berlack, H. R., *Software Configuration Management*, New York: John Wiley & Sons, 1992.

Dart, S., "Concepts in Configuration Management Systems," Technical Report, Software Engineering Institute, Carnegie-Mellon University, 1994.

Feiler, H. P., "Software Configuration Management: Advances in Software Development Environments," Technical Paper, Software Engineering Institute, Carnegie-Mellon University, 1990.

Quality Management—Guidelines for Configuration Management, ISO 10007:1995(E), Geneva, International Standards Organization, 1995.

Magnusson, B. (Ed.), *System Configuration Management: ECOOP'98 SCM-8 Symp. Proc.*, Berlin: Springer-Verlag, 1998.

Configuration control

Introduction

IEEE [1] defines *configuration control* as an element of configuration management, consisting of the evaluation, coordination, approval or disapproval, and implementation of changes to configuration items after formal establishment of their configuration identification. So once the configuration items of a project or system have been identified, the next step is to bring in some degree of control. Restrictions have to be implemented and rules regarding who can do what to these configuration items have to be formulated. This aspect of SCM is handled by the configuration control function or the "change management and control system."

Changes to all items identified in the configuration identification phase—configuration items (CIs)—should be controlled. To properly control change, procedures have to be established, guidelines have to be implemented, roles and authorities have to be defined, and all workflow processes of the change management system—change identification, change requisition, change approval/disapproval, change implementation, testing, and so on—have to be designed, documented, and implemented. How these procedures and guidelines apply to the different configuration items such as source code, documents, specifications, third-party software, and subcontracted items also has to be established. These activities fall under the purview of configuration control.

Of the SCM functions, configuration control is the one that is performed most often. Configuration identification, as we saw in the previous chapter, is done only once at the beginning of the SCM implementation. Status accounting, that is, recording and reporting of the SCM activities, is done on a regular basis. Configuration audits are performed when a configuration is complete or before a system is released. But the configuration control activities have to be done whenever a change request is initiated. Requests for changes will be quite frequent during the software development phase and after the system is released. Requests for new features, functional enhancements, and bug and defect reports can all initiate a change.

The different activities of configuration control lend themselves to automation. For example, all activities from change initiation to change disposition can be easily automated. Thus configuration control is one SCM function that can be automated very efficiently and effectively. In fact, it is imperative that one use some sort of change management tool, because except in the case of very small single-person projects, change management and control is too repetitive, monotonous, and hence more prone to error and not worth the effort for manual processing. Many software tools are available, covering almost all available platforms and development environments, that can be used to automate configuration control. In fact it was one of the first functions of configuration management that was automated, which is evident from the number of change management tools available on the market.

Configuration control is not an easy task. It involves a lot of people and a lot of procedures, making it difficult to manage. The configuration control activities will increase as the project evolves, because more and more items will undergo change, more and more people will be inducted, requirements will change, new modules and subsystems will be added, different versions will have to be maintained, and so on. However, if designed intelligently, planned properly, and supported well by a good software tool it can be an easy if not exciting task.

Change

Change is one of the most fundamental characteristics in any software development process. All phases of the software development process from requirements analysis to production or maintenance are always subject to change. Making changes to software is easy. In fact, it is one of best features of software—that it can be changed at will. But if changes are made at will, without any proper planning, chaos will result. Making changes is easy; managing those changes—the uncontrolled changes—is not, because there is no way of knowing what was changed and hence what to manage.

Software development is a continuously evolving process. You cannot freeze one phase of software development and then go to the next phase. Even though early development models like the waterfall model were developed based on the compartmentalization of the various phases, the real-life situation is quite different. You cannot freeze analysis and go to design and freeze design and then go to development. A great deal of overlap occurs between these phases. This is because software development is a complex process that involves many variables, all of which can change. Changes to the requirements drive the design, and the design changes affect the code. Testing then uncovers problems that result in further changes, which might force us to return to the requirements phase. So change is something that cannot be avoided. Managing the change process is a complex but essential task.

Change and configuration control

Change is inevitable during the software development life cycle. Changes to the software come from both external and internal sources. External changes originate from users, from evolution of operational environments, from improvements in technology, and so on. Internal changes come from improved designs and methods, from incremental development, from correction of errors, and so on. A properly implemented configuration control process is the project manager's best friend and provides potential salvation when coping with change.

Configuration control (or change management and control) is thus the process of evaluating, coordinating, and deciding on the disposition of proposed changes to the CIs, and implementing the approved changes to baselined software and associated documentation and data. The change control process ensures that changes that have been initiated are classified and evaluated, approved or disapproved, and that those that are approved are implemented, documented, tested, verified, and incorporated into a new baseline.

Configuration control is the set of techniques used to ensure that the components in a system achieve and maintain a definite structure (where the relationships between the components are established) throughout the system life cycle. To this end, change management and control provide the necessary procedures, documentation, and organizational structure to make sure that all items identified in the configuration identification phase, the details of the changes made to them, and other related information are available to all who need to see it (or have the necessary authority) throughout the system life cycle. In other words, configuration control provides the necessary mechanism to orchestrate change—but in a controlled manner.

Problems of uncontrolled change

We have seen that uncontrolled or unmanaged change can create problems serious enough to create project failures. In its mildest forms, these changes can create confusion and chaos. Change management and control solves the four most common (and dangerous) software development/maintenance problems: communications breakdown, shared data, multiple maintenance, and simultaneous update problems.

In any development environment, the same code, say a program, function, or subroutine, is often shared by different programmers. This sharing of common items—source code or data or documentation—reduces development costs because it avoids the problem of reinventing the wheel. If a function or a program or a component library that suits one's needs is already available, then it is prudent to use it, rather than coding it again. Similarly in the case of documentation, such as RDD or SDD, the entire project uses the same document. So what is wrong with sharing data, code, or documents? As long as nobody makes any changes to these shared items, there are no problems. But if changes are made to any shared item without a proper control mechanism trouble can arise. We have already discussed these problems in detail in Chapter 3.

In the case of a properly implemented change management system, all changes made to the components of a software system are made after proper analysis and review. Because changes can be made only with proper authorization and the authorization is done by a separate entity that is responsible for managing the changes to all the items, the chances of effort getting duplicated or two people solving the same problem in isolation do not occur. Also the problem of one person overwriting another person's efforts also does not occur because the changes are made to items that are stored in a controlled environment, where records of who is making change to what items are kept. So if a person is making some changes on some item, then that fact is known to all the people in the project. Also the information regarding a change is reported to all concerned. Thus a good change management system solves the above-mentioned software problems and can bring discipline into the development process and improve the development productivity, because a lot of time that would otherwise be spent on debugging and reworking can be saved. The following sections describe how this is accomplished.

Configuration control

We have seen the dangers and problems of unmanaged and uncontrolled changes. So how do we to avoid them? We should have a good change management and control system. The system should define a process and the necessary procedures to ensure that all events—from the identification of a change to its implementation and baselining—are done in a systematic, scientific, and efficient manner (i.e., following the SCM principles).

To make this happen procedures should be established for requesting a change once the need has been identified and people authorized to decide whether the requested change needs to be implemented. Once the decision to implement the change has been made, a mechanism should be in place for analyzing which other resources are impacted by the proposed change and then assigning the task of effecting the change to the resource (and if necessary to any impacted resources). The necessary facilities to test, verify, and validate the changed resources also need to be in place; or, in other words, the changed function or program needs to be tested, verified, and approved so that it can be incorporated or promoted as the new version.

An orderly change process is necessary to ensure that only approved changes are implemented into any baselined document or software. Figure 8.1 shows a simple overview of the change management and control process. The steps mentioned here are very generic and will vary from one company to another and even from one project to another.

The steps within the overall process can be grouped into the following categories:

1. Change initiation;

2. Change classification;

3. Change evaluation or change analysis;

4. Change disposition;

5. Change implementation;

6. Change verification; and

7. Baseline change control.

These seven steps in change control are individually discussed in the following sections. But if one is using a change management tool or SCM tool, then most of these processes will be done automatically. For example, the change requisition, verification of the details, assignment of CR numbers, intimation of the change request evaluators, intimation of the change control board members, voting on the change request, informing the result, and so on, could be done automatically. But we first look at how configuration control is done manually.

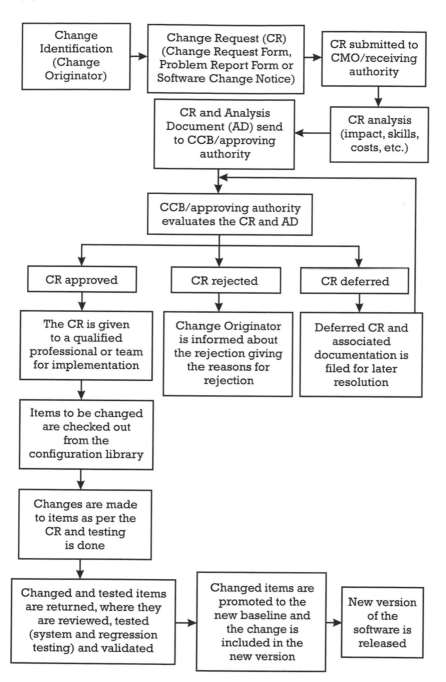

Figure 8.1 Overview of change management and control process.

Change initiation

Requests for change to software and documents come from many sources. A change request (CR) can be submitted by the developer, a member of the QA team, a reviewer, or a user. Each project should set up a CR form for documenting the proposed change and its disposition. Sometimes a change request is also called a problem report (PR) or a software change notice (SCN).

Problem reports are a special kind of change request where the cause of the change is a defect or bug in the system. We will discuss problem reports later in the chapter. But problem reports necessitate change, so the procedures for resolving the problem reports and for requesting an enhancement or a new product feature are the same. Figure 8.2 shows a sample CR form. The sample contains the basic information that should be included in a CR/PR/SCN form; however, the actual form for a particular project must correspond to the planned SCM process. Note that electronic forms, containing the same information, are being increasingly used as direct interfaces to SCM support tools.

Each project should also name an individual—the configuration management officer (CMO) or a member of the SCM team—to receive the CR form, assign it a tracking number and classification, and route it for processing. This person receives the CR and reviews it for clarity and completeness. If the CR is not complete, it is returned to the originator. Once complete, the CR is assigned a unique identifier for tracking purposes and the information about the CR is recorded in the change request tracking database or files.

Change classification

Changes to software and associated documentation are classified according to the impact of the change and the approval authority needed. Depending on the criticality, impact, and cost involved, there will be a hierarchy of people who can approve the changes. At the top of the hierarchy is the change control board or CCB, which is discussed in more detail later in this chapter. Major changes need the approval of the CCB, whereas minor changes can be done with the approval of the CMO or a designated SCM team member. The exact mechanism of the change classification and the approval should be defined in the SCM plan. (See Chapter 11 for more on SCM plans.)

CHANGE REQUEST

CR No.: _____

Analysis Document No.: _____

System/project: _____ Item to be changed: _____

Classification: Enhancement / Bug fixing / Other: _____

Priority: Immediate / Urgent / As soon as possible / Desirable

Change Description:

Status		Date	By	Remarks
Initiated				
Received				
Analyzed				
Action (A / R / D)*				
Assigned				
Check-out				
Modified and tested				
Reviewed				
Approved				
Check-in				
Baselined				

Figure 8.2   Sample change request form.

The changes are classified into different categories with different priorities. Classification methods can be based on severity or importance or impact or cost involved and so on. For example, a change request for fixing a bug that could result in system failure will have higher priority than a request for a cosmetic change. A functional enhancement request that comes from a user may not be in the same category as a change request from a member of the development team. But the classification criteria (how to classify a change) should be spelled out very clearly in the SCM plan.

The individual who proposes the change may suggest a classification for that change. The CMO or the receiving authority reviews suggested classes and assigns a working/tentative classification. After assessment of the impact of the CR, the CCB or the approving authority will assign the final class.

Change evaluation/analysis

One important aspect of the configuration control process is that it provides adequate analysis of changes in terms of impact to system functionality, interfaces, utility, cost, schedule, and contractual requirements. Each change should also be analyzed for impact on software safety, reliability, maintainability, transportability, and efficiency. The project CMO routes the CR to the software engineering staff for evaluation.

In some cases, project procedures require that the CR be screened before it is analyzed. Some change requests will not have any chance of approval due to some considerations (costs or schedules) of which the change initiator may not be aware. In some cases, management may decide not to take any action in the case of changes that fall into some category or meet some predefined criteria. This information might not be or need not be communicated to all the people involved in the project. So when such CRs—the CRs that do not have any chance of approval are submitted—they will get rejected in the preevaluation screening. This approach saves the cost of analysis for changes that do not have any chance of approval.

The analysis produces documentation (like that shown in Figure 8.3), which describes the changes that will have to be made to implement the CR, the CIs and documents that will have to be changed, and the resources required to effect the change. This documentation becomes part of the change package, along with the CR. After completion of the analysis, the change package is sent to the CCB.

Change disposition

Disposition of changes to baselined items are usually done by a CCB. The CCB evaluates the desirability of a change versus the cost of the change, as described in the documentation of the analysis. The CCB may approve, disapprove, or defer a change request. Sometimes the CCB may have to request more information and additional analysis.

Items for which decisions have been made are sent to the CMO for action. Rejected items are sent to the originator along with the CCB's

Change Analysis Document

No.: _____

CR No.: _____

Date: _____

System/project: _____   Item to be analyzed: _____

Analyzed by: _____

┌───┐
│ Implementation alternatives: │
│   │
│   │
│   │
│   │
└───┘

Items affected

Item ID	Item description	Version no.	Nature of change

Estimated effort: _____

Impact on schedule: _____

Impact on cost: _____

┌───┐
│ Recommendation: │
│   │
│   │
│   │
└───┘

Figure 8.3   Sample change analysis document.

rationale for rejection. CRs needing further analysis are sent back to the analysis group with the CCB's questions attached. Deferred CRs are filed, to be sent back to the board at the proper time.

Remember that in all cases the CCB may not be the change approving/disapproving authority. In some cases the project leader, the CMO, or any other designated person could make the decision. The exact mechanism of change disposition varies from one organization to another and will be usually documented in the SCM plan.

The CMO sends approved items to the development team. The CMO also prepares and distributes the meeting minutes and records the current status of the CR. This information is added to the tracking database or recorded in files.

Today, with the use of change management tools, physical CCB meetings are rare. In today's development environment, e-mail or some other messaging system connects everybody in the organization. So it is possible to hold CCB meetings without the CCB members actually meeting. The change requests and the necessary information (such as evaluation reports and impact analysis reports) can be sent electronically to all CCB members, and the CCB members can convey their responses in the same way. Thus today it is possible to hold virtual CCB meetings and have on-line voting on change requests. The SCM tools take care of all the technological issues, thus making change disposition and management an easy task.

Change implementation

Approved CRs are either used directly as a change authorization form or result in a change directive being prepared by the CMO. In either case, approval results in the issuance of instructions that authorize and direct the implementation of the change in the software and associated documentation.

The development team schedules the resources to make the change. It must get official copies of the baselined component to be changed from the program library. For code changes, design has to be developed, code has to be written, and testing has to be done and the correctness of the change verified. Moreover, the associated documentation has to be revised to reflect the change. Once the change has been made and local testing completed, the revised component and documents are returned to the control of the program library. After verification, the new version takes its place in the sequence of baselines.

Change verification

The implemented changes, which have been tested at the unit level, must be verified at the system level. This may require the rerun of tests specified in the test plan or the development of additional test plans. Regression testing will usually have to be included in the test to ensure that errors have not been introduced in existing functions by the change. Once the verification is complete, the reviewing team submits evidence of it to the program library, which will then accept the changed items for inclusion in the SCM controlled files that make up the new version of the baseline.

After the successful implementation and testing of the change described in the CR, the CMO will record the occurrence of this process into the change request tracking database or files. Also something called a *change history* (or *patch history*) is maintained. The change history is a recording of the events that occurred to an item from the state before change to the one after. The details to be incorporated include (but are not limited to) name of the originator and receiving authority, date received, analysis done by, date of analysis, approving authority's name, date, names of the persons who effected the change, testing, review and audit, reasons for change, and a short description of change.

If an SCM or change management tool is used, then the process of recording the change implementation information, the task of changing the status of the change request, and so on do not have to be done manually. All of these activities will be taken care of by the tool. As mentioned before the tools capture all the information as and when the events are happening and will record them automatically. So details such as when the change was initiated, when it was evaluated, when it was reviewed, who initiated the change, who reviewed it, who approved it, when the implementation started, when it was finished, who performed the implementation, and so on will automatically be captured by the tool. So in a project where the SCM tools are used the above-mentioned activities (the activities that are performed by the CMO or SCM team members in a manual SCM system) are done automatically and without human intervention.

Baseline change control

Changes to software are not complete until the code and data changes have been implemented and tested and the changes to associated documentation have been made and all of the changes verified. To minimize the number of versions and the frequency of delivery of software components, changes to software are usually grouped into releases. Product release is the act of making a product available to its intended customers [2]. Each release contains software and documentation that has been tested and controlled as a total software system.

There are other reasons for product releases. One would be to satisfy a customer by customizing a software system to meet the specific needs of that customer. This is called a *customer-specific release*. For properly incorporating emergency fixes (a fix that was done without following any change management procedures due to the urgency of the problem or situation), a release might be made after the emergency fix has been properly incorporated. Alpha and beta releases are also used for alpha and beta testing.

Companies also do major and minor releases. Major releases are done when there is a significant increase in the product's functionality, whereas minor releases are done when the release is to correct a bug or fault in the program or system. The decision on the when and how of the releases is usually made by the CCB because it is the ultimate authority for making decisions about configuration control and is represented by all functions of the organization.

File-based versus change-based change management

In a file-based change management system, to make a change the change initiator identifies the file he wants to change and initiates the change management process. The change request is then analyzed, the impacted files are identified during the change request evaluation phase, and the decision to approve or reject the change request is made. If the change request is approved then the file (or files if more than one file is impacted) is checked out and the necessary changes are made to it. Then the file is tested, verified, and checked in. So if there is more than one file for the same change request then they are not associated with one another except for what is recorded in the evaluation report.

The major drawback of the file-based system is that it fails to capture the relationships between the items that are changed due to a change request. In real life, a typical change is rarely limited to a single file; in most cases more than one file needs to be changed to implement a change request. But the problem with a file-based change management system is that once the files are checked in there is no way to determine which files were modified as a result of a particular change request. Yes, the person who has implemented the change might know or there might be some informal records somewhere. But there are no formal methods to track all the files that were modified in response to a single change or change request. This creates a lot of problems because people often forget the details of all the files they changed and often forget to include some of them during the system building, resulting in build failures.

To avoid the drawbacks of file-based change management, SCM practitioners started to use change-based change management. In this system all the files required to perform a task or to implement a change request are considered to be a single entity. Here we are tracking logical changes rather than individual file changes. But the technology of making all the files of a change request into a single logical unit is not new. Some mainframe systems tracked changes in this manner as early as the 1970s, and companies such as IBM, Control Data Corporation, Unisys, and Tandem have used logical-change-based software tracking systems for years [3]. In 1983, SMDS (now True Software) released Aide-de-Camp as the first commercial SCM system that tracked logical changes rather than physical file changes [4].

Since then many commercial SCM systems have added the ability to track logical changes rather than individual file changes, including Continuus/CM from Continuus Software Corporation, CCC/Harvest from Platinum Technology, and ClearGuide (ClearCase) from PureAtria. SCM tools like Merant's PVCS and StarBase's StarTeam have the ability to mark a source code change with the corresponding defect report or enhancement request.

The method of tracking software by units of logical change is a more logical and practical model because the items that are changed because of a single change request are logically linked. They are checked out together, they are tested together, they are reviewed and approved as a group, and checked in and promoted together. According to Weber [5], not all SCM systems use the same name for the logical unit of change. For example, ADC/Pro uses the term "change set," CCC/Harvest uses "package," Continuus/CM uses "task," ClearGuide uses "activity," PCMS uses "work package," and StarTeam uses "subproject."

Also not all SCM systems implement the ability to track changes in the same way. Two very different implementations have emerged—

change sets and change packages. Systems that treat a logical change as the individual lines of code typically refer to the unit of change as a *change set*. Systems that treat a logical change as the set of file versions that contain the code changes are called *change packages*. A detailed discussion on change sets and change packages is not intended in this chapter. But the reader is referred to the following documents to get a comprehensive idea about change sets and change packages:

1. Burrows, C., S. Dart, and G. W. George, *Ovum Evaluates: Software Configuration Management*, London: Ovum Limited, 1996.

2. Cagan, M., and D. W. Weber, "Task-Based Software Configuration Management: Support for 'Change Sets' in Continuus/CM," Technical Report, Continuus Software Corporation, 1996.

3. Weber, D. W., "Change Sets Versus Change Packages: Comparing Implementation of Change-Based SCM," *Proc. 7th Software Configuration Management Conf. (SCM7)*, Boston, MA, May 1997, pp. 25–35.

4. Weber, D. W., "Change-based SCM Is Where We're Going," Technical Report, Continuus Software Corporation, 1997.

Escalation and notification

Escalation can be defined as the process of increasing the intensity or magnitude of an issue. In the change management process, there are times when issues need escalation. For example, consider a change request for which the evaluation report was forwarded to all CCB members for their decision. If a CCB member has not conveyed a decision within the specified time period, then the person has to be reminded about it. But if, even after the reminder, nothing happens, then the issue has to be brought to the attention of the senior member of the CCB, so that necessary corrective action can be initiated.

The escalation process is equally applicable for most of the change management processes such as change evaluations, impact analysis, and change implementation. Also we have seen that the change requests can be accepted, rejected, or deferred. In the case of deferred change requests, a time period can be set after which it has to be revisited. So once the specified time is over, the change request is again reviewed. This process of keeping track of the deferred change requests and then bringing them back for review is another form of escalation.

Today's change management tools are capable of performing problem escalation and notification automatically based on predefined rules and criteria. For example, the change management tools could be programmed to escalate an issue (like failure to convey the decision on a change request) after a specified number of days. Multiple levels of escalation are also possible. For example, if the CCB member fails to respond to the reminders, then the issue could be escalated to her superior and if there is still no action after a specified period, the next person in the organizational hierarchy could be informed about the issue. Here the levels of escalation, the time period before escalation, the people who are to be informed, and so on can be predefined and the tools will do the rest. This is an important aspect that will improve the efficiency and productivity of the SCM team because they do not have to keep track of each and every change request; the tools will automatically perform the necessary actions when something is not happening according to the rules and schedules.

Emergency fixes

Some change requests or problem reports need immediate action and will not allow enough time to follow all change management and control procedures. For example, an emergency request from a client or a distress call from a customer cannot wait for the change evaluation, CCB meeting, change disposition, and so on. Efforts to correct these difficulties are referred to as *emergency fixes*. These are not change management processes in the conventional sense, because the sole focus of an emergency fix is to resolve the customer's difficulties right away. The most important distinction is that these emergency fixes invalidate the version of the component that they fix because these are temporary measures taken when there is not enough time or resources to process them in the proper manner. When time permits, these emergency fixes will be undone and the changes will be implemented following the proper change management procedures.

Problem reporting and tracking

We have seen how the change management and control process works, starting with the initiation of the change request and the subsequent processing to effect the change. A change request can result from many things. It can be the result of a user needing a new feature, it can be the result of some enhancements of the existing functionality, or it can be due to an anomaly in the software system. An anomaly is any condition that deviates from expectations based on requirements specifications, design documents, user documents, and so on or someone's perceptions or experiences. Anomalies may be found during, but not limited to, the review, test, analysis, compilation, or use of software products or applicable documentation [6]. In common usage the terms *error, fault, flaw, gripe, glitch, defect, problem,* and *bug* are used to express the same meaning. In this section we deal with problem reports (PRs) or software problem reports (SPRs). The SPR or PR is a type of change request—a request that is the result of an anomaly in the system.

Problem reports and change requests

A SPR usually will get more and immediate attention than a CR because it is the result of a problem and the problem has to be fixed. It is not some cosmetic change that can wait. Also a single SPR can create or result in more than one CR. This is because a problem or bug (for example, navigation not working properly) can be the result of faults in two different subsystems that require different skills to fix and thus need two different persons or teams to do the job. Also it might be better to keep the two subsystems separate if there are no direct relationships or dependencies between the two. So it is quite possible that a PR or SPR can initiate more than one CR.

We saw that SPRs can result in one or more CRs. In the author's opinion, the disposition of a fault or problem report should follow the same process as that of the enhancement requests once the CRs associated with the PR has been created. Or in other words, the processing of the problem report and the enhancement request become the same. But in the case of a problem report, before the creation of the CR and after the change management process is set into motion, some activities need to done. These activities are intended to prevent the same type of mistakes from recurring and also to create a knowledge base of the anomalies. Figure 8.4 shows the problem reporting and tracking process.

Problem identification

We know that a problem, bug, or defect can go undetected and can remain in the software system. It is not possible to say that a software system is 100% defect free. What we should do is try to reduce the number of defects in a system and, more importantly, reduce the number of critical defects. We know about the existence of a defect when something goes wrong, or when the system starts misbehaving, or when the performance of the system is not what it is supposed to be, or when the system stops performing, and so on.

Once the problem is identified it should be reported and fixed and the fixed version should be reviewed, approved, and baselined. So the first

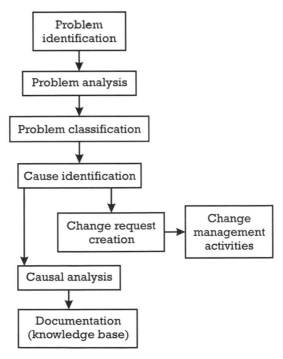

Figure 8.4 Problem reporting and tracking process.

step after the detection of an anomaly or defect is to report it. Figure 8.5 shows a problem report form. Problem reports are usually handled by the SCM team, so the problem report is also received by the CMO or a representative of the SCM team. Once the problem report is received, it is checked for clarity and completeness and if the necessary details are specified, the problem report is assigned a PR number. This number serves as the identifier for the problem report.

Once the problem is known and the report is received, the report is given to qualified professionals (people from the project team or QA department who have the necessary technical knowledge of the system and the problem analysis methodologies) for analysis. These people will analyze the problem with the objective of determining the severity of the problem, its nature, its impact, the cause, the category, place of origin, the items affected, cost, time, and skills required for fixing the problem. The analysis will also classify the defect (based on its seriousness and impact) and will create the CRs for fixing the problem. As we have mentioned before, a PR can result in more than one CR.

The analysis team will report their findings in the problem analysis document. Figure 8.6 shows a sample problem analysis document. This document forms the basis of causal analysis, which is discussed later in this chapter. The CRs that are created as a result of the problem analysis are processed as discussed in the previous sections.

Problem Report

PR No.: _____

Analysis Document No.: _____

System/project: _____

Place where the problem occurred: _____

Problem description:

Received by: _____   Date: _____

Figure 8.5   Sample problem report form.

Problem Analysis Document

No.: _____

PR No.: _____

Date: _____

System/project: _____

Analyzed by: _____

Severity: Critical / Fatal / Non-fatal / Cosmetic

Classification: _____

Cause of the problem:

Items affected

Item ID	Item description	Version no.	Nature of change

Impact on cost: _____   Time: _____

Skills required in fixing the problem: _____

Implementation alternatives:

Recommendation:

CR(s) created: _____

Figure 8.6   Sample problem analysis report.

Defect classification

The classification of a defect is dependent on the phase in which it occurs. The following is a general classification of defects during the various phases of a project.

Requirements analysis

▶ *Incorrect requirements.* This occurs when a requirement or part of it is incorrect. This may result from a misunderstanding of the user expectations.

▶ *Undesirable requirements.* The requirement stated is correct but not desirable due to technical feasibility, design, or implementation cost considerations.

▶ *Requirements not needed.* The user does not need the stated functionality or feature. Adding this requirement does not significantly increase the utility of the project.

▶ *Inconsistent requirements.* The requirement contradicts some other requirement.

▶ *Ambiguous/incomplete requirements.* The requirement or part of it is ambiguous. It is not possible to implement the stated requirement.

▶ *Unreasonable requirements.* The requirement cannot be implemented due to cost, hardware, or software considerations.

▶ *Standards violation.* The standards set for analysis have not been followed.

Design phase

Design defects may relate to data definition, the user interface, the module interface, or processing logic. Each of these may be incorrect, incomplete, inconsistent, inefficient, undesirable, or violate standards.

Coding and testing phase

Coding and testing defects may relate to logic, boundary conditions, exception handling, performance, documentation, standards violations, and so on.

The above classifications are very general and depending on the nature of the project and degree of detail required, a defect classification system should be designed for each project.

Defect severity

Severity of a defect is a measure of the impact of the defect. During the analysis, design, and coding phases the defects might be classified as follows:

▶ Major defects, which have substantial impact on several processes or subsystems. The correction activity involves changing the design of more than one process or subsystem.

▶ Minor defects that impact only one process or subsystem. The correction activity will be local to that process or subsystem.

▶ Suggestions toward improvements.

During the testing phase the defects may be classified as follows:

▶ *Critical.* These are fatal errors that cause system failure.

▶ *Fatal.* These are fatal errors that result in erroneous output.

▶ *Nonfatal.* These are errors that are not fatal but will affect the performance or smooth functioning of the system.

▶ *Cosmetic.* Minor errors like cryptic error messages, or typos in messages or screens or user documentation, and so on.

During problem analysis, the analysis team classifies the defect and decides on its severity and these findings are recorded in the problem analysis document.

Defect prevention

The primary objective of the problem report is to identify the fault and fix it. The problem analysis and CR generation and change management process achieve this. The secondary objective (maybe one that is more critical in a long-term perspective) is to prevent faults from recurring. This area of problem identification and tracking is called *defect prevention.*

One of the main methods of defect prevention is causal analysis. The other method is the creation of a knowledge base that contains the classified and categorized defects, so that a programmer or designer can browse the knowledge base before he starts the analysis, design, or development, so that he can be forewarned of the problems that could occur.

Causal analysis

The objective of causal analysis is to analyze defects and problems to determine and record the cause and initiate corrective actions so that the defects will not occur again. The primary document or the basis of the causal analysis is the problem analysis document. This document contains the causes of the defects, where they occurred, the severity, and so on.

By studying the analysis reports, the person doing the causal analysis will be able to come up with cause patterns. For example, some of the causes for the defects are insufficient input during the analysis stage, inadequate standards, inadequate skill levels, lack of training, lack of documentation, lack of communication, oversight, and inappropriate methodology or tools. For example, in a project if the causal analysis reveals that the reason for most of the defects is lack of knowledge of a tool that is used to generate the code, the team members can be given training on the tool so that the problem can be prevented. Thus causal analysis plays an important role in defect prevention.

Defect knowledge base and help desks

When a problem analysis document is submitted, it should result in the creation of CRs and problems being fixed. It will also form the basis of causal analysis. Its contents should also find their way into the defect knowledge base—a knowledge base that stores defects in an organized way, classified and categorized. This knowledge base should have a search facility where one can search for defects by category, phase of origin, cause, severity, and so on. The details about the defects such as the project, the defect description, the cause, the solution, how it was fixed, and so on should be in the knowledge base.

This knowledge base will be of tremendous value because it will serve as a road map and guidebook for analysts, designers, programmers, and people who do the testing and maintenance. For analysts, designers, and programmers, it will serve as a guide in telling them what to do, what to avoid, what mistakes can happen, and so on. The people who do the testing can create better test cases and test data if they know about the defects that escaped testing and how that happened. People who do the problem fixing will find similar problems and can see how they were fixed. This information will be very useful for people who are managing the help desks and for the technical support team. Also as new problems get added to the system, it will become more and more comprehensive and its usefulness will increase.

Change control board

We have seen that once the configuration items are identified, acquired, and baselined they come under the purview of configuration control, and formal change control procedures come into effect. This means that once the items are brought into the SCM system, the changes to it are done through a formal change management process. We have seen the exact mechanism of this process in the previous sections.

We also saw that there should be a body for deciding what changes should be made to a configuration item, which change request should be rejected, and so on. This approving authority is called the change control board (CCB) also known as the change control authority (CCA). IEEE [1] defines CCB as a group of people responsible for evaluating and approving or disapproving proposed changes to configuration items and for ensuring implementation of approved changes.

CCB composition

The name change control board has the connotation of being a very bureaucratic setup with many people. The composition of the CCB can vary anywhere from a single person to a highly structured and very formal setup with many people. For example, in small projects, the project leader alone will perform all the functions of the CCB, but in the case of large projects like a defense project there will be a highly structured and formal CCB setup with well-defined procedures.

The composition, the nature of functioning (formal or informal), the number of people in the CCB, and so on depends on the complexity, size, and nature of the project. In some very large projects there can be multiple levels or hierarchies of CCBs (CCBs for handling different types of problems) or multiple CCBs (each dealing with a subsystem of the project). In some cases there can be a super CCB to coordinate the activities of the CCBs and to act as an arbitrator to solve conflicts between CCBs of equal status and authority.

But irrespective of the size and nature of the CCBs their function is the same—to control and manage change. To manage and control change in a software system, the CCB should be constituted with people who have knowledge about the system (its technical, managerial, and economic aspects) and the effect and consequences of their decisions on the system.

The CCB should contain a representative from the SCM group (preferably the CMO), representatives from the project team (project leader or his representative), QA group, company management, and marketing. In some cases the CCB must include the client's representatives. The members of the CCB should be senior people who can speak for their respective departments. Also there should be a provision by which the CCB can summon anybody (like the change initiator, or the person who conducted the analysis or some outside experts) if their presence is required for better decision making.

Functions of the CCB

As stated in the IEEE definition, the main function of the CCB is to evaluate and approve or disapprove the change requests and problem reports that have been initiated or filed. The CCB will also see to it that the approved changes are implemented in the correct manner. The change requests and problem reports are evaluated before submitting them to the CCB. This evaluation is necessary because it will save a lot of time and effort. Also there are some tasks that are better accomplished by a single person than a team. So the presubmission evaluation should be done by a qualified professional, who knows the subject well. Assigning the right person to this task is the duty of the CMO. The evaluation report along with the change request or problem report is submitted to the CCB.

The CCB is constituted by members who are quite senior and have other responsibilities and whose time is valuable. So speedy resolution of the issues is a must. To attain speedy resolution and better decision making, the facts should be presented to the CCB in a clear and concise manner. It is a good idea to circulate the agenda of the CCB meeting and the issues and the supporting documents to the members so that they can come prepared for the meeting. This is a task that has to be done by the

CMO. The CCB members will evaluate the requests for their technical feasibility, economical viability, impact on marketing, and other factors. Depending on the pros and cons, the committee will decide to approve, reject, or defer the change requests.

During the presubmission evaluation the focus of the analysis is on the impact of the program on other programs, the cost of implementation, skills required for implementing the change, the time required, and so on. During the CCB meeting, these factors, along with other issues such as how a particular change is going to affect the system release schedule, how the change will affect the marketing strategy, and how it will affect the quality of the system, will be evaluated. In other words, the CCB members will decide on each request looking at the overall picture.

For example, a change request if implemented will delay the system release; but it is a user interface change that the marketing department feels will improve the sales. So the CCB has to decide whether to delay the release for better sales or to go ahead with the release and incorporate the change request in the next version. So the decisions made in a CCB meeting are strategic in nature, even though a good technical understanding is necessary to make those decisions.

Functioning of the CCB

The CCB should have a chairman. Usually the CMO is given this post. But in some organizations, the members are assigned this post on a rotating basis. The CCB should meet at the intervals specified in the SCM plan. There should be a provision to call an emergency meeting if need arises. This is because certain change requests may require immediate action and cannot be delayed until the next scheduled CCB meeting.

The minimum number of people who can make a decision must also be specified. The rules for the functioning of the CCB should be formulated. How will the CCB decide on an issue? Is it by vote and if it is by vote what will be done in the case of a tie? These things should be specified in the SCM plan. If they are not specified in the SCM plan, then these issues should be addressed at the first meeting of the CCB.

Another important point is that all transactions that happen during the CCB meetings should be recorded. The minutes of the meeting should be circulated among the CCB members. The format and the style of the meeting minutes can be formal or informal, but they should contain at least the following information:

▶ Members present;

▶ Date of the meeting;

▶ Agenda of the meeting;

▶ Action taken report (ATR) by the CMO (status of the CRs and other SCM activities since the last CCB);

▶ Change requests (CR number and evaluation document number) discussed at the meeting;

▶ Discussion details and decisions;

▶ Other issues discussed, if any; and

▶ Distribution list.

The approved changes will be assigned to a qualified person or team for making the changes. If a CR is rejected, then the change initiator will be notified about the decision and the reasons for rejection. The initiator can resubmit the request or file an appeal, if she feels that the reasons are not satisfactory. The deferred change requests are filed for later dissuasion and the decision is conveyed to the initiator.

In the case of approved changes, the CCB will assign the task of implementing the change to someone or assign the change management process to the CMO. In such a situation, the CMO will assign the task to qualified person(s) and perform the necessary actions to complete the change management process (review, approve, promote, baseline). In the next meeting of the CCB, the CMO will present the ATR on the change requests that were approved and implemented.

As we saw earlier, with the growing popularity of SCM tools, which allow CCB meetings to be conducted electronically, the need for and importance of physical CCB meetings are decreasing.

Conclusion

We have seen what configuration control is, why it is needed, and how it is done. We saw the reasons for change and how a change is requested, processed, and implemented. We also saw the benefits of automating the change management process.

We also saw the problem reporting and tracking process and discussed a little about defect prevention. Strictly speaking, defect prevention does not come under the purview of SCM. But in the author's opinion, because it is closely related to SCM, the SCM team must perform these tasks.

An integral part of any configuration control system is the change control board (CCB). We saw the composition, functions, and working of the CCB.

We have seen that as change management and SCM tools become more and more popular, a lot of activities that were performed by the SCM team members are being automated. This automation will reduce the monotonous and repetitive nature of change management and will help make the configuration control function easier and improve development productivity because automation will allow people to concentrate more effort on developmental activities.

References

[1]   *IEEE Standard Glossary of Software Engineering Terminology* (IEEE Std-610-1990), *IEEE Standards Collection (Software Engineering)*, Piscataway, NJ: IEEE, 1997.

[2]   Bays, M. E., *Software Release Methodology*, Upper Saddle River, NJ: Prentice-Hall PTR, 1999.

[3]   Cagan, M., and D. W. Weber, "Task-Based Software Configuration Management: Support for 'Change Sets' in Continuus/CM," Technical Report, Continuus Software Corporation, 1996.

[4]   Burrows, C., S. Dart, and G. W. George, *Ovum Evaluates: Software Configuration Management*, London: Ovum Limited, 1996.

[5]   Weber, D. W., "Change Sets Versus Change Packages: Comparing Implementation of Change-Based SCM," *Proc. 7th Software Configuration Management Conf. (SCM7)*, Boston, MA, May 1997, pp. 25–35.

[6]   *IEEE Standard for Software Anomalies* (IEEE Std-1044-1993), *IEEE Standards Collection (Software Engineering)*, Piscataway, NJ: IEEE, 1997.

Selected bibliography

Berlack, H. R., *Software Configuration Management*, New York: John Wiley & Sons, 1992.

Ben-Menachem, M., *Software Configuration Management Guidebook*, New York: McGraw-Hill, 1994.

Davis, A. M., *201 Principles of Software Development*, New York: McGraw-Hill, 1995.

Humphrey, W. S., *Managing the Software Process*, New York: Addison-Wesley, 1989.

IEEE Standard for Software Configuration Management Plans (IEEE Std-828-1998), Piscataway, NJ: IEEE, 1998.

IEEE Standards Collection (Software Engineering) 1997, New York: IEEE, 1997.

"NASA Software Configuration Management Guidebook," Technical Report SMAP-GB-A201, NASA, 1995.

Pressman, R. S., *Software Engineering: A Practitioner's Approach*, New York: McGraw-Hill, 1997.

"Quality Management—Guidelines for Configuration Management," Technical Report No. ISO 10007:1995(E), Geneva, International Standards Organization, 1995.

"Software Configuration Management for Client/Server Development Environments: An Architecture Guide," White Paper, Intersolv, 1998.

Sommerville, I., *Software Engineering*, Reading, MA: Addison-Wesley, 1996.

Weber, D. W., "Change-based SCM Is Where We're Going," Technical Report, Continuus Software Corporation, 1997.

Whitgift, D., *Methods and Tools for Software Configuration Management*, Chichester, England: John Wiley & Sons, 1991.

Contents

Status accounting

Introduction

Configuration status accounting is an element of configuration management that consists of the recording and reporting of information needed to manage a software system and its characteristics effectively. This information includes a listing of approved configuration identifications, the status of proposed changes to the configuration, and the implementation status of approved changes [1]. In other words, the status accounting function is the recording and reporting of information needed to manage configuration items (CIs) effectively, including, but not limited to, a record of approved configuration documentation and identification numbers, the status of proposed changes, the implementation status of approved changes, and the build state of all units of the CIs.

A good status accounting system should be able to answer questions like these:

▶ What is the status of an item?

▶ Has a particular CR been approved? What is its status?

▶ What items were affected by a particular CR?

▶ When was the CR approved and who approved it?

▶ Who performed the change for a particular CR and when was it completed? Who reviewed it? Who approved it?

▶ Which version of an item implements an approved CR?

▶ What is different about a new version of a system?

▶ How many CRs are initiated each month and what is the approval rate?

▶ How many PRs are filed each month and what is the status of each of them?

▶ What are the major causes of the problems/defects?

The status accounting of the CIs can be compared with bank accounts, where each CI is an individual account. All transactions that happen to the CI and all activities that are performed on the CI are recorded. So individual transactions can then be tracked through each account as they occur.

Status accounting information gathering

The procedure of tracking the status of the CIs should be established early enough in the software development process to allow for data gathering. Also the system should be designed in such a way that the SCM activities will update the status accounting database rather than the person in charge of the status accounting function collecting the data regarding each and every change that is happening.

If control mechanisms are built into the process that make updating the status accounting database a prerequisite for further processing, the data in the database will be current and complete. For example, when a CR is initiated, that information is recorded in the database and if a check is made to ensure that the details of the CR have been entered in the database before it is forwarded to the CCB, the status accounting function can be performed more effectively.

For this process to happen, people should be aware of what to do and how to update the status accounting database. This is beneficial to the people who update the information because they are the same people who will be asking for information about the status of the various items at a later stage.

Importance of status accounting

Status accounting refers to the information management (or data management) functions in the SCM system. For each CI designed, developed, reviewed, approved, released, and distributed, the activities that are done, how they were done, and why, where, and when they were done, who did them, and so on have to be recorded.

These details will be useful for everyone involved in the project in various ways. The information needs of a developer are different from that of a project manager; but each and every member of the project team and the support functions will need at least some of the information. Status accounting is the information gathering and dissemination component of SCM. It is also used by management in decision making to monitor the progress of the project and can help identify problems before they become critical so that project management can take corrective actions.

The information provided by the status accounting function helps project management identify problems, pinpoint the source of the problem, and take corrective action before the situation gets out of hand. From the reports that are produced and by making ad hoc queries, project management can determine how the project is performing and compare the performance against the plan. One can also look at the types of changes, the rate of changes, causes for the changes, cost, and many other factors and take the necessary actions.

The status accounting reports are invaluable during the maintenance phase. To understand and identify the cause of a problem, one needs to know the history of the CI. For example, consider a program that was working until last week but is not working now. The easiest way to find out why is to identify the changes that were made to the program since last week. In situations like this, the information provided by status accounting helps resolve the problem faster.

The information provided by the status accounting function is useful in determining the performance characteristics of the project such as number of change requests, approval rate, number of problem reports, average time for a change resolution, average implementation time, cost of implementing a change, and so on. This information will help when evaluating the performance of the project and when comparing different projects. Also, these details will help to fine-tune the estimation and costing procedures of the organization.

So when the SCM system is designed, the information that has to be gathered by the status accounting function should be identified and selected, keeping in mind all of the uses mentioned here. A good status accounting system should provide information that is accurate, relevant, and timely.

Status accounting reports

As we saw earlier, the major functions of status accounting are to record and report information needed to manage a software system and its characteristics effectively. Even though it is not possible to anticipate all possible information requests, there are several reports that every system must have. These include the change log, progress report, CI status report, and transaction log. We will look at each of these reports in some detail a little later.

The factors that should be considered while designing the reporting requirements and reports of a system include these:

▶ Audience for the report;

▶ Information contained in each report;

▶ Need for a routine report or need on an ad hoc basis;

▶ Frequency of the report; and

▶ Distribution list.

Examples of routine reports are, as we have seen, the change log and transaction log. Some examples of ad hoc reports are given next:

▶ List of all CRs that have been approved but not implemented;

▶ List of all CRs initiated in the last 4 months;

- List of how many people are working on a particular CR;
- Record of how much time was needed to implement a particular change; and
- Record of how many CRs are pending.

Ad hoc reports are generated when a user requests particular information not included in the routine reports.

Let's take a look at some of the most common routine reports.

Change log

The change log should contain all information about the CRs in the system. The usual distribution frequency is monthly. This report should contain information such as change request number, status, originator's name, impacted items, origination date, description of change, and implementer's name. A sample change log is shown in Figure 9.1.

Progress report

The progress report is a summary of development progress since the last report was issued and is used primarily by management to monitor the progress of the project. This report should include the reporting period (from and to dates), task ID,[1] a brief description of the work performed during the period on the task, status of the task (complete, percent completed), and so on. A sample progress report is shown in Figure 9.2.

CI status report

This report is prepared to summarize the status of all CIs in the system and should include information such as a list of the CIs, description, and location of the CIs (the controlled library where they are stored). The CI description should include the name, version number, and details of dependent items as shown in Figure 9.3.

---

1. A task is the result of a CR implementation. An approved change request can result in one or more tasks, which can be assigned to one or more persons or teams. When the task is created the CMO creates a task ID and associates it with the CR.

CR number	CR status	Initiated by	Initiation date	Impacted items	Implemented by	Change description

Figure 9.1 Sample change log.

Progress report for the period mm/dd/yyyy to mm/dd/yyyy			
Task ID	Associated CR	Work description	Status

Figure 9.2 Sample progress report.

CI name	Description	Location

Figure 9.3 Sample CI status report.

Transaction log

This log contains the transactions that have happened to items, recorded in chronological order. The log should contain details such as transaction number, date, originator (person who is making the entry), nature of the entry (the entry is regarding what), affected items, activity (change request, CCB approval, analysis, problem report, and so on), description, participants (people who are involved), impacted items (items affected by the activity), and remarks.

The objective of the transaction log is to find out what happened during a specific period, say, "What were the activities done on mm/dd/yy?" Here the idea is not to provide a detailed description on how things were done, but to give someone a snapshot of what happened during a given period.

Status accounting and automation

The SCM tools fully automate the status accounting function. We have seen that the SCM tools capture all SCM-related information as and when it happens and does so automatically. The SCM tools store this information in a database so retrieval of the information is fast and efficient. Also, the information can be generated in any format the user wants. The SCM tools can be used to generate the routine reports.

When ad hoc reporting is required, however, is when the use of an SCM tool delivers its full potential. The user can query the system for any information that she requires and get the answers immediately and in the format that she wants.

Increased capability, flexibility, and customizability

If an SCM tool is not used, the SCM team will have to go through change logs, defect logs, change requests, transaction logs, and so on to correlate and collate bits and pieces of information from different sources to create a report that satisfies the user's requirements. This is a tedious and time-consuming process and will increase the workload of the SCM team if the users start asking complex queries that involve more than one source.

An SCM tool is an ideal solution to this situation. It is quick, it is accurate, and it is customizable. In the case of an SCM tool, all SCM-related information is stored in relational databases, which makes information retrieval easy and quick. Also, in the case of a tool, the information will be up to date as the events are recorded and the information is captured as the activities occur.

Another advantage of using tools is the variety of information that can be retrieved. For example, one can obtain information about all pending CRs, all completed CRs, all CRs completed between such-and-such a date, all CRs initiated by a particular developer, all CRs implemented by a particular person, and so on. The beauty of this system is that no additional cost or extra effort is required to produce these different reports. Most SCM tools will have a set of standard reports and then the facility to query the SCM database for other details. Most tools have the facility to display the information in graphical form also.

Thus SCM tools greatly enhance the capabilities of the status accounting function because they can record and retrieve minute details with speed and accuracy to satisfy ad hoc queries. This is especially true when different users of the SCM system have different needs. The project manager's information requirements are different from that of the developer's. What the change initiator wants to know will be different from what the project leader or a QA person wants to know. With a manual system, people will have to wait while the information is compiled from records, whereas with a computerized system, retrieval is merely a matter of running a query.

Another advantage of a software tool is that the people concerned can be given read-only access so that they can query the system and get the answers they need. Here once again, the author would like to stress the need for a computerized system. The manual systems are fine for the routine reports. But an interactive system can reduce the workload of the SCM staff because the people who want the information (and have the necessary authority) can log on to the system and get the information required. Also, routine reports provide static information. But if the users have access to the interactive system, they can view the reports and if they require more information, they can drill-down and get the details they want. In this way, SCM information is more effectively used, leading to better and well-informed decisions being made.

If an SCM tool does not support flexible and customizable reporting features then it is of limited value. We next look at some of the common report categories that are supported by most SCM tools.

Change/problem tracking reports

These reports contain details such as who made the change, when, who initiated it, change history, and CR status. Here the advantage, as mentioned before, is that the user can tailor the information retrieved in any format that he wants. So one can generate reports of all unassigned CRs, all pending CRs, all CRs assigned to a particular person, CRs sorted by date, severity, priority, classification, completion date, status, and so on.

Difference reporting

It is important to keep track of the differences between versions and releases because doing so will make it easier to incorporate changes from one version to the next. Most SCM tools have the facility to generate difference reports, which will contain the differences (changes) between two versions of an item or set of items.

Ad hoc queries

The usefulness of having ad hoc querying capabilities can never be overstated. Ad hoc queries allow the users of an SCM system to get the information they want, when they want it, and in the form they want. The reporting tools are so advanced that many of them have graphical user interfaces that help the users write their own queries by choosing the items in which they are interested. Also these reporting tools have drill-down features, so that a user can drill-down from a summary report to the level of detail required. This feature is particularly useful for project leaders and management.

Journals

The journal feature is what makes SCM tools stand apart from the manual status accounting process. A journal records all events that happen to all configuration items as they occur, thus providing the users with a complete and comprehensive picture of what happened during a particular period in time. This is a much advanced and more comprehensive version of the manual transaction logs.

Journals provide audit trails that can be used for a variety of purposes including configuration audits. The advantage of having the journal details in a database is that the information contained in it can be manipulated at will. So one can recreate all of the events that happened during the transition of a configuration item from, say, version 1 to 6 or the details of activities performed by a certain developer. The advantage here is that the information can be retrieved quickly and without any extra effort.

Conclusion

Status accounting is the recording activity and serves as a follow-up to the results of the SCM activities of configuration identification and change control. It keeps track of the current configuration identification documents, the current configuration of the delivered software, the status of the changes being reviewed, and the status of the implementation of approved changes.

The status accounting function plays a vital role in the efficient management and control of projects by providing the necessary information to project management and the project team. SCM tools automate the status accounting function and help provide users with information that is accurate, timely, and relevant.

Reference

[1]   *IEEE Standard Glossary of Software Engineering Terminology* (IEEE Std-610-1990), *IEEE Standards Collection (Software Engineering)*, Piscataway, NJ: IEEE, 1997.

Selected bibliography

Babich, W. A., *Software Configuration Management: Coordination for Team Productivity*, Boston, MA: Addison-Wesley, 1986.

Ben-Menachem, M., *Software Configuration Guidebook*, London: McGraw-Hill International, 1994.

Berlack, H. R., *Software Configuration Management*, New York: John Wiley & Sons, 1992.

Bersoff, E. H., V. D. Henderson, and S. G. Siegel, *Software Configuration Management, An Investment in Product Integrity*, Englewood Cliffs, NJ: Prentice-Hall, 1980.

IEEE Standards Collection (Software Engineering), Piscataway, NJ: IEEE, 1997.

"Software Configuration Management: A Primer for Development Teams and Managers," White Paper, Intersolv, 1997.

"Software Configuration Management for Client/Server Development Environments: An Architecture Guide," White Paper, Intersolv, 1998.

Contents

Configuration audits and reviews

Introduction

The purpose of the configuration audits and reviews is to verify that the software system matches the configuration item description in the specifications and documents and that the package being reviewed is complete. Once the software has been designed, developed, and tested, it is necessary to establish that the software product has been built in accordance with the requirements and that the software is correctly represented in the documentation that is shipped along with the software. So a configuration audit is a check to verify that the product package contains all of the components it is supposed to contain and performs as promised.

Audits are the means by which an organization can ensure that software development has been performed in the correct way, that is, in conformance with the development standards and guidelines. Audits vary in formality, but all audits perform the same function—they provide a check on the completeness of the software system or product. Any anomalies found during an audit should not only be corrected but the root cause of the problem should be identified and corrected to ensure that the problem does not occur again. (Here the defect prevention methods that we mentioned in Chapter 8 are quite useful.)

Before the release of a product baseline, a functional configuration audit (FCA) and a physical configuration audit (PCA) of the CIs are usually conducted. The FCA ensures that the functions defined in the specifications are all implemented in the correct manner. The PCA determines whether all the items identified as being part of the configuration item are present in the product baseline.

When, what, and who of auditing

An audit is usually done at the end of a phase in the development life cycle. Before the development proceeds to the next phase, it is a good practice to conduct an audit so that the development team has the satisfaction of knowing that they are working on something that is complete and approved. But the reality is that audits are usually performed only before a system release. This is because the system release is the one that will go to the customer.

Conducting the audit prior to final release gives the company and the customer the satisfaction of knowing that what they are delivering/getting is complete in all respects and meets the requirements specified. The configuration audit can be performed before the final release for projects done in-house and when the organization is following all the development standards and guidelines and other QA procedures are in place. But even then, every final major baseline or release must be audited. Items supplied by subcontractors must be subjected to a formal auditing process.

Who should perform the configuration audits? Audits are usually performed by a representative or team of representatives from management, the QA department, or the customer/client. In some cases the auditing is done by an external agency. It is best to have the configuration audit performed by an external auditor. This is because the auditing activity requires a very high degree of objectivity and professionalism. The person who conducts the audit should be knowledgeable about SCM activities and functions and technically competent to understand the functionality of the project.

Functional configuration audit

The objective of the FCA is to verify that a CI's actual performance agrees with the requirements specified in the requirements definition and system design documents. IEEE [1] defines FCA as an audit conducted to verify that the development of a configuration item has been completed satisfactorily, that the item has achieved the performance and functional characteristics specified in the functional or allocated configuration identification, and that its operational and support documents are complete and satisfactory.

The FCA team reviews the test plans, the test data, and the testing methodology to verify that all functional parameters were tested and the test results were satisfactory. The audit team[1] may ask for additional tests to be conducted if deemed necessary. Functional audits normally involve a structured and well-defined sequence of tests designed to ensure that the performance of the new or modified item conforms to the requirements in the specification.

The form of the FCA will vary according to the type and extent of change involved. In most cases the FCA represents a review of the qualification of the item, to ensure that it not only meets the specification requirement but that there are no unintended consequences associated with the change. This process may include some or all of the following forms of test, analysis, or demonstration: environmental tests, to ensure that the new design is suitable for operation within the extremes of the operational requirements; reliability tests; user trials; interfaces with other systems; software testing; and stress testing.

Physical configuration audit

The objective of the PCA is to verify that a configuration item as built conforms to the technical documentation that defines it. When a PCA is completed, the product baseline is established. The audit team examines

---

1. As mentioned, the audit team consists of representatives from management, QA, external experts, and/or client representatives. An audit team can be an ongoing part of the organization or it can be constituted on an as-needed basis. Sometimes audit teams are from an external agency that specializes in conducting audits. The composition and structure of the audit team depends on the company and the auditing standards that the company is following.

the design documentation with the source code and user documentation and any other items that will accompany the final software system. The PCA is usually done after successful completion of the FCA.

Auditing the SCM system

SCM system audits are carried out to ensure that the implementation of SCM remains consistent with established policy and procedures. System audits are essential to ensure that defined processes are being properly applied and controlled. General aspects that may be considered part of a system audit are as follows:

- ▶ The operational change control processes, including the CCB function;

- ▶ The implementation of change requests;

- ▶ The traceability of approved changes to the original specification and requirement;

- ▶ The availability of design data and documentation in support of approved changes; and

- ▶ The traceability of design decisions to the initiating requirement.

The auditing of the SCM system is done by management's representatives, QA personnel, or SCM experts. It is better to have the SCM system audits done by the people who reviewed the SCM plan, because they are familiar with the SCM system that is being practiced and thus are able to do a better job. The SCM system will be audited against the SCM plan and the standards mentioned in the SCM plan. The purpose of auditing the SCM system is to ensure that the SCM system and SCM functions and procedures are being practiced as specified in the SCM plan and to find out areas in the functioning of the SCM system that need improvement.

Role of the SCM team in configuration audits

It is the responsibility of the SCM team to schedule the audits and find qualified personnel to perform them. The SCM team also acts as the liaison between the audit team and the development and testing team and ensures that the audit team gets full support from the development and testing team to carry out the audits successfully.

Sometimes the auditors need to question the development or testing team members as part of the audit. The SCM team should act as a facilitator of such meetings and should record the points discussed in such meetings; these minutes should form part of the audit report. The SCM team should arrange for the infrastructure facilities such as room(s), furniture, machine access, documents, and any other items required by the audit team.

After the FCA and PCA have been completed, the SCM team will review the auditor's comments and nonconformance reports (NCRs) and will initiate the necessary corrective actions.

Configuration audits and SCM tools

SCM tools makes the auditing process a totally painless one. As we have seen, SCM tools capture all SCM-related information in a very comprehensive manner as the activities occur. We have seen that the journal reports created by the SCM tools record all events that have happened to the configuration items, thus creating an audit trail, which can be used by the auditors to perform the auditing. Also the querying facility of the tools will help in getting any other information that is needed by the auditing team.

The automated information gathering abilities of the SCM tools make auditing into an incredibly simple process because any necessary information can be generated for verification purposes and because they can confirm whether the system or product that is being audited is complete and meets all the requirements.

Conclusion

Configuration audits are carried out to ensure that the software system is functioning correctly and to ensure that the configuration has been tested to demonstrate that it meets its functional requirements and that it contains all deliverable entities.

The two types of audits are physical configuration audits and functional configuration audits. Whereas the functional configuration audits authenticate that the software performs in accordance with the requirements and as stated in the documentation, the physical configuration audit authenticates that the components to be delivered actually exist and that they are complete in all respects and contain all of the required items.

The SCM system should also be subjected to auditing to ensure that the implementation of SCM remains consistent with established policies and procedures. The SCM tools automate most of the auditing tasks and make auditing an easy and painless task.

Reference

[1]   *IEEE Standard Glossary of Software Engineering Terminology* (IEEE Std-610-1990), *IEEE Standards Collection (Software Engineering)*, Piscataway, NJ: IEEE, 1997.

Selected bibliography

Ben-Menachem, M., *Software Configuration Management Guidebook*, New York: McGraw-Hill, 1994.

IEEE Standards Collection, Software Engineering, 1997, New York: IEEE, 1997.

Pressman, R. S., *Software Engineering: A Practitioner's Approach*, New York: McGraw-Hill, 1997.

Sommerville, I., *Software Engineering*, Reading, MA: Addison-Wesley, 1996.

Whitgift, D., *Methods and Tools for Software Configuration Management*, Chichester, England: John Wiley & Sons, 1991.

11

Contents

Software configuration management plans

Introduction

We have seen that once the SCM system is designed it should be documented so that the working of the SCM system, the procedures, and the functions, duties, and responsibilities of each member are transparent and known to all members of the SCM team, project team, the subcontractor's team (if any), and others. This document is called the *software configuration management plan (SCMP)* or simply the *plan.*

An initial draft of the SCM plan should be created and circulated among the various groups involved in the project during the initial phases (i.e., during the analysis or design phase). Once the feedback from the various groups—project team, QA team, management, and others—is obtained, it can be incorporated and the approved SCM plan can be made available so that everybody is clear about the various SCM procedures and their duties and responsibilities.

According to Bounds and Dart [1], the CM plan is one of the three keys to the success of attaining a CM solution (the other two are the *CM system* and the *CM adoption strategy*). It is generally the case that an SCM solution is part of a corporate-wide process improvement plan and, as such, the solution is coordinated with that effort. This means that the SCM plan needs to be in agreement with any other plans related to the corporate improvement effort.

The objective of the SCM plan is to create and document a system that will describe and specify, as accurately as possible, all tasks that are to be performed by the agency that is responsible for the configuration of the system or product. Thus the main function of the SCM plan is to create an awareness among the various groups involved in a software project about the SCM functions and how they are to be performed in that project.

SCM is not a well-known subject and in most cases people—even people who have been in the software profession for many years—are not aware of SCM and how an SCM system works. So in order to create awareness among the project team members, SCM team members, and other people who are in some way related to the project (such as the QA personnel), a document that describes how SCM will be practiced for the project is needed. Thus the SCM plan forms the basis of training the personnel who are part of the project team and SCM team. It will be used as a reference manual for the SCM functions. It will also be used in the resolution of conflicts regarding the practice or implementation of SCM functions in the project.

The SCM plan can be either created for the organization or for each project. If the plan is created for the entire organization, its suitability should still be assessed for each project and necessary modifications should be made. In the case of organizations where the projects that are carried out differ in nature, complexity, and size, it is desirable to create separate plans for each project tailored to suit the needs and characteristics of the project.

SCM plan and the incremental approach

Some companies adopt what is called the *incremental approach* to SCM implementation. In the incremental approach, SCM functions are implemented in stages. The system starts with just some of the components, say, a change/problem tracking system or a source code control and revision management system. Then slowly, as time progresses, the other components are introduced until the full spectrum of SCM functionality is achieved.

The natural question when considering the incremental approach is that of how an SCM plan can be developed when the full SCM system is not being implemented. Another question is that of why an SCM plan is needed since many of the components will not be part of the plan during the first phase of implementation.

In the author's opinion, irrespective of whether the company chooses the big-bang approach (where full SCM functionality is implemented in one shot) or incremental approach, it is always better to have an SCM plan. This is because, even for the incremental approach, the broad outline of what the final system will be like, must be decided at the outset. There is no need to go into the finer details of the portions that are not being implemented in the first phase, but a very high-level outline of how these missing components will fit into the final system and the chosen implementation strategy (the when and how of implementing those functions) should be documented. This is important because, if the different functions of the SCM system are implemented without considering the overall picture (that is, the effect of each subsystem on the overall SCM system), then the integration of the different subsystems will not be seamless.

So, even when the incremental approach is used, the full SCM system should be designed and the SCM plan prepared based on a full implementation. Otherwise, as components are added and full SCM functionality finally reached, the SCM tools will not be well integrated.

SCM plan and SCM tools

Another question that is often asked about SCM plans by companies using SCM tools is that of whether the SCM *plan* is really necessary. Here also the answer is "yes." The SCM plan is the document that records how the different SCM functions will be performed. Only after analyzing and deciding how the SCM system should function, what its functions will be and which functions will be automated, and the peculiarities of each organization/project can the decision about which tool to use be reached.

The SCM plan has a section on SCM resources in which details are given about the software tools, techniques, equipment, personnel, and training necessary for the implementation of the specified SCM activities. The SCM plan, as we have seen earlier, is the basis for SCM training and auditing of the SCM system. So it is still very important to have an SCM plan. In fact, the author strongly advocates training the employees in the fundamentals and concepts of SCM and on how the SCM functions are carried out before training them on the tools. This will give the users a better understanding of what they are doing and how their actions will affect others in the project. In practice, if one is using a tool he can perform the SCM functions without knowing the SCM concepts—the tool's user manual is enough. But if he wants to know why he is performing a function, he will need to be aware of the SCM concepts.

So even though it is possible to use SCM tools without knowing much about the SCM concepts and functions, it is the author's opinion and experience that a person who knows the SCM concepts is a better user of the SCM tool than a person who has been told just to perform certain activities. There is always a difference between doing something just because somebody is told to do it that way and doing something after knowing why a task has to be performed and what will be the effect of that action.

SCM plans and standards

Almost all configuration management standards advocate some sort of a document or plan. Except for some minor differences, the format specified by most of the standards for the SCM plan is similar. According to a study conducted by Bounds and Dart [1], in which they compared three standards (by IEEE, NASA, and DOD) based on six criteria (ease of use, completeness, tailorability, consistency, correctness, and life cycle connection), the IEEE standard had the best rating.

As mentioned before, many standards exist for SCM plans. We will examine three of them, which is a representative sample of the lot. They are:

1. ANSI/IEEE Std-828-1998, *IEEE Standard for Software Configuration Management Plans,* and ANSI/IEEE Std-1042-1987, *IEEE Guide to Software Configuration Management;*

2. DOD-Std-2167A, *Defense System Software Development;* and

3. ISO 10007, *Quality Management—Guidelines for Configuration Management.*

ANSI/IEEE Std-828-1998 and ANSI/IEEE Std-1042-1987

ANSI/IEEE Std-828-1998 is the standard for configuration management plans. Complementing this standard is a guide—*IEEE Guide to Software Configuration Management* (ANSI/IEEE Std-1042-1987)—that contains an explanation of the standard and sample SCM plans for different kinds of projects. In the author's opinion these two standards together form the most comprehensive standards available on SCM and SCM plans.

The IEEE standard is a very comprehensive standard on SCM and it is very tailorable (that is, it can be customized easily to suit one's needs). This standard intentionally addresses all levels of expertise, the entire life cycle, other organizations, and the relationships to hardware and other activities on a project.

The ANSI/IEEE Std-828-1998 provides a format for creating the SCM plan. According to the standard the SCM plan should consist of six sections as shown in Table 11.1.

ANSI/IEEE Std-1042-1987, the guide to SCM plans, explains how Std-828 should be implemented. This guide has several appendixes for different types of SCM plans (real-time, critical projects, maintenance projects, and so on) that can be customized very easily to suit individual needs and requirements.

DOD-Std-2167A

The purpose of DOD-Std-2167A is to establish requirements to be applied during the acquisition, development, or support of software systems. This standard requires configuration management procedures to be used for the acquisition, development, or support of software systems to be documented. According to the standard, the contractor (the person who

Table 11.1
Format of SCM Plan per ANSI/IEEE Std-828-1998

No.	Section Name	Description
1	Introduction	Purpose of the plan, scope, definition of key terms, and references.
2	SCM Management	Describes the allocation of responsibilities and authorities for SCM activities to organizations and individuals within the project structure.
3	SCM Activities	Identifies all functions and tasks required for managing the configuration of the software system as specified in the scope of the SCM plan. Both technical and managerial SCM activities must be identified.
4	SCM Schedules	Establishes the sequence and coordination for the identified SCM activities and for all events affecting the SCM plan's implementation.
5	SCM Resources	Identifies the software tools, techniques, equipment, personnel, and training necessary for the implementation of the specified SCM activities.
6	SCM Plan Maintenance	Identifies the activities and responsibilities necessary to ensure continued SCM planning during the life cycle of the project.

is doing the development) must document and implement plans for performing the configuration functions. In this case the SCM plan is constructed as a part of the software development plan (SDP).

This standard was developed for the Department of Defense (DOD) environment but can be tailored to handle rapidly evolving software technology and to accommodate a wide variety of state-of-the-practice software engineering techniques. This standard allows the user to incorporate the SCM plan into the SDP or to treat it as a separate document. The benefit of handling the SCM plan in this manner is that for those projects where SCM is either tied tightly to project management and the life cycle, or where the SCM function is relatively small, it allows the plan to be placed in the SDP where it is more appropriate.

This standard is widely used by all NATO countries and also in many countries that purchase their weapons systems from the United States. Note that this standard is by no means limited to defense systems or to military purposes. This standard is now in the public domain and easily obtainable. One thing to remember about this standard, however, is that it is for a specific project. So if you are developing standards for an entire organization, you should not use this one.

Also, the format of the configuration management plan, which is embedded in the SDP, is determined by the data item description called Software Development Plan—DI-MCCR-80030A. So DOD-Std-2167A is for project-specific software development and configuration management and is not for plans, which are developed for the entire organization.

ISO 10007

This international standard gives guidance on the use of configuration management in industry and its interface with other management systems and procedures. This standard defines a configuration management plan as a document that sets out the organization and procedures for the configuration management of a specific product or project. The standard states that the CM plan provides the CM procedures that are to be used for each project, and states who will undertake these and when. The standard also states that the plan should be subjected to document control procedures.

This standard specifies a format for the CM plan (Annex A—Recommended Structure and Content of a Configuration Management Plan). According to ISO 10007 a configuration management plan should have the six chapters listed in Table 11.2.

The standard also specifies that whenever an existing procedure or standard is used, reference be made to it rather than giving the details so that duplication can be avoided and simplicity can be maintained. In the author's opinion this is a good practice to follow irrespective of which standard you are using, because it will make the SCM plan simple and short and, as mentioned before, data duplication can be avoided. For example, according to the preceding standard the audit procedures that will be followed have to be mentioned in Chapter 6, Configuration Audit. If the audit is conducted per the ISO guidelines for auditing quality systems, instead of mentioning the auditing process the plan can just say that the SCM auditing will be done in accordance with the ISO 10011-1:1990, ISO 10011-2:1990, and ISO 10011-3:1990 (ISO guidelines for auditing quality systems, Parts 1, 2, and 3).

Table 11.2
Format of SCM Plan per ISO 10007

No.	Chapter Name	Description
1	Introduction	Description of the system or CIs to which the plan applies, a schedule of the CM activities, the purpose and scope of the plan, list of related documents, and so on.
2	Policies and Procedures	CM policies, CM organization and structure of the CCB and the other committees, selection criteria for the CIs, frequency, distribution, and control of reports and agreed terminology.
3	Configuration Identification	Family tree of the CIs, numbering conventions, baselines to be established, and so on.
4	Configuration Control	Organization and composition of the CCB, change management procedures, and so on.
5	Configuration Status Accounting	Procedures for collecting, recording, processing, and maintaining the data for status accounting reports, definition of all CM reports, and so on.
6	Configuration Audit	List of audits to be conducted, the audit procedures, the authorities and disciplines involved, format of the audit reports, and so on.

In a study conducted by Bounds and Dart [1], the users of the CM plans were asked whether CM procedures should be part of the CM plan or separate. The overwhelming response was that the procedures should be kept separate from the plan, but that the plan should reference the procedures. Although many reasons were cited for this, the most common reasons were that separating the procedures allows the users to focus only on what applies to them, and makes maintenance of the procedures and plan much easier. Respondents also stated that procedures should focus on how to do something, whereas a plan should focus on what is to be done.

The same study recommended the use of IEEE standards as the best standards to use in developing SCM plans for these reasons:

1. The IEEE standard was written explicitly for use by anyone within the industry, whereas the NASA and DOD standards were written for their specific segments of industry.

2. The IEEE standard is, by far, more complete than the other two standards, and is the only standard that can be treated as a stand-alone document.

3. The IEEE standard has greater potential for timely updates than the other standards since it is used by the general industry.

Audit of the SCM plan

An SCM plan is a controlled document as well as a configuration item. So all document control procedures that are applicable to a controlled document and all the change management procedures that are applicable to a configuration item are applicable to the SCM plan also. This means that the distribution of the SCM plan should be controlled. There should be a distribution list that contains the names of persons having a copy of the plan. Also, access to the plan should be controlled—the level of control is decided based on the nature of the project. If the plan is hosted on the company intranet or bulletin board, then the access to that should be controlled.

Another aspect is that changes to the plan should be done in accordance with the change management procedures mentioned in the plan. When a change is implemented the new versions should be made available to all who are in the distribution list. If the plan is hosted on the intranet then it should be updated.

The SCM plan should be subject to auditing. Like any other configuration item, the plan should undergo the functional and physical configuration audits. The purpose of the auditing is to ensure that the plan is complete and correct and satisfies the requirements as described in the standard or standards on which it is based.

How to write a good SCM plan

Writing the SCM plan is not an easy task. It takes time; good knowledge of SCM functions, the peculiarities of the project, and the organization; and knowledge of other procedures such as auditing and testing to write a good SCM plan. It is also not a task that should be taken lightly because the practice of the SCM function in a project or organization is based on the procedures and tasks specified in the SCM plan. It is not too strong a statement to say that the SCM plan can make or break a project. A bad and improperly designed SCM plan will create unnecessary and cumbersome procedures and instead of assisting the development process and improving productivity will result in creating confusion and increasing the workload of the project team as well as the SCM team. In the following paragraphs we look at some practices and tips that will help in the creation of good SCM plans.

The most important decision that affects the quality of an SCM plan is the capability and knowledge of the person or the team that writes the plan. Ideally the plan should be written by the people who have designed the SCM system for the project/organization. Here we are talking about experienced people who have a good understanding of the project/organization and the SCM system. Once they have written the plan, the technical documentation team can copyedit it so that typos and grammatical mistakes are eliminated. This is a good practice to follow, because the writing skills of the technical people may not be on par with their technical skills. The copyeditors should be given clear instructions not to touch the structure of the plan, just to check for grammatical and spelling errors. Maybe it would be a good idea to have the editor sit with the technical team during the writing process, so if any issues arise they can be resolved immediately.

The second most important decision is selecting the standard on which the SCM plan is going to be based. As mentioned earlier, the IEEE standards emerge as the best and most popular choice. But it is good practice to see what other standards have to offer and it may not be a bad idea to borrow good ideas from them. There is nothing wrong with formulating an SCM plan based on more than one standard, because all standards will have some weak areas and adapting that area from another standard is not a bad idea. Some of the standards that could be referenced include the following:

1. ANSI/IEEE Std-828-1998, *IEEE Standard for Software Configuration Management Plans*, IEEE, 1998.

2. ANSI/IEEE Std-1042-1987, *IEEE Guide to Software Configuration Management*, IEEE, 1987.

3. ISO 10007, *Quality Management—Guidelines for Configuration Management*, ISO, 1995.

4. NASA-Sfw-DID-04, *Software Configuration Management Plan Data Item Description*, NASA, 1986.

5. NASA D-GL-11, *Software Configuration Management for Project Managers*, NASA, 1987.

6. DOD-Std-2167A, *Military Standard for Defense System Software*, U.S. Department of Defense, 1985.

7. DOD DI-MCCR-80030A, *Data Item Description for the Software Development Plan*, U.S. Department of Defense, 1986.

8. DOD MIL-STD-973, *Military Standard for Configuration Management*, Department of Defense, 1995.

9. DOD MIL-STD-483A, *Configuration Management Practices for Systems, Equipment, Munitions, and Computer Programs*, U.S. Department of Defense, 1985.

One can get a feel for how to write the SCM plan by studying some sample plans and also reading books on software configuration management. Today, getting sample SCM plans is not a difficult task. IEEE Std-1042-1987 has four appendixes consisting of sample SCM plans for different types of projects. Also hundreds of SCM plans—of all types and sizes—are available on the web. A simple query for configuration management plans on the web by the author produced more than 1000 results.

The next step in writing the SCM plan is to identify the procedures that should be followed in the practice of SCM. If the SCM system is using procedures that are from standards or are part of other standards, then as we have seen before, it is quite sufficient just to give references to those standards. These standards can be industry standards or the organization's internal standards or even the project's own standards. But before giving reference to a standard, it is a good idea to ensure that all the standards are available and if possible bring them under document control, so that they are readily available for reference.

We have researched the standards and literature, discussed the sample plans, and identified the procedures that will be followed and the documents that define these procedures. The next step is to write the plan using any of the existing templates that are available. Many SCM plan templates are available on the web, the IEEE standard provides a very customizable template, and the ISO has a reasonably good template. The choice of template is a matter of taste and convenience. The contents of both the IEEE and ISO templates are almost the same, but the IEEE template is more comprehensive. But if the company is using ISO standards, then the ISO 10007 template can be used. You just have to choose a template that is suited to your purpose (and similar to your project/organization) and customize it to your specific needs. Once the template or the table of contents is ready, the next step is to fill in the blanks or put the procedures and other details in place to complete the plan. The resulting document is considered the initial draft of the SCM plan. Copies of this document—the initial draft—should be circulated to all groups who will be involved in implementing the SCM system and performing the various SCM functions. This process—involving everyone who matters in plan development—is very important. SCM is a team effort. So in order to implement and manage an SCM system successfully, the SCM team will need cooperation from all quarters. One way to ensure that cooperation is to get others involved by sending them copies of the initial draft and asking for feedback.

Once the feedback from the various groups is received, the SCM plan's authors can review it, accept valid comments, and incorporate them into the plan. Once the final draft is ready, it is a good idea to get it reviewed by an external agency—a person or team of experts. This review can throw light on issues that the plan might have failed to address or bring up inadequacies or even detect errors that the internal reviews have missed. The external audit also provides a stamp of approval from a body that is supposed to be an expert in this area, which will help to increase the credibility and acceptance of the plan. Once the SCM plan is reviewed and approved, then it can be baselined.

Contents of a typical SCM plan

The SCM plan can be written in any format as long as it contains all necessary information. The standards offer considerable latitude and freedom to the person who writes the SCM plan. All standards require you to address certain topics such as scope, purpose, definitions, SCM organization, SCM functions, responsibilities, resources, and so on. But how this material should be presented is decided by the author of the plan. The degree of detail, the amount of additional information, and so on that you include in the SCM plan depends on the nature of the project.

A sample outline for an SCM plan is given next. All items, sections, and subsections need not be present in all projects. Some will have additional information. This structure relies heavily on the IEEE standards. The explanation of each section and subsection is given at the end.

Cover Page

Copyright Page

Distribution List

About the Document

1.0 INTRODUCTION
   1.1 Purpose
   1.2 Scope
   1.3 Definitions
   1.4 References
2.0 SCM MANAGEMENT
   2.1 SCM Organization
   2.2 SCM Responsibilities
   2.3 Relationship of CM to Software Process Life Cycle
   2.4 Interfaces to Other Organizations on the Project
   2.5 SCM Responsibilities of the Organizations
3.0 SCM ACTIVITIES
   3.1 Configuration Identification
      3.1.1 Identification of Configuration Items
      3.1.2 Naming Configuration Items
      3.1.3 Acquiring Configuration Items
   3.2 Configuration Control
      3.2.1 Change Initiation
      3.2.2 Change Evaluation
      3.2.3 Change Management—Approval Process

3.2.4 Change Implementation

3.2.5 Change Control Boards (CCBs)

3.3 Configuration Status Accounting

3.3.1 Identifications of Information Needs

3.3.2 Information Gathering Mechanisms

3.3.3 Reports, Their Contents, and Frequency

3.3.4 Access to Status Accounting Data

3.3.5 Status Accounting Information Dissemination Methods

3.3.6 Release Details

3.4 Configuration Auditing

3.4.1 Audits to Be Performed

3.4.2 CIs Under Audit

3.4.3 Audit Procedures

3.4.4 Audit Follow-Up Activities

3.5 Interface Control

3.6 Subcontractor/Vendor Control

4.0 SCM SCHEDULES

5.0 SCM RESOURCES

6.0 SCM PLAN MAINTENANCE

Cover Page: This page should have the title "Software Configuration Management Plan" and the details regarding the project, the organization, the authorities, the version number, release date, and so on.

Copyright Page: Copyright information of the SCM plan.

Distribution List: Name and number of copies distributed. Also a description of how the documentation control activities will apply to this document.

About the Document: A short description about the document and its sections.

1.0 INTRODUCTION: This section provides an overview of the plan, the SCM activities, the audience for the plan, and how to use the plan, so that the user will have a clearer understanding of the plan. The introduction should contain at least the following four topics—purpose, scope, definitions, and references.

1.1 Purpose: This section addresses the need for the plan and the intended audience.

1.2 Scope: The scope covers the plan's applicability, limitations, and assumptions. This section provides an overview of the software development process in the project/organization and how the SCM functions and activities fit into the project.

1.3 Definitions: This section defines the key terms used in the document.

1.4 References: This section identifies all documents, standards, procedures—both internal and external—to be used in the plan. This section also identifies where the documents can be found so that the readers of the plan can retrieve them.

2.0 SCM MANAGEMENT: This section gives information about the organization of the SCM team, allocation of responsibilities to teams and individuals, and so on.

2.1 SCM Organization: This section describes the organizational structure of the SCM team and how it fits into the organizational structure with respect to other groups such as the project team, the QA team, and top management. Also included in the structure are clients/customers and vendors/subcontractors, if any are involved in the SCM activities. An organization chart depicting the structure is very useful in this section. This section also describes the composition of the CCB and other auditing and review teams that will be part of the SCM activities.

2.2 SCM Responsibilities: This section describes the duties and responsibilities of all those involved in carrying out the SCM activities. This section identifies the responsibilities of the CCB and other committees and boards necessary for configuration management, the structure of which has been defined in the previous section.

2.3 Relationship of SCM to the Software Process Life Cycle: This section relates the SCM activities to the different phases of the software development life cycle. It spells out what SCM activities need to be performed during each phase of the life cycle.

2.4 Interfaces to Other Organizations on the Project: Describes how the SCM team will interact with other organizations in the project such as vendors and subcontractors.

2.5 SCM Responsibilities of the Organizations: This section describes the responsibilities of the vendors, subcontractors, and other organizations in relation to the carrying out of SCM functions. Or in other words, this section describes what is expected from them.

3.0 SCM ACTIVITIES: This section identifies the tasks and functions that are required to manage the configuration of the system as specified in the scope of the plan. This section deals with the core SCM activities and how they are performed in the project.

3.1 Configuration Identification: This section describes how to identify, name, and document the functional and physical characteristics of the configuration items. Once the items are identified, they are acquired and moved into the controlled environment.

3.1.1 Identification of Configuration Items: Identifies the items to be selected as configuration items that will be controlled by the SCM activities. This section gives a list of configuration items in the project. Inclusion of a tree structure showing the various configuration items and their inter-dependencies is ideal.

3.1.2 Naming Configuration Items: This section of the plan specifies the identification system, naming conventions, version numbers, and letters used to identify the configuration items.

3.1.3 Acquiring Configuration Items: This section describes how the configuration items are to be stored, how access to them will be controlled, the details of the configuration libraries, the procedures for check in and check out of configuration items from the library, and so on.

3.2 Configuration Control: This section describes the change management processes such as change initiation, change disposition, change implementation, reviews, approval, and baselining.

3.2.1 Change Initiation: Describes how to initiate a change. A change can be the result of a fault or problem or the result of an enhancement or new feature. This section describes the procedures to be followed to initiate a change request or problem report so that the change management activities are started.

3.2.2 Change Evaluation: This section describes how the evaluation of a change request is carried out. This section also details how to handle the problem analysis, problem classification, and so on. The section gives details on how to classify the changes/problems, how to do an impact analysis, and so on. The section also specifies the qualifications of the people who will be doing the change/problem evaluation.

3.2.3 Change Management: This section describes how a change request is processed. It spells out clearly the procedure for the receiving of the change requests, assigning the change requests for evaluation, the CCB meetings, how to disposition the change requests carried out, and so on.

3.2.4 Change Implementation: Once the change request is approved it has to be implemented. How to select the change implementation team or person, how to conduct the verification and validation, and how to promote the item to the new baseline are described in this section.

3.2.5 Change Control Boards (CCBs): This is the apex body that decides the fate of the change requests. This section describes the functioning of the CCB. If multiple CCBs are present, the authority of each CCB must be specified and if more than one CCB of the same authority is present in the project, then conflict resolution mechanisms also should be documented.

3.3 Configuration Status Accounting: This section deals with the details of recording the status of the configuration items and reporting them to people who need to know about them.

3.3.1 Identification of Information Needs: This section describes the information requirements of the project. What kind of information is required, who requires it, the nature of the requirement (routine, ad hoc), the frequency of the reports, and so on.

3.3.2 Information Gathering Mechanisms: Describes how the status accounting information is gathered. Ideally the information should be entered into the configuration management database by the initiators of the SCM activities rather than by the SCM person chasing the activities and updating the status accounting data. For example, when a change request is initiated, if the person who initiates the change request creates a record of that in the database, then the job of information gathering is easy. But to accomplish this, the necessary forms and access privileges should be given to the different users of the system. This section describes the exact mechanism of how the information is captured for status reporting.

3.3.3 Reports, Their Contents, and Frequency: Describes the various reports that will be created, their contents, and the frequency of each report.

3.3.4 Access to Status Accounting Data: The status accounting function cannot anticipate all of the information requirements of users and produce reports to meet all requirements. Also in many cases, information requests will be for ad hoc reports, which may be generated only once. If the status accounting system is computerized, then an interactive query facility can be made available to the users to get this information. If such a facility is available, this section will describe the procedures for using that facility. In the case of manual processing, this section will describe how the manual records can be accessed for ad hoc information needs.

3.3.5 Status Accounting Information Dissemination Methods: This section describes how and to whom the status accounting information will be disseminated.

3.3.6 Release Details: Details information such as what is contained in a release, to whom the release is being provided and when, the media the release is on, known problems with the release, known fixes in the release, installation instructions, and so on.

3.4 Configuration Auditing: This section describes what types of audits are to be performed, the audit procedure, frequency, and the auditing authority, and so on.

3.4.1 Audits to Be Performed: Describes the different types of audits that will be performed and when they will be performed. The typical audits include functional configuration audits (FCA), physical configuration audits (PCA), subcontractor audits, and external audits.

3.4.2 CIs Under Audit: Specifies the list of CIs that are to be audited.

3.4.3 Audit Procedures: Describes the procedure to be followed for each audit—the auditing authority, the documents required, how the audit should be conducted, the format of the audit report, and so on.

3.4.4 Audit Follow-Up Activities: This section describes the activities that should be carried out after the audit such as resolution of nonconfirmation reports (NCRs) and so on.

3.5 Interface Control: This section describes the coordination of the changes to the CIs with the changes to the interfacing items outside the scope of the plan like the hardware system, off-the-shelf packages, support software, and so on. The plan must identify each of these external items and should define the nature of the interface, the affected groups, how the interface items will be controlled, and how the interface items will be approved to be included as part of a baseline.

3.6 Subcontractor/Vendor Control: This section describes the activities necessary to incorporate the items developed outside the project environment into the project environment, in particular, items that are the responsibility of subcontractors and vendors. This section should describe the SCM functions and activities that should be followed by the vendor/subcontractor, mechanisms to ensure that they are followed, procedures to audit the items that are submitted by the vendor/subcontractor, and the items that must be supplied by the vendor/subcontractor. This section also describes how the items will be received, tested, and placed under SCM, how change requests to this items will be processed and implemented, and so on.

4.0 SCM SCHEDULES: This section describes the sequence of the SCM activities, their interdependencies and relationship to the project life cycle, and project milestones. The schedule will identify the life cycle phases or project milestones where the different baselines (functional baseline, allocated baseline, product baseline, and so on) will be established. This section also establishes the schedule for the different configuration audits. Graphical representation using PERT charts or Gantt charts help to enhance the usefulness of this section.

5.0 SCM RESOURCES: This section identifies the software tools, techniques, equipment, personnel, and training necessary for the implementation of the specified SCM activities.

6.0 SCM PLAN MAINTENANCE: This section describes the activities that are required to keep the plan current during the life cycle of the project. The plan should be monitored and synchronized with the activities of the project. This section describes the mechanism for the synchronization and identifies the person or team responsible for those activities.

Sample SCM plans

We have just looked at a generic structure for SCM plans, which can be tailored to suit the needs of the individual projects. We have also discussed tips for writing good SCM plans. As mentioned before it is a good idea to go through a few sample SCM plans of similar projects before you start writing the SCM plan.

The sample SCM plans can be obtained from a host of sources, but two of the easiest sources are listed below:

1. *The Internet.* Thousands of SCM plans covering a spectrum of projects—military, government, research, commercial, and so on—of various sizes and complexity are hosted on the Internet. You can use a search engine to locate them. By spending a few hours on the Internet you can browse through the different types of SCM plans.

2. *ANSI/IEEE Std-1042-1987.* This is the IEEE *Guide to Software Configuration Management.* There are four appendixes for this document, which are sample SCM plans for different types of projects.

Also, in the author's opinion, anyone who is writing an SCM plan will benefit tremendously from the document "CM Plans: The Beginning to Your CM Solution" by Nadine M. Bounds and Susan Dart of Software Engineering Institute, Carnegie Mellon University. This is an excellent primer for SCM plans.

Conclusion

The SCM plan is the document that defines the SCM system and how SCM is to be practiced in a project. The SCM plan documents what SCM activities are to be done, how they are to be done, who is responsible for doing specific activities, when they are to happen, and what resources are required.

The SCM plan should be prepared irrespective of whether the organization is using an incremental approach or using SCM tools. Preparing a good SCM plan requires knowledge of the SCM concepts and functions, SCM tools, SCM standards, software engineering and quality assurance procedures, and standards and knowledge of the organization or project for which the standard is being written. The SCM plan can be based on a single standard or can be based on more than one standard. The SCM plan is a configuration item and should be updated and reviewed whenever required. The SCM plan should be prepared with the cooperation of all those who will be involved in the functioning of the SCM system and should be audited by external SCM experts. It is a good idea to go through some SCM plans before starting to write the plan. Hundreds of sample plans are available on the Internet. Anyone who is writing an SCM plan will benefit tremendously from the document by Bounds and Dart [1].

Reference

[1]   Bounds, N. M., and S. Dart, "CM Plans: The Beginning to Your CM Solution," Technical Report, Software Engineering Institute, Carnegie-Mellon University, 1998.

Selected bibliography

Babich, W. A., *Software Configuration Management: Coordination for Team Productivity*, Boston, MA: Addison Wesley, 1986.

Ben-Menachem, M., *Software Configuration Guidebook*, London: McGraw-Hill International, 1994.

Berlack, H. R., *Software Configuration Management*, New York: John Wiley & Sons, 1992.

Bersoff, E. H., V. D. Henderson, and S. G. Siegel, *Software Configuration Management, An Investment in Product Integrity*, Englewood Cliffs, NJ: Prentice-Hall, 1980.

IEEE Standards Collection, Software Engineering, 1997, New York: IEEE, 1997.

Whitgift, D., *Methods and Tools for Software Configuration Management*, Chichester, England: John Wiley & Sons, 1991.

Contents

SCM organization

Introduction

Configuration management—like any other management function—needs people to perform the various activities and to produce results. Configuration management is a discipline that applies technical and administrative direction and surveillance to (1) identify and document the functional and physical characteristics of a configuration item, (2) control changes to those characteristics, (3) record and report change processing and implementation status, and (4) verify compliance with specified requirements [1]. As you can see, this definition states a lot of tasks—configuration identification, change management, change disposition, change implementation, configuration control, status accounting, and configuration audits, to name a few—that have to be performed for the SCM system to function properly.

To perform all of these functions effectively and efficiently, one needs procedures and resources. We looked at the various SCM procedures in the last few chapters and we saw that the most important resource is people. So for any SCM system to function properly there should be enough qualified people to do the various functions.

The number of people on an SCM team will vary depending on the nature, size, and complexity of the project. In the case of large and complex projects with hundreds of programmers and thousands of programs, the SCM team will be big with lots of full-time members, whereas in the case of small projects the project leader himself might do all the SCM functions. Also there are people whose services will be required on an as-needed basis. For example, for a change request evaluation, an outside expert might be called and once the evaluation is over and the report is submitted she will leave. There might also be permanent personnel on the SCM team who are in charge of receiving the various change and problem reports, ensuring the completeness of these forms, assigning them to the right people for evaluation, coordinating the CCB activities, and so on.

In this chapter we review the structure of a typical SCM team based on the different functions. But as SCM tools become popular and more and more SCM tasks are automated, the number of people required to perform SCM effectively is diminishing.

SCM and the organization

We know that SCM is a support function, so let's take a look at where and how SCM fits into the organizational structure. Different organizational structures in different organizations will require the SCM team to be structured or positioned differently. In many cases there will be a central SCM team that will take care of all the SCM activities of the different projects in the company. The SCM team here will act as a support function and will use the members of the project team to get the SCM activities done.

The main responsibilities of the SCM team in such an arrangement are to complete the SCM activities of the different projects such as receive the change requests, assign the implementation, and convene the CCB meetings. The advantage of this kind of setup is that the central SCM team can have standardized procedures and policies enforced for all projects and can prioritize the SCM needs of the different projects based on the overall company objectives. This kind of an arrangement is shown in Figure 12.1.

Some companies have a central SCM team along with individual teams for each project. The central team creates the guidelines and policies and the general organization-wide SCM plan and is responsible for the proper functioning of the SCM system in the company as a whole. The individual teams associated with each project customize the plans and procedures to suit the needs of the particular project and are responsible for the SCM activities in the project. These SCM teams in the different projects usually have a dual reporting arrangement in which they report to the central SCM team leader and also to the project leader of the project

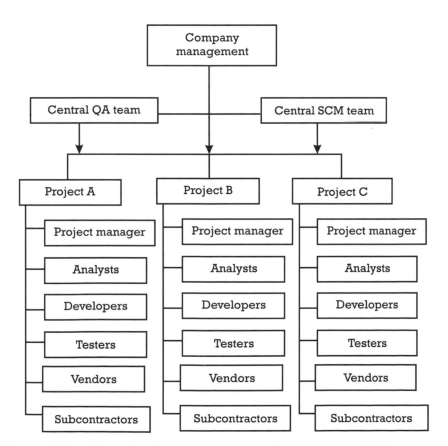

Figure 12.1 Organizational structure in which a central SCM team deals with the different projects.

with which they are associated. This type of arrangement is shown in Figure 12.2.

In a third situation, there may be no central SCM team, but each project will have its own SCM team. This is usually applicable to large projects, where the size and complexity of the project warrants a full-fledged SCM team of its own. This type of arrangement is shown in Figure 12.3.

The SCM team needs strong support from management, because it does not have the necessary muscle power to enforce its decisions like the line functions do. But if proper awareness is created about the importance

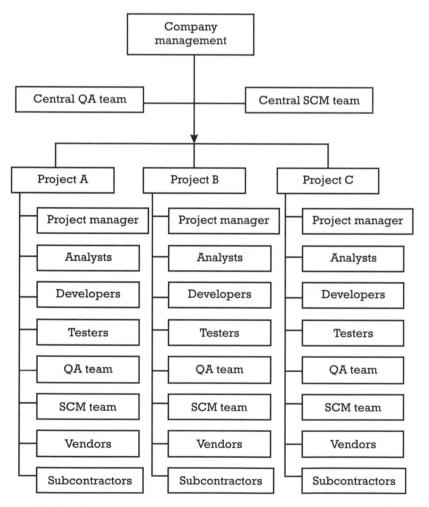

Figure 12.2 Organizational structure when a central SCM team and individual SCM teams are used.

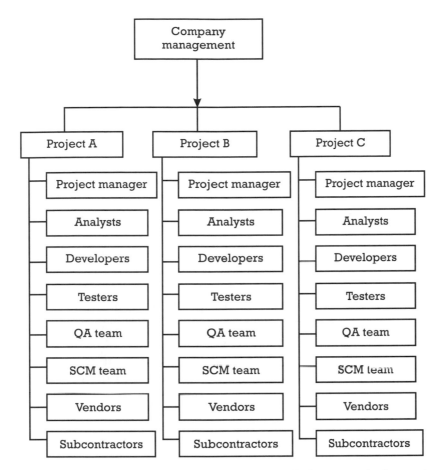

Figure 12.3 Organizational structure in which there are independent SCM teams for each project.

of SCM and its benefits and if the SCM system is designed in such a way that SCM approval is a prerequisite for moving from one phase to another, the SCM team can get the necessary cooperation from the project team and other support functions to carry out its tasks.

Another important aspect that should be remembered is that the SCM team will have to enlist the help of other professionals in the organization. The SCM team will require help from the management team, the QA team, the project team, and others to carry out the various functions. For example, the CCB's permanent members include management, QA, marketing, and project team representatives. Also for conducting

CR evaluations or causal analysis, outside help might be required. So a mechanism should be in place for determining how these human resources will be made available to the SCM team. Ideally the SCM team should make a request to the concerned group and the group should cooperate. But if the cooperation is not forthcoming, the SCM team might need management support to get the required personnel.

SCM organization

The configuration management officer (CMO) is the head of the SCM team. She is usually the person who was part of the SCM system design team and has most probably written the SCM plan. This person is responsible for all SCM activities in the project and reports to the CCB. The main responsibilities of the CMO include setting up the SCM system, training the SCM team, assigning duties and responsibilities, constituting the CCB or CCBs as the case may be, coordinating between the project team and the CCB, managing the change control activities, setting up the SCM libraries and other control mechanisms, and coordinating between the audit team and the project team. She will be part of the CCB and will ensure that the CCB meetings are convened according to the schedule or whenever the need arises (emergency meetings).

Other members of the SCM team have the responsibility of assisting the CMO in performing the SCM tasks. These include both technical people and administrative personnel. The technical people will be concerned with tasks like configuration identification, change management, version control, release management, configuration audits, causal analysis, and updating the configuration knowledge base. The administrative staff will ensure that meeting information is sent on time, the minutes of the meetings are sent to the people on the distribution list, the decisions made in the meetings are conveyed to the appropriate people, the status accounting reports are delivered, the skill inventory database is updated regularly, and so on.

Then there will be people who work for the SCM team on an ad hoc basis. These people include those who conduct the change request evaluation, problem analysis, causal analysis, and configuration audits and who serve as subject experts in the CCB meetings and so on.

So in a typical SCM setup, different people will carry out the various SCM functions. Some of the people in an SCM environment are listed next and a brief description given about what they do.

- ▶ *Developers.* Developers are the project team members who develop the software system or product. They do the analysis, design, and coding.

- ▶ *Testers.* Testers conduct the testing of the programs developed by the developers. In most cases the developers do the unit testing and hand over their programs to the testers. The testers do the module testing, the integration testing, and the system testing. These people are responsible for coordinating the alpha and beta testing phases. The testers originate the defect or problem reports, make enhancement suggestions, and collect and collate the feedback from the alpha and beta testing programs. Then they initiate the problem tracking and change management process for each of the defects/enhancements found. The role of the testers varies slightly from project to project (for example, in some projects, there will be separate teams for alpha and beta testing), but their main responsibility is to find the bugs and report them.

- ▶ *Quality assurance representatives.* The goal of a good QA program is to prevent defects from occurring or recurring. So the main responsibility of the QA personnel is to develop standards and guidelines for the different activities in the project such as design, coding, and testing. They must also make sure that these policies and standards are followed by everybody on the team. To ensure this, they conduct quality audits. QA personnel also form part of the CCB and play a vital role in the change disposition. In many organizations it is the QA team members who perform the change request evaluation, problem analysis, casual analysis, and the knowledge base and help desk maintenance.

- ▶ *Assigners.* An assigner is the SCM team member responsible for scheduling the tasks that are to be performed based on their severity and impact and assigning these tasks to the other people in the team. Assigning the change requests for evaluation, giving the problem reports for analysis, giving the task of implementing a change to somebody, and ensuring that all activities are performed on schedule is the assigner's responsibility.

▶ *Build manager.* This is another SCM role and the responsibility of the person is to handle the various builds and releases. He is the person who is responsible for ensuring that the configuration items are given the correct version numbers, proper baselines are established, build files are accurately kept, branching and merging of the file or files is done properly, and so on. The primary goal of this person is to take all the necessary steps to ensure that the SCM system is capable of configuring and building the system or its components completely and accurately at any time.

▶ *Administrator.* This is the person who does the database administration of the various SCM databases and repositories, assigns access privileges to the different team members, makes backups, and so on. This person works very closely with the build manager to ensure that the build process proceeds without any problem.

We have already seen that many other people are involved in the SCM team. The roles just mentioned are generally full-time jobs and are usually present in every project that has SCM. The other personnel in the SCM team, possibly with the exception of the CMO and a few administrative people, are called in as needed. For example, the CCB members are called only when a change request has been submitted that needs to be resolved or a decision has to be made about the release of a product and so on.

With configuration management tools automating every possible aspect of configuration management, the number of people required to manage the SCM functions is decreasing. But some areas—analysis, evaluation, audits—still require human intervention. Also, not all projects will use totally automated SCM tools; some projects will use tools that automate certain areas such as change management, version control, build management or system building, and status accounting. Projects will also arise in which all SCM functions are done manually. So depending on the nature of the project and level of automation, the organization of the SCM team will vary.

Skill inventory database

We have seen that the SCM team relies heavily on professionals from other groups in the organization to carry out its various functions. So the SCM team should know whether the people (with the necessary qualifications) whom they want are available and if available where are they located and so on. The author has worked on many projects where one of the main problems faced by the SCM team was tracking down the right people to do particular functions such as impact analysis, problem evaluation, and causal analysis.

In one particular project where the author was the CMO, this problem—the task of finding the right people—was very acute. The company had more than 1500 employees in five or six different offices. The skills and availability of people was difficult information to get. So the idea of a skill inventory database was used and it was successful. The idea was borrowed from industrial engineering. (The author worked as an industrial engineer before becoming a software professional.)

This technique of creating a skill inventory of the shop floor workers has been used for implementing modern production systems like Toyota production system and small group manufacturing where finding the people with the right skills fast is a necessity. So that technique was used in the SCM system and it worked so well that the author has since used it in many projects with equal success. So it is a good idea for the SCM team to have a skill inventory database of the company's personnel. The database can store the details of each and every professional whose services will be required by the SCM team. This includes top management, the QA team members, the project team members, the SCM team members, the vendor/subcontractor team members, the members of the hardware group, and other support functions. A sample of such a database is shown in Table 12.1.

The skill inventory database captures the skills of every person in the company. The SCM team should decide which skills need to be captured. For example, knowledge of SCM procedures, experience in conducting quality audits, causal analysis, change evaluation, and knowledge of programming languages and database management systems are all skills that could be captured in the database.

Table 12.1
Sample Skill Inventory Database

Name	Thomas	Barbara	Ishtar	Bob
Location/project	L1/P1	L2/P2	L2/P2	L1/P2
SCM activities	7	2	0	0
Quality audits	4	0	3	0
Causal analysis	3	4	3	0
COBOL	10	0	5	2
DB2	7	0	3	2
CICS	7	0	3	2
Oracle	0	4	0	0
Visual Basic	0	5	0	0

The numbers in the columns in Table 12.1 represent the experience in years for each skill. The number of years of experience in a particular field is not always a good guide, however, to a person's knowledge level and expertise in that field. But this is the most easily available yardstick. Other criteria can be used such as a merit rating or point rating system. If the company has a good personnel evaluation system, then those ratings could be used instead of the number of years of experience.

Although it is perfectly fine to store this information on an electronic spreadsheet, it would be ideal if it were stored in a relational database, because this makes the identification of the right people an easier task. For example, if you need a person to do an evaluation of a change request that involves a program developed in the COBOL-DB2-CICS environment, then you need a person who is familiar with the SCM activities and who has good knowledge of COBOL, DB2, and CICS. If you were using a spreadsheet or a manual log, it would be a very time-consuming job to locate the people you want. But if the data is stored in a relational database you can get an answer by simply querying the database:

```
SELECT name, location
FROM skill_inventory_table
WHERE SCM ≥2 AND COBOL ≥2 AND DB2 ≥2 AND CICS ≥2;
```

This query will bring up the names of all people who have 2 or more years experience in SCM, COBOL, DB2, and CICS. Then you merely choose from the resulting list.

The relational database should always be kept current. People leave the company, new people join, and people learn new skills, all of which should be reflected in the database. The SCM team can get the data from employee records and update the database or ask the employees to update their records.

CCB organization

The CCB or change control board is the apex body that decides on whether or not to carry out a change. Depending on the size, complexity, and nature of the project, there will be a single CCB, multiple CCBs, or even multilevel CCBs. In most projects there will be only one CCB. For small projects, there may not even be a CCB; in which case, the project leader will decide whether to accept or reject a change request. For projects having a CCB, the CCB will have both permanent and ad hoc members. The permanent members include the representatives of the management, project team, QA team, marketing team, SCM team, and in many cases client representatives. The ad hoc members are people who are called (and whose expertise is required) in to resolve issues that the CCB is not able to resolve or needs expert advice to resolve. Sometimes the CCB may summon the change initiator or evaluator for clarifications. A sample structure for the CCB is shown in Figure 12.4.

In some large and complex projects, more than one CCB will be required, with each handling different modules of the project. This situation arises when the project is very large and may be distributed geographically, so that a single CCB will not be able to handle the disposition of all the change requests and problem reports. In cases where multiple CCBs are present, there should be a "super CCB" (SCCB) to oversee the functioning of the CCBs and to resolve conflicts, if any, between the CCBs. This type of setup is shown in Figure 12.5.

In some cases, multilevel CCBs will be required as shown in Figure 12.6. Here the difference is that each level of CCB will handle a particular kind of change request or problem report. For example, a level 3 CCB will handle problems with low severity. Here the CCBs are classified based on the types of change requests they handle, whereas in the case of multiple CCBs they are classified based on the module or subsystem they handle.

So in the case of a multiple CCB environment all the change requests from a particular module will be handled by the same CCB, but in a

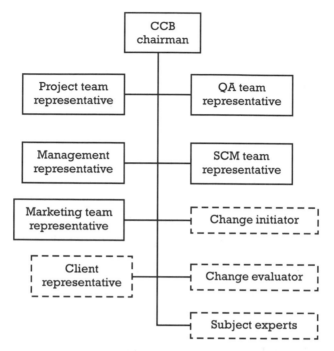

Figure 12.4   Sample CCB organization.

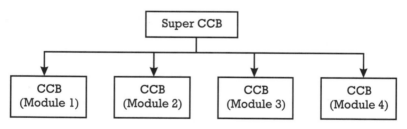

Figure 12.5   Multiple CCBs.

multilevel CCB all the change requests with the same severity level will be handled by a CCB. Multiple CCBs are useful when the project is large and has many modules and development takes place in different locations. Multilevel CCBs are applicable to large projects that are complex in nature but the development takes place in one place. Here the multiple levels help to resolve simple problems faster because the lower level CCB would be constituted by the module leader and an SCM representative, who can make decisions faster rather than waiting for the full CCB meeting to happen. Thus the load on higher level CCBs is reduced and they can

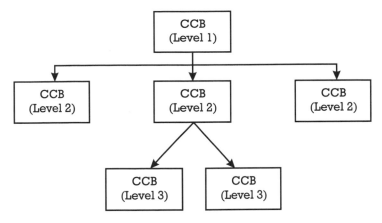

Figure 12.6 Multilevel CCBs.

focus their attention on critical and severe problems that will have huge impacts on costs and project schedules.

Conclusion

The place of the SCM team in the organizational structure depends very much on the organization and varies from one organization to another. We have seen the different organizational structures. But irrespective of the position in the organizational hierarchy, the SCM team performs the same functions. We also saw the organization of the SCM team and the different people who play significant roles in the functioning of the SCM activities. We saw the different types of CCBs and how they function.

Because SCM tools are automating more and more tasks the role of the SCM team and the tasks they have to perform are being reduced. So in the future we can see reductions in the size of the SCM team, except in some areas such as analysis, evaluation, and audits, where human intervention is still required.

Reference

[1]   *IEEE Standard Glossary of Software Engineering Terminology* (IEEE Std-610-1990), *IEEE Standards Collection (Software Engineering)*, Piscataway, NJ: IEEE, 1997.

CHAPTER

13

Contents

Software configuration management tools

Introduction

Software configuration management tools are becoming more important in today's complex software development environments. Today a typical software development project consists of multidisciplinary teams, spread across different parts of the globe, and working in networked environments and in different time zones. To avoid chaos and to bring in discipline and improve development productivity, the role played by SCM tools is becoming more and more important.

Software configuration management tools are nothing new. They have existed in the mainframe and UNIX environments for many years and now they are available for every platform and every kind of development environment. In fact, hundreds of SCM tools are available in the marketplace.

But it is important to remember that no SCM tool is a panacea for all SCM problems.

The purchase of a sophisticated tool is just one step toward effective SCM. Using the wrong tool, or using the right tool ineptly or insensitively, makes SCM problems worse, not better [1]. In this chapter we look at exactly what SCM tools are and what they can do to automate the SCM process and improve development productivity. We also discuss how to select an SCM tool that is best for your project/organization and take a look at the question of whether to make or buy your organization's SCM tools.

Evolution of SCM tools

Initially, SCM was just a means of controlling changes to the source code. Tools like Source Code Control System (SCCS) and Revision Control System (RCS) under UNIX were created for that purpose, but their function was quite limited. Eventually, the ability to manage revisions, compress deltas, handle binary file types, and increase security levels were added—and source code control turned into version control.

SCM evolved into a more comprehensive process as developers realized the need to track more than just changes to the source code. Today, SCM tools include such diverse features as build management, defect and enhancement tracking, requirement tracking, release management, software production control, software packaging and distribution control (licensing and generation of serial numbers, CD keys, codes), and site management. The ability to identify components, recreate deliverables, monitor problems and change requirements, and deliver a product of consistently high quality is the current goal of SCM. Thus it involves monitoring every phase of a software product's life cycle.

SCM tools have come a long way from just managing the source code. They are now one of the critical functions of software engineering that help to keep projects on track and manage them effectively. According to Mosley and others [2], today's SCM tools are getting *bigger, better,* and *bolder*. They are bigger because they no longer manage just code; they can manage the development of any object in the system's life cycle. They are better because they support parallel as well as incremental development. They are bolder because they have expanded their functionality beyond the control and management of objects and into the control and management of processes.

Reasons for the increasing popularity of SCM tools

There is no question that the market for SCM tools is very hot. Industry analysts are forecasting steady growth rates for the SCM tools market. Why have so many companies replaced their manual or semiautomated SCM systems with SCM tools? Why are so many companies, which were using old SCM tools like SCCS or RCS, changing to more sophisticated tools? Here are some reasons:

▶ *Development time reduction.* SCM tools reduce development time by improving development productivity and reducing mistakes.

▶ *Increased business agility.* Improved productivity and reduced development time means less time is needed to get a product to market. This coupled with the SCM tool's ability to manage and track problems, fix them, rebuild the systems easily, accurately, and quickly, and release them faster results in improved customer satisfaction. So the company can be more agile and more responsive to the needs of the customer without compromising product quality.

▶ *Error reduction.* The SCM tools automate most of the monotonous and repetitive tasks that were done earlier by people. Thus SCM tools almost eliminate the chance to make errors.

▶ *Information integration.* One of the major functions of SCM is to provide sufficient, relevant, and accurate information about the software system to the different people in the project—programmers, managers, analysts, auditors, and so on—so that the software development and maintenance processes proceed smoothly. Earlier, people had to rely on reports provided by the status accounting function. These reports were not capable of answering ad hoc queries. But today's SCM tools have all the information the user needs and can deliver them to the user in any format that she wants almost instantly. This information integration capability and flexibility is one of the most important advantages of SCM tools.

▶ *Automation.* SCM tools automate many processes such as configuration control, defect tracking, status reporting, version control, and build management. These were the tasks that were considered the "necessary evils" of manual SCM systems. By automating these tasks, SCM tools have improved development productivity and given people more time for the system development process.

These are some of the reasons for the increasing popularity of the SCM tools market. As more and more companies join the race, the competition is getting hotter and the SCM tool vendors are gearing up to meet the competition by offering more features and better capabilities for their products. So the future will see a fierce battle for market share and mergers and acquisitions aimed at gaining strategic and competitive advantage. The ultimate winner in this race will be the customer, who will get better products and better services at affordable prices.

Advantages of SCM tools

Installing an SCM tool has many advantages, both direct and indirect. The direct advantages include improved development efficiency (people will have more time to work on developmental activities), information integration for better decision making, faster response time to customer queries, and so on. The indirect benefits include a better corporate image, improved customer goodwill, and customer satisfaction.

Some of the direct benefits are (1) information integration, (2) flexibility, (3) better analysis and planning capabilities, and (4) use of latest technology. These benefits are discussed next.

Information integration

The first and most important advantage lies in the promotion of integration. The reason SCM tools are called *integrated* is because they have the ability to automatically update data between related SCM components. For example, you need only update the status of a change request at one place, say, in the change management system; all the other components will automatically get updated. So when a developer checks in a component after making changes, the status of a change request automatically changes from "Assigned" to "Complete." The new files or files that are checked in are automatically assigned the new version numbers. The dependency details are updated to reflect the new change. The new versions are designated as the latest versions of the items and so on. The next time you create a status report all of these modifications will be reflected in that report.

The beauty of this system is that information updating happens instantaneously. So you get up-to-the-minute information at your fingertips. This information integration leads to better decision making and resolution of problems.

Another advantage of this integration is that the people who are involved in a project are also connected to each other. This integration has tremendous potential for improving productivity. For example, one can have virtual CCB meetings, on-line polls, automatic notification, and so on.

Flexibility

The second advantage of SCM tools is their flexibility. Diverse multinational environments are covered in one system, and functions that comprehensively manage multiple locations and distributed and parallel development can be easily implemented. To cope with globalization, distributed development, and sophisticated development projects (development of large, complex, and mission-critical systems), this flexibility is essential, and one could say that it has major advantages, not simply for development and maintenance, but also in terms of management.

Better analysis and planning capabilities

Yet another advantage is the boost to the planning functions. By enabling the comprehensive and unified management of related SCM functions (such as configuration control, status accounting, configuration audits) and their data, it becomes possible to utilize fully many types of decision support systems and simulation functions, what-if analysis, and so on. For example, we could simulate the impact on the project cost and schedule of using more than one person on a change implementation. Furthermore, it becomes possible to carry out flexibly and in real time the filing and analysis of data from a variety of dimensions. The decision makers can get the information they want, thus enabling them to make better and more informed decisions.

Use of latest technology

The fourth advantage is the utilization of the latest developments in information technology (IT). SCM tool vendors realized that in order to grow and to sustain that growth, they would have to embrace the latest developments in the field of information technology. So they quickly adapted their systems to take advantage of the latest technologies such as open systems, client/server technology, and the Internet/intranets. It is this quick adaptation to the latest changes in IT that makes the flexible adaptation to changes in future development environments possible. It is this flexibility that makes the incorporation of the latest technology possible during system design, development, and maintenance phases.

Why many SCM tool implementations fail

SCM tools—if chosen correctly, implemented judiciously, and used effi-ciently—will raise productivity, shorten development times, improve responsiveness, and result in better customer satisfaction. To use the tool efficiently, it has to be the right tool (right in the sense that it integrates well with the organization's business processes), the people who use the tool have to be properly trained, and so on. But many a project/organiza-tion fails in this because they use the wrong product, conduct an incompetent and haphazard implementation, and suffer inefficient or ineffective usage.

SCM is *first an attitude; second, a process; and only third, a set of tools* [3]. Attitude refers to the feeling or mood of the people in the organization toward SCM. So the users of the SCM system have to be convinced about the real benefits of using SCM. This can be done by educating the people about its benefits and exposing the misconceptions about SCM. This is important because, if people believe SCM is unnecessary, they will try to bypass it. And unless a consistent SCM process is integrated into the development methodology, no one will know when to apply the SCM tools, or even what those tools are.

To work successfully, the SCM solutions need a lot of factors to click. There should be good people who know the SCM concepts and the proj-ect/organizational details, the vendor should be good, and the vendor's package should be the one best suited for the company's needs. The implementation should be planned well and executed perfectly and the end-user training should be done so that the people understand the system and the effect of their efforts on the overall success of the program.

SCM can be implemented in a variety of ways. It can be implemented in a phased manner (the incremental approach) or it can be implemented in one shot (the big-bang approach). Irrespective of the implementation methodology chosen, the development process has to be mature and the development environment and the organizational culture must be conducive for the implementation of SCM and its tools. If the implementation is done in an environment where the people are not ready for SCM and the work culture is not suited, then the implementation will fail. So the first step in the SCM implementation process is to make the organizational environment suitable for SCM.

Organizations exist in different levels of process maturity. The ease and correctness with which they can execute a process depends on their maturity. As such, it is generally not fruitful to impose a very sophisticated process on an organization whose maturity is low. The maturity of an organization not only depends on the skill sets of the individuals, but also on the chemistry of the team. This makes improvement an incremental process. The lessons, habits, and practices learned doing simple tasks provide the foundation to take the organization toward more sophisticated tasks [4]. So the maturity level of the organization is very critical in the success of an SCM implementation.

Also many SCM tool implementations fail because they try to implement SCM in the "tool" way rather than in the "process" way. As we saw earlier, SCM is first an attitude, then a process, and only third a set of tools. One can implement sophisticated, all-encompassing SCM tools, loaded with features, but if the people who are using them do not know why they are doing a particular task or what happens when they do something or the effect of their actions (or lack of it) on others, then the chances of such an implementation succeeding are slim.

Thus for an SCM tool implementation to succeed, the implementation has to be planned well, the people must be ready for SCM, the development process must be in place, the selected tool should be well integrated with the process, and finally everybody involved in the project should understand the importance of SCM and the role each one of them has to play to make the implementation a success.

SCM tools and SCM functions

The days when a single programmer developed an application all by himself are a thing of the past. Today's software development is a team effort. When more than one person is involved in the development of a software system, it can lead to communications breakdowns, shared data problems, simultaneous update problems, and so on. We have seen how an SCM system could help solve these problems. But manual SCM is a tedious, monotonous, and time-consuming process. Many tasks like change management, record keeping, and status reporting are repetitive in nature. So we need to automate these tasks. A good SCM tool should automate the project coordination and management tasks, should support repeatable processes, should manage changes and issues, and should automate the system builds.

In a manual SCM scenario a developer or programmer spends more time on nondevelopmental activities such as documentation, modification, and revision of the requirements and design documents, bug fixing, and so on. Another portion of the nonprogramming time is spent on handling change requests, tracking user requirements, doing causal analysis, creating status reports, and so on. Even though all of these tasks are necessary for the smooth functioning of the project, spending the precious time of the programmers and developers on these mundane tasks, which could easily be automated, is a cardinal offense—and this is where automated SCM tools can be invaluable.

SCM tools automate the manual tasks and hence set the development teams free to actually develop. Also today's software systems are more sophisticated, highly complex, support multiple platforms (sometimes they are cross-platform), use complex technologies, and are developed in distributed environments by diverse (different cultural, social, educational, and ethnic backgrounds) development teams. Managing a project of this kind manually is almost impossible. So today SCM tools are no longer a luxury, but a necessity. Not having an SCM tool can become a strategic disadvantage and can lead to the catastrophic consequences of failed projects, cost and time overruns, customer dissatisfaction, and others.

We have seen that SCM tools automate most of the SCM functions. We now look at the features of SCM tools that help automate the SCM functions, reducing human intervention and improving productivity.

Version management

Version management is a critical function of SCM and is the basis on which other functions are built. Version management is the storage of multiple images of the development files or set of related files in an application. With a good version management system one can get an image—a snapshot in time of the development process—and recreate the file or files as they were at that discrete point in time.

Any good SCM tool will support version management activities such as creating, working, and changing versions. A version consists of a file or a set of files, each with a particular version label. The SCM tools have the capability to define what file or files make up a version. Once a version is defined, the user should be able to check out the files that make up a version. The SCM tool should be able to identify the changes to the components of a version and then create or define a new version. In this area—identifying the changes and creating new versions—and in the system building (or build management) area the version management system works in conjunction with the change management system and build management system so that the correct versions are incorporated into the system builds.

Change management

Most SCM tools completely automate the change control procedures. They manage the repositories. When a change request is made, the information about it goes to all the concerned personnel (like CCB members) so that they can send their approval or disapproval immediately by e-mail or some other messaging system. This eliminates the time lag between change initiation and disposition. Virtual CCB meetings and on-line polls are now standard with almost any good SCM tool. The change management system can be configured (a rule-based system) to automatically receive the change requests, process them based on a set of rules, get the responses from the appropriate sources regarding the disposition, and allocate the implementation work to qualified professionals and notify them regarding the work allocated to them. All of these things can be done without human intervention. This kind of workflow automation helps to improve productivity and shorten the change process. Also when a developer checks out the file or files,[1] the change management systems will begin the tracking of the activities that affect those file or files.

The change management system is also notified when the task of implementing a change is allotted to someone. So only authorized personnel can check out or make changes to the specific files. So the change management system keeps track of the modifications made to the change set and its components and when the change is completed and the items are checked in, the system can compare the before and after images and create the change history, the delta, and store the items in the most efficient manner. Also the details of the change process, such as who initiated the change, which people were involved in the decision making, who implemented the changes, how much time was taken for implementing the change, how the change was implemented, and a host of other details are captured automatically. This information is very relevant to the status accounting function and helps in managing the project more effectively.

We have seen that the configuration identification function is an element of configuration management, consisting of selecting the configuration items for a system and recording their functional and physical characteristics in technical documentation. In an automated environment this type of information can be captured and updated automatically. The parsing tools can determine the interdependencies of the various configuration items so that when shared components get modified, the system can alert the users about the other impacted items. This automatic capturing of the component interdependencies saves a lot of time that would otherwise be spent on impact analysis when a change request is initiated. With this information already in the system, the users just have to query the system repository to determine the impacted items.

Most change management systems support team development, parallel development, and distributed development. Many of the modern tools allow more than one person to work on the same file or set of files. In parallel development, two or more users may need to work on the same file, just as they would do in concurrent development. In the case of

---

1. A person can check out more than one file because a change request implementation is
   rarely confined to a single file and even if it is confined to a single file, the associated
   analysis and design documentation, user manuals, and so on also have to be updated.

concurrent development, the branches are eventually merged into a single item, whereas in the case of parallel development the branches will go ahead without merging. Parallel development is necessary when the development teams are producing versions of the same component for different hardware platforms or operating systems (also called variants).

Multiple development paths are usually supported with branches. Branching allows users to store more than one path for the same file. In the case of concurrent development, once the changes are made and the different people check in their files, the system will compare the changes and do an automatic merging of those changes. There is also the facility to do interactive merging, where the system will highlight the changes made by the different people with respect to the ancestor object. The systems can be configured to do automatic merging or interactive merging depending on the user's preferences.

The change management systems keep a chronological record (or *journal*) of all activities that are applied to the system components so that at any point any object or component in the system can be brought back to any of the previous states. This is helpful in cases where you need to unwind the impact of an emergency fix that was done in the middle of the night, so that it can be thoroughly checked, tested, and repromoted.

Another important and very useful feature of the SCM tools is their graphical interface. The tools use different colors, icons, and other features to help the users absorb information quickly and determine patterns and exceptions easily.

Problem tracking

Problem reporting and tracking is one of the activities that takes a lot of time and effort. The problem has to be reported, analyzed, fixed, and the defect prevention methods have to be carried out. The existing problem records (the knowledge base) can be scanned for similar incidents that may have been solved already. This searching is best done by a computer, especially when we are talking about large knowledge bases. The computer can easily find the records that match the search criteria, in a fraction of the time taken by a manual process.

The problem tracking components of the SCM tools track the problem from its origin to completion and capture the details of the problem, such as originator, date of problem identification, cause of the problem, how and when it was fixed, how much time was taken, what kind of skills were needed, and so on. These details are captured automatically as the activities happen. Modern problem tracking tools are very sophisticated and have advanced features like automatic receiving of the problem reports, automatic categorization of the reports, rule-based actions, automatic notifying, and alerting mechanisms.

Many tools are capable of automatically notifying the concerned personnel by e-mail or pager messages about the arrival of a problem report depending on predefined criteria chosen, such as severity and/or impact. These tools are also capable of creating alerts (automatic notification and problem escalation) based on the promotion of the problem through stages of resolution.

Promotion management

As the software system is being developed, it goes through the software development life cycle process. Depending on the life cycle model chosen, the phases will differ, but all software components have to go through the various phases of analysis, design, development, testing, release, maintenance, and so on. The promotion management tools automatically record the phases through which the configuration items in the system go through and the various details such as when each phase started and when it was finished. This is one advantage of the SCM tools. They can capture a lot of information and create trails, which will be very useful when one needs to know exactly what happened or needs to recreate an event or an item before or after a particular event. For example, if we know exactly what was done just after alpha testing, we can recreate an item so that it is in the state it was in before the test, when it did not have any problems.

Obtaining this information and these facilities are possible in the manual systems also, but with an SCM tool the degree of detail that can be captured is almost infinite.

System building

When the components of a software system are ready to be tested or shipped, we do what is called *system building*. We combine all files and may compile them, link edit them, and create an application. This build can be done for a subsystem, a module, or an entire system. This build can be done for integration testing, alpha or beta testing, and for system releases.

At this stage, capturing the details of each and every build and the building process is of paramount importance—which components were used in the build, what versions of the components were used, which operating system was used, which version of the operating system, what compiler and linker options were in effect, and so on. This is important because each build should be reproducible and repeatable, and that reproduction has to be reliable and accurate. One must be able to recreate, say, the alpha test version of the system, say, 1 year after the actual testing was done. For doing this one needs the information mentioned above.

The SCM build management tools capture this information (in most cases automatically) and help provide reliable, repeatable builds. The automatic source code scanning, the dependency analysis capabilities, and the creation of build audit trails (footprinting) are just some of the features of the SCM tools that save time, shorten build cycles, and eliminate build errors by providing repeatable, automated builds of software projects. The SCM tools make the cross-platform builds that span multiple platforms, operating systems, and development environments easier, faster, and more accurate.

Also many of these systems maintain the history of the previous builds and releases in their repositories. This helps when monitoring conflicts between the new releases and any of the previous releases that are still in use.

Status accounting (querying and reporting)

Status accounting consists of the recording and reporting of information needed to manage a configuration efficiently. With manual systems one has to record all events that will be needed later. This record keeping is a tedious and monotonous job and requires effort by the many people who perform the different SCM functions. There is also a limit to which the details can be captured. Also the manual reporting function basically relies on routine reports to satisfy the information needs of the various participants in the software development process. Ad hoc queries are always time consuming and difficult to accommodate.

When one uses an SCM tool, however, as we have seen earlier, the information integration happens. There is no need for active record keeping; the system monitors all activities and keeps a record of them to the level of detail specified by the user. Once the information is in the SCM tool's database, it can be managed at will. The powerful querying tools allow the users to get accurate answers to their numerous and varied information needs, when they need them. The reports can be generated in any format specified by the user. She can use graphical interfaces and templates or wizards to create a query and get the answers. This accurate and immediate access to information is one of the best features of the SCM automation.

Configuration audits

Auditing means validating the completeness of a product and maintaining consistency among the components by ensuring that the product is a well-defined collection of components. For auditing requirements one needs a history of all changes, traceability between all related components in the product and their evolution, and a log containing all details about work done [5]. The reporting features of the SCM tools provide this information.

The differences reporting feature of the SCM tools reports the differences between the versions and releases. The ad hoc query facility of the tool helps answer any specific questions that the auditor has. The SCM tools automatically record all activities happening to the configuration items, and thus provide a comprehensive audit trail of the activities performed on an item and the events that have happened. These reports and logs help a great deal in automating the auditing process and make the configuration audits a painless process.

Access and security

The information contained in the SCM tool is sensitive and should not be available to all. Also the items in the repository should be accessible only to those who have the necessary authorization. In the case of manual systems the configuration managers will have to take action to prevent unauthorized access to files or information. But the SCM tools have features that aid in managing access to the system.

The system can be configured so that only people with the necessary authorization will get to see the information or will have access to the files. These access privileges and security mechanisms can be enforced using the user ID and login password of the users, so that the exact mechanism is transparent to them.

A user can log in to the system and access all information he is authorized to see, and what he is authorized to see can be set based on the user ID (or designation, title, role). With distributed development scenarios, where developers access the SCM information and files using the Internet, encryption methods are used to ensure secure transmission of data and information across the Internet.

SCM tools

In the previous section we discussed the general characteristics of the modern SCM tools and their advantages. More than 50 major SCM tools and vendors were on the market as of early 2000 and new players are entering the market. A list of the SCM tools and details about the vendors are given in Appendix A.

As we saw earlier, SCM tool selection is one of the critical factors for the success of the SCM implementation. The success of a company lies in selecting an SCM tool that suits its needs and matches its profile. In the next section of this chapter we look at how to select the right SCM tool for your organization/project.

SCM tool selection

SCM tools have gained popularity and their usefulness has increased to a point where software development without an SCM tool is almost non-existent. Also, a manual SCM system is not acceptable, except for very small, single-person projects. All other projects can really benefit from the use of SCM tools.

SCM tools are now available in all sizes and shapes for all platforms and development environments. Evaluating the SCM tools available in the marketplace and then selecting one for your organization/project are critical parts of the process. This decision can make or break an organization. If the choice is not right then the organization will pay dearly for it.

Of the more than 50 SCM tools available, the features they offer vary, as do the technologies they support, the technologies they use, the architecture on which they are built, and the available platforms. Each tool has its own strengths and weaknesses. For example, some are better at change management, whereas others have excellent build management and versioning capabilities. There are SCM tools that cover the entire spectrum of SCM functionality and there are tools that just do source control.

Deciding which tool is suited to your organization is a difficult task. Each piece of marketing literature of the tool vendors claims that their product is the best among the lot and has all of the features that you will ever need. So if you go by what is written in the product brochure or what the salespeople say, you will find it very difficult to make a decision and might end up with the wrong choice. According to Dart [6], "… such literature (the marketing literature of the tool vendor) is valuable for giving the reader an overview of functionality and a glimpse at the differentiator for that vendor's offering. But, if you compare the literature or listen to a vendor's presentation, it would be very difficult to evaluate which package is the best or which would be most suitable for your organization." So tool selection is something that should be done in a systematic and scientific manner. In this section we examine how to select an SCM tool that will suit your needs.

The most important factor to keep in mind when analyzing the different packages is that none of them is perfect. The idea that there is no perfect package needs to be understood by everyone on the decision-making team. The objective of the selection process is not to identify a package that covers each and every requirement (a perfect fit). The objective is to find a package that is flexible enough to meet the company's needs. Or in other words, to find a tool that can be customized to obtain a "good fit."

Because there are so many, analyzing all SCM packages before reaching a decision is not a viable solution. It is also a very time-consuming process. So it is better to limit the number of packages that is evaluated to less than five. It is always better to do a thorough and detailed evaluation of a smaller number of packages, than to do a superficial analysis of dozens of packages. So the company should do a preevaluation screening to limit the number of packages that is to be evaluated by the committee. The preevaluation process should eliminate those packages that are not at all suitable for the company's business processes. One can zero in on the few best packages by looking at the product literature of the vendors, getting help from external consultants, and most importantly finding out what package is used by similar companies. It is a good idea to look around to find out how the different packages are performing in environments similar to yours. Once you select a few packages after the screening, you can call the respective vendors to request presentations/ demos.

Dart [6] classifies the SCM tools into three categories: version control tools, developer-oriented tools, and process-oriented tools. According to her the evaluation process can be narrowed down to a few tools if the company knows which category of tools they are looking for. The tools vary in features, complexity, and functionality, with the process-oriented tools being the most sophisticated and having more functionality than the other two.

According to Dart [6], a version control tool would typically suit a small company, or a research and development group that has a small number of releases and possibly no variant releases. A developer-oriented tool would typically suit a medium- or large-sized company that does not have a lot of formal processes defined and is not focused on standards certification. The company might have many variant releases, and would need strong support for parallel development and build management, as well as more reliability from the CM repository. A process-oriented tool would typically suit a large corporation with formal processes that need to be automated, that is focused on process improvement in general, and that has sophisticated build management and change management needs. The categorization of the SCM tools by Dart can be used to narrow the list of candidates in the preevaluation screening process.

After the decision to buy an SCM tool has been made, the company needs to develop selection criteria that will permit the evaluation of all the chosen packages on the same scale. To choose the best system, the company should identify the system that meets the business needs, that matches the development process, and that identifies with the development practices of the company. It will be impossible to get a system that performs its development and maintenance functions in exactly the same way as the company does, but the goal is to get the system that has the least number of differences.

Selection process

The selection process is one of the most important phases of SCM implementation, because the tool that you select will decide the success or failure of the project. Because SCM tools involve a huge investment, once a package is purchased, it is not an easy task to switch to another one. So it is a "do it right the first time" proposition. There is no room for error.

Selection committee

It is a good idea to form a selection or evaluation committee to do the evaluation process. The selection committee should be entrusted with the task of choosing a package for the company. The package experts or the consultants can act as mediators or play the role of explaining the pros and cons of each package.

According to Dart [7], the evaluation committee should be made up of various representatives of the user community. It can include developers, testers, QA people, technical leaders, build managers, and project managers. All provide perspective and ensure their needs are addressed, while providing their own experiences, skill set, and processes to address the three important areas apart from functionality requirements: usability, performance, and scalability requirements.

Working with vendors

Once you decide to buy an SCM tool, the marketing executives of the different vendors will swamp you. Each will have colorful and superbly produced brochures and presentations claiming that their product is the best one for you. They will try eagerly to convince you of that. So you should have a strategy in place for working with these vendors.

As mentioned, you should conduct a detailed evaluation of, say, five packages that meet your preselection criteria. When the vendors arrive for their presentations, you should be thoroughly prepared; otherwise they may overwhelm you with their presentations and you will not have time ask questions. This point is being stressed again and again because most vendors are able to make presentations that leave potential users dazzled, and without proper consideration of all aspects, the selection may end up being based on a set of factors that is insufficient for arriving at a well-informed and judicious decision.

So instead of just listening to presentations, you should be prepared to ask questions. The questions should be prepared beforehand and should address all of your concerns. The responses that you get to your questions will help you either eliminate a vendor or strengthen his case. The questions, if properly prepared and asked, will expose the weak/problem areas, if any, that exist in the vendors' products. Also when you are asking questions, it means that you are not taking anything for granted. It is a good idea to prepare minutes of the meeting and ask the vendors to sign off on them. This will prevent the vendors from making false claims and you can make them accountable if they fail to deliver what they have promised.

The vendors should be asked to show testimonials and practical demonstrations of the system. The vendor should provide references for organizations where the system has been implemented successfully. But all vendors will also have customers where the tools have failed. In the author's opinion, getting those names and reasons for the failure is more important than the success stories. Also it is the author's experience that while vendor representatives are well prepared for the success stories, the questions about failed implementations usually reveal points and issues that the vendor is trying to downplay. So it important to ask about failed implementations.

Role of technology

The existing technology will play a very important role in the SCM tool selection process. Each organization has its own technological environment—how the development process works, what kind of hardware and software are used, a particular database management system that is preferred, and so on. These factors can greatly influence the selection process in the sense that they can limit the number of packages available for evaluation. So management must decide whether the SCM tool will be selected taking the existing infrastructure into consideration or whether the existing systems will not be considered (in which case some of them will have to be scrapped). This is a hard decision, and it is always a better idea to find a package that is compatible with the hardware, software, and technology the company already has in place. Also if the organization has the necessary infrastructure, then it can think of buying the required components from the vendors and integrating them with the existing system.

For example, if an organization is using the operating system's library management system and is quite satisfied with it, then it can go in for a change management and problem-tracking tool and not the complete offering from the vendor. Later if the organization wants to switch from the operating system's library management, it can then purchase the remaining modules of the package. So it is not imperative that all the components offered by the vendor be bought. The evaluation committee in association with the vendor can select the required components and then integrate them with the existing infrastructure. But do not forget here to get the vendor's assurance (in writing) that the existing system will integrate smoothly and seamlessly with the purchased components.

Selection criteria

SCM tools come in all sizes and shapes, with all of the frills, bells and whistles, gizmos and gadgets that you can imagine. So it is a good practice to specify selection criteria for evaluating the packages that survive the preevaluation screening. The criteria can be in the form of a question-naire and a point system can be implemented. This will help make the selection process more objective.

The questions should address the organization's needs and concerns and each issue or question should be given a weight according to how critical that function is for the company. For example, if the company is doing distributed development and has development centers in different countries, then the ability to handle distributed development and web features becomes an important criterion. Likewise the selection criteria should be divided into categories—vital, essential, and desirable—and points should be given to each criterion. This point rating system simpli-fies the evaluation process; but remember that the importance of human intuition (gut feeling) and judgment should never be underestimated.

The best method for preparing the selection criteria is to con-duct a requirements analysis—find out what the company needs. The requirements must reflect those factors that the company considers indispensable for the successful running of the business according to the company's work culture and practices. A set of questions that could form part of the selection criteria can be found in the following documents:

Mosley, V., et al., "Software Configuration Management Tools: Getting Bigger, Better, and Bolder," *Crosstalk: The Journal of Defense Software Engineering*, Vol. 9, No. 1, Jan. 1996, pp. 6–10.

Firth, R., et al., "A Guide to the Classification and Assessment of Software Engineering Tools," Technical Report CMU/SEI-87-TR-10, Software Engineering Institute, Carnegie-Mellon University, 1987.

Berlack, R. H., *Evaluation and Selection of Automated Configuration Management Tools,* Amherst, NH: Configuration Management International, 1995.

Here are some examples of selection criteria:

▶ The package should have distributed development support.

▶ The package should support parallel development of variants.

▶ The package should have both automatic and interactive merging facilities.

▶ The package should have a customizable report generation facility and the facility to export the reports to other systems.

▶ The tool should support a footprinting feature for build management.

▶ The change management and problem tracking system should have the facility to conduct virtual CCB meetings, on-line polls, automatic notification, and so on.

▶ The system should have a graphical user interface.

▶ The performance of the system should be within in such-and-such limits.

▶ The vendor should have been in the business for at least "x" years.

▶ The package should have at least "x" number of installations out of which at least "y" should be in organizations similar to your organization.

▶ The cost of the package with all the necessary modules should be less than "x" dollars.

▶ The package should support incremental module addition. For example, the company should be able to buy the core modules initially and then purchase additional modules as and when desired.

▶ The vendor should provide implementation and postimplementation support.

▶ The vendor should train the company employees on the package.

▶ The package must be customizable and the customization process should be easy (something that could be done in-house).

▶ The package should be scalable or should be capable of growing with the organization.

▶ The vendor's policy and practices regarding updates, versions, and so on should be acceptable.

In this way, the issues, concerns, and expectations that the company has regarding the package can be consolidated and made into a list. Then the items in the list should be divided into the "vital–essential–desirable" categories. Then using this list each package should be evaluated. Many items in the list will have descriptive answers. The committee should analyze these issues and assign points to these items.

One important thing to keep in mind is that whenever a decision is made, the committee should discuss it and a consensus must be reached. In doing so, the chances of conflict between different functions (like the development team, QA team, and other support teams) are reduced. Remember that the SCM tool belongs to all functions, so it is better for decisions to be arrived at via a consensus. This will create the notion that the tool belongs to everyone, and it furthers the idea that a commitment from everyone is needed to make it happen. Most importantly, because both the SCM experts (people who know the tools well) and project team members (people who know the project and work culture well) are involved, they can point out areas and issues that should be given more importance and the aspects that should be scrutinized more thoroughly.

Another source from which the evaluation committee can get information about the tools is independent research agencies and companies.

These sources supply information, comprehensive analyses, and comparison reports about the leading tools. But these reports, although excellent sources of information and a single-point reference about the leading SCM tools, are not totally unbiased, completely accurate, and totally objective and therefore should not be taken as gospel truth. But these reports can provide valuable information about the tools. So, at least a few reports by these research groups should be studied along with the vendor's literature, so that you get a complete picture of the SCM tool marketplace. These reports analyze and compare the tools and their features, predict market trends, forecast the position of the different players in the coming years, and so on. A number of companies and consultants do this kind of analysis. Prominent among them are Ovum Limited (*http://www.ovum.com*), The International Data Corporation (*http://www.idc.com*), and The Butler Group (*http://www.butlergroup.com*). Sometimes the trade magazines like *IEEE Computer* and *Application Development Trends* publish articles about SCM and its current state. This information is also worth looking into because it is independent and not biased.

Once the committee has evaluated all the tools that have cleared the preevaluation stage, listened to the vendor presentations and demos, and cleared pending issues, a decision is reached on which tool to buy.

Once the committee has reached a decision on a tool, it is a good idea to visit a few companies that have installed the particular package to see it in action. But many people will not admit when they have made a mistake, so anything the existing owners say about a package should be taken with a grain of salt. But visiting four or five installations should give the committee members a good idea about the package. If the committee members feel that their decision is right and what they thought is what they have seen, then the company can proceed with the purchase and implementation of the chosen tool.

If anybody is uneasy about some aspect or does not feel that the product meets the expected standards, then the committee members should revisit the question of which tool to choose and be prepared to do the analysis once again. The package that received the maximum score in the point rating system need not be the one that is best suited for the company. So the extra time spent on analysis and evaluation is not a waste; in fact, it could save the company from a potential disaster.

Tool implementation

Once the right tool has been selected, then the next step is implementation. According to Dart [8], making a major change in a company, such as
changing over to a new automated configuration management (CM)
tool, is both a significant opportunity and a major responsibility. It is an
opportunity because it enables a company to address its CM problems and
improve processes to result in better management of its data and its development and maintenance activities. But changing over is a major responsibility because of the ramifications and the resources required to make
the change. Many tricky technical, political, organizational, cultural,
process-oriented, risk-related, and personnel issues need to be addressed
in making the change and people need to be committed to the change.

So to adopt an SCM tool successfully or to make the changeover from
one tool to another, careful planning is a must. All possible aspects of the
implementation should be addressed satisfactorily before starting the
implementation/changeover. This includes the implementation of new
procedures, the changing responsibilities of the users (with SCM tools the
users get more freedom than with a manual system, like the ability to
check out and check in files and interactively merge the changes), the
changing responsibilities of the SCM team (because most of the processes
become automated, a significant reduction is seen in the size of the team),
and the role of the CCB members, QA members, and the audit team (they
will have to be trained in the new technologies, which enable them to
conduct virtual CCB meetings, on-line polls, and audits), and so on.

Many people will need to be trained or retrained on the new tool.
Many will have to be trained on the concepts of SCM and its functions. In
the author's experience, it makes a tremendous difference if the people
are first trained regarding the concepts of SCM and then trained on the
tool. In this way, they can correlate what they are doing with the tool
with the actual SCM concepts and functions. If staff are just trained to use
the tool without understanding the underlying SCM concepts, then they
will be doing their tasks without knowing how their actions affect other
staff. Yes, it is possible to implement an SCM tool and use it without
actually knowing anything about the SCM concepts, but in the long run it
is better to do it the right way—that is, provide training in the tools
along with a training on the SCM concepts and how the concepts are
implemented in the tool.

According to Dart [8], the following issues need to be addressed before the SCM implementation/changeover begins: process, culture, roles, risk management, environment, application, requirements, management, and planning.

The organization should address the current process and new SCM process and how the new tool will be different. The work environment and work culture of the organization and whether they have to be changed or adapted to meet the needs of the new tools need to be analyzed. This is important because a new tool will bring about changes in the roles of the users and give them more power, freedom, and responsibility. The people and the organization should be geared to handle this change.

The new roles of the staff need to be clearly defined. Because most processes are automated by the introduction of the SCM tool, many existing jobs will no longer be needed, and many job profiles will change. The implementation team should make the staff aware of the postimplementation scenario and what exactly will happen to their jobs after the tool is implemented. This is important to secure the cooperation of the users, which is a critical success factor for the tool.

The organization should also identify and assess the potential risk factors in making the transition to the new tool and try to reduce/resolve them. The tool implementation team should also consider which projects are going to use the tool and which project will be the pilot project. If the tool is implemented for a single project and not for the entire organization, then the team should identify which subsystems of the project are to be under control of the tool, whether the work given to the subcontractors will be put under the control of the tool, which module is going to be chosen for the pilot implementation, and so on.

The organization should also have a realistic knowledge of what they can expect from the tool and what its limitations are. This information should also be given to the users of the tool, because overexpectations about a tool can turn into dissatisfaction, misuse, lack of use, or noncooperation when the tool fails to deliver what the user expects it to deliver. So the users should be educated about the capabilities and limitations of the tool. During and after the implementation, management support is essential for the success of the tool. So management must take active interest in the tool and should designate one of the top executives who has the necessary authority and firepower as the leader of the tool implementation team. As Dart [8] says, many brave decisions need to be taken and resources have to be used, schedules have to be altered, and so on and for this one needs a senior person at the helm of the implementation team. Finally all of these issues should be documented and plans, cost estimates, budgets, time schedules, and so on should be prepared before the implementation begins.

Once the planning stage is over, the implementation team in association with the vendor's representative can start the implementation. The tool can be first implemented on the pilot project. Selecting the pilot project is another critical factor, because failure in the pilot project can end the implementation process. So the pilot project must be carefully chosen, considering the project members, the project environment, and other variables. The users in the pilot project have to be given thorough training on the tool and the SCM concepts, how it is going to affect the work environment, how the processes are going to be automated, and so on.

Choosing a high-profile project for the implementation is advantageous and at the same time dangerous. Advantageous in the sense that if the pilot project is an unqualified success, then winning over company-wide acceptance is easy. Dangerous because if it fails, then everybody will know about it. So if the implementation team is sure about making the pilot implementation a success, then in the author's opinion it is better to choose a high-profile project. If the tools have been chosen correctly, if the implementation is well planned, if the project team is well prepared and well trained, then there is no reason why the project should fail. Also with constant monitoring during the initial phases, any signs of a disaster can be easily detected and corrected. The pilot project will also give information about the organization and its peculiarities that will be very useful when the company-wide implementation is done.

Any organization that is going to implement an SCM tool or change over to a new SCM tool will benefit greatly by reading the technical paper "Adopting an Automated Configuration Management Solution" by Susan A. Dart [8].

Finally, a caveat: The most critical factor that decides the success of any SCM tool implementation is the support of the people who use the system. Even the best tools will fail if there is no user support. So the decision of the committee should be a consensus decision. If some people's views are overridden by majority vote, then management should make every effort to make them understand the reasons for the decisions and should spare no effort to win them over. Disagreements are common in any group discussion, but the success of the group lies in the fact that the decisions made by the group are owned by all members of the group, everybody emerges as a winner, and the choice was made by the group as a whole. This feeling is very important, because the company will need everyone's goodwill and support to achieve success during implementation and after implementation.

SCM tools: Make or buy?

So far we have seen three possible scenarios for implementing an SCM system:

1. The manual system;

2. The semiautomated system, in which some components like change management system or build management system are automated; and

3. The integrated system where the configuration management tools are integrated into the development process.

Except for the first case, the other implementation scenarios use some sort of an SCM tool. The question is whether to make the SCM tools in-house or to buy them.

Why can't companies develop their own SCM tools? Developing an SCM tool is a very complex and time-consuming process that requires a lot of skilled manpower and other resources. Many companies have personnel on their payrolls who can absorb the necessary knowledge and who have experience in developing sophisticated systems. The problem is that SCM tool development is not the main business of these companies. They should be directing all of their available resources into improving their own products or services so that they can remain competitive and better serve their customers and continue to grow.

SCM tool vendors are people who have invested huge amounts of time and effort in research and development to create packaged solutions. SCM tool vendors spend billions of dollars in research and come up with innovations that make the packages more efficient, flexible, and easy to implement and use. Also with the evolution of new technologies, the vendors will be able to constantly upgrade their product to take advantage of the best and latest advancements in technology because their main focus is on improving the capabilities of their tools.

Because designing and implementing SCM tools is not the business of most companies, or a focus of their executives, the systems an in-house team comes up with will never equal in quality, scope, functionality, or technology those created by software firms whose business this is. These software firms (SCM tool vendors) can produce sophisticated packages and provide their clients with products that allow them to maintain a focus on their own chief activities, thus improving revenues, profits, and shareholder returns.

But situations do exist in which a company will have to develop or make its own SCM tools. The main reasons are nonavailability of tools suited for the company, the peculiar nature of the company or the project, and so on. For example, an organization the author worked with had more than 2500 professionals spread around the globe in more than 54 offices in more than 15 countries. The main development was carried out in the headquarters with dedicated lines connecting the client sites in different continents. The professionals were constantly moving from one project to another, from one country to another. The company had a central SCM team and individual teams within each project. The company personnel were connected via e-mail. The main problem the SCM team of the company faced was finding the appropriate people to deal with a change request evaluation, problem evaluation, or auditing. Because the people were always on the move, a person who was on a project today could be on another continent the next day. So the configuration team was finding it difficult to allocate the tasks to the right people. The solution was to create a skill inventory database of all the employees (as described in Chapter 16) that was always kept current and up to date. The information was stored in a relational database. The company had something called a Manpower Allocation Task Committee (MATC) which assigned the various professionals to the various locations and projects. The MATC records were always current and updated because MATC did the allocation and coordinated the travel plans. So these details (the availability details) were imported from the MATC database to the configuration management database.

The company also had a good performance evaluation system, which included asking the employees to update their skill inventory—that is, how many years of experience they had in each of their skills. The skills included programming languages, DBMS, GUI design, testing, and auditing, to name a few. For each skill, for which the employee had more than 6 months of experience, he or she was asked to take an on-line test. The test scores were multiplied by the experience in months to arrive at a point rating system. So the configuration database had the employee availability, the skill set, the competency level, and other details of the employee such as her work phone number, e-mail ID, and so on. The configuration team could query this database and obtain details about people who were available currently for a task. Because the contact information was also available in the database, the concerned person could be contacted immediately and the task assigned. This was a requirement that no tool supported and the company had to make the tool in-house. The company already had tools for most of the other SCM functions like change management and system building. This employee tracking tool integrated seamlessly with the other tools and proved very effective in eliminating the delays in change request processing, problem report evaluation, auditing, and so on.

In another company the problem was quite different. The company had a workflow automation system based on Lotus Notes. All the users in the company were very familiar with the Lotus Notes environment. Bringing in an SCM tool was discussed but discarded, because it would not integrate well with the existing infrastructure. The author was in charge of the SCM implementation. The SCM implementation team discussed the various options and found that the most cost-effective solution was to build a tool in-house. Lotus Notes's inherent strengths in workflow automation, security administration, and web features made it easier to design and develop the SCM tool. The SCM tool that was finally developed integrated seamlessly with the existing environment and was a huge success. Also there was no need for extensive training; the project members needed training only on the concepts of SCM and how it was implemented in the system. Because all of them were comfortable with the environment, the transition was almost painless.

To conclude, it is always better to buy SCM tools. Many tools are available free of cost; but the main problem with them is lack of technical support. Also these tools will not be updated to take advantage of the latest technological developments. But the commercial tools are getting better, bigger, and have more features. Also they have been developed by people who specialize in developing those types of tools. Most of the tools could be customized to suit your needs. So unless, and until, your project or organization has a need that cannot be fulfilled by the available tools, it is better to buy the tools rather than make them.

Conclusion

This chapter discussed SCM tools and their selection. Except for very small, single-person projects, SCM tools can dramatically improve development productivity. This chapter also discussed how to choose a tool that is right for an organization and how to deploy the tool in that organization. We also looked at making a decision about whether to make or buy SCM tools.

References

[1]   Whiftgift, D., *Methods and Tools for Software Configuration Management*, Chichester: England, John Wiley & Sons, 1991.

[2]   Mosley, V., et al., "Software Configuration Management Tools: Getting Bigger, Better, and Bolder," *Crosstalk: The Journal of Defense Software Engineering*, Vol. 9, No. 1, Jan. 1996, pp. 6–10.

[3]   Weatherall, B., "A Day in the Life of a PVCS Road Warrior: Want to Get PVCS Organized Quickly in a Mixed-Platform Environment?" Technical Paper, Synergex International Corporation, 1997.

[4]   Jasthi, S., *"SCM Without Tears,"* http://pw2.netcom.com/~sjasthi/index.html, 1997.

[5]   Dart, S., "Concepts in Configuration Management Systems," Technical Report, Software Engineering Institute, Carnegie-Mellon University, 1994.

[6]   Dart, S., "Not All Tools are Created Equal," *Application Development Trends*, Vol. 3, No. 9, 1996, pp. 45–48.

[7]   Dart S., "Achieving the Best Possible Configuration Management Solution," *Crosstalk: The Journal of Defense Software Engineering*, September 1996.

[8]   Dart S., "Adopting An Automated Configuration Management Solution," Technical Paper, STC'94 (Software Technology Center), Utah, April 12, 1994.

Selected bibliography

Alder, P. S., and A. Shenhar, "Adapting Your Technological Base: The Organizational Challenge," *Sloan Management Review*, Fall 1990, pp. 25–37.

Bochenski, B., "Managing It All: Good Management Boosts C/S Success," *Software Magazine Client/Server Computing Special Edition*, Nov. 1993, p. 98.

Bones, M., "Technology Audit: True Software Suite," White Paper, Butler Direct Limited, 1998.

Bouldin, B. M., *Agents of Change: Managing the Introduction of Automated Tools*, Englewood Cliffs, NJ: Yourdon Press, 1989.

Cagan, M., and D. W. Weber, "Task-Based Software Configuration Management: Support for 'Change Sets' in Continuus/CM," Technical Report, Continuus Software Corporation, 1996.

"Change Management for Software Development," Continuus Software Corporation, 1998.

Chris, A. "Why Can't I Buy an SCM Tool?" *Proc. ICSE SCM-4 and SCM-5 Workshops (Selected Papers)*, Berlin, Springer-Verlag, 1995, pp. 278–281.

"Cost Justifying Software Configuration Management," PVCS Series for Configuration Management White Paper, Intersolv, 1998.

Dart, S., "Past, Present and Future of CM Systems," Technical Report, Software Engineering Institute, Carnegie-Mellon University, 1992.

Dart, S., "Spectrum of Functionality in Configuration Management Systems," Technical Report, Software Engineering Institute, Carnegie-Mellon University, 1990.

Dart, S., "To Change or Not to Change," *Application Development Trends*, Vol. 4, No. 6, 1997, pp. 55–57.

Feiler, P. H., "Configuration Management Models in Commercial Environments," Technical Report, Software Engineering Institute, Carnegie-Mellon University, 1991.

Fichman, R. G., and C. Kemerer, "Adoption of Software Engineering Innovations: The Case of Object Orientation," *Sloan Management Review*, Winter 1993, pp. 7–22.

Hurwitz, J., and A. Palmer, "Application Change Management—True Software, Inc.," White Paper, Hurwitz Group, 1997.

Kolvik, S. "Introducing Configuration Management in an Organization," *Proc. ICSE '96 SCM-6 Workshops (Selected Papers)*, Berlin, Springer-Verlag, 1996, pp. 220–230.

Mason, R. P., "Enterprise Application Management in the Age of Distributed Computing: The True Software Approach," White Paper, International Data Corporation, 1998.

Parker, K., "Customization of Commercial CM System to Provide Better Management Mechanisms," *Proc. ICSE SCM-4 and SCM-5 Workshops (Selected Papers),* Berlin, Springer-Verlag, 1995, pp. 289–292.

"Software Configuration Management: A Primer for Development Teams and Managers," White Paper, Intersolv, 1997.

"Software Configuration Management for Client/Server Development Environments: An Architecture Guide," White Paper, Intersolv, 1998.

Weber, D. W., "Change Sets Versus Change Packages: Comparing Implementation of Change-Based SCM," *Proc. 7th Software Configuration Management Conf. (SCM7),* Boston, MA, May 1997, pp. 25–35.

Contents

SCM implementation

Introduction

Implementing an SCM system in an organization is not an easy task. It is not an easy task because the implementation needs support from a lot of departments, from top management to the developer/programmer. It involves changing the way the organization is doing software development and maintenance. The SCM system will introduce new procedures and controls and people will have to follow those procedures to get something done—something that could have been done in the past without somebody looking over one's shoulder.

For example, in a non-SCM scenario, changes could be made at will, but once SCM is implemented change management procedures have to be followed. SCM also brings accountability because all events are recorded and these records could be used to trace the person who made a particular change or modified a program's source code. Thus the resistance to SCM will be a factor that can create many a problem during an SCM implementation.

As with any project, SCM implementation also cannot succeed without the complete cooperation of all people involved, whether it is the top managers who will use the status accounting reports to monitor the project or the developer who has to follow the SCM procedures. In this chapter we look at some of the techniques that will help overcome resistance to SCM and any other problems during an SCM implementation.

SCM implementation plan

Before implementing an SCM system in an organization or project, it is very crucial that the implementation process be planned. Implementation planning includes developing the implementation strategy and implementation schedule and organizing the implementation team. The implementation plan should address all concerns such as the existing procedures, the effect of the SCM implementation on the procedures, how it will affect the employees, the work environment of the organization, the SCM awareness of the employees, creation of SCM user manuals, and so on.

Implementation strategy

The plan should identify the implementation strategy, that is, whether the incremental approach or the big-bang approach will be used and whether SCM will be implemented in all projects simultaneously or instead introduced in a pilot project.

When the incremental approach is used, full SCM functionality is not implemented in one step. The different functions are introduced one by one. For example, the organization might choose to implement the change management system first and then the other functions at a later date. The advantage of the incremental approach is that the company can get feedback on the implementation and how it is received and possibly fine-tune the implementation strategy based on the feedback received. Another advantage is that it can spread the investment over a period of time.

The advantage of the big-bang approach is that the company can start reaping the full benefits of SCM soon after implementation. The big-bang approach is effective if the organization is mature and conducive to SCM and the people are ready for the SCM. Here there is no room for error—it is a "do it right the first time" proposition. Implementing SCM in a pilot project is a good idea because it will give the implementation team a feel for the issues in an actual implementation, the peculiarities of the organization, its work environment, and so on. A successful pilot project can be used as an effective tool for convincing staff and alleviating any doubts and eliminating fears about SCM. But the pilot project must be selected carefully—it should be a project where the team members are willing to face the challenge of doing something new, have an open mind, and can adapt to new systems. There is nothing like a successful pilot project implementation to convince others why they should also implement SCM in their projects.

SCM implementation team

The SCM implementation project is a joint effort of many groups of people—the in-house implementation team, package vendor's team, outside consultants, end users, and company management. In this section we discuss how to organize the internal resources of the company for an SCM implementation.

The most frequently asked question is "Who within the company should participate in the project?" The natural response is everyone who is involved in the SCM process—developers, QA team, project leaders, support personnel, marketing team, and top management. Because the SCM system is an integrated package, almost everyone in the company must participate in one way or another. The functionality of today's sophisticated SCM systems will extend to practically every sector of the company.

But just because everyone in the company should be involved in the project, we do not mean that everybody should stop their jobs and join in the SCM implementation effort, thus virtually stopping the company's day-to-day functioning. But the company will need an owner or sponsor for the project—somebody who is going to lead the implementation. This should be a senior person who has the knowledge of the SCM system and the organization and the necessary authority to make decisions and implement them. Then the company will need at least one professional from each major department to carry out a specific project function. Roles will vary in complexity and time involved, but all are equally important for the success of the implementation.

It is very important for all business functions having some relation to the SCM system to be represented adequately in the project team—from the top level to the lowest level of operation. This is important because these are the key people who will make the SCM system acceptable to everyone in their own departments. So if the implementation team is comprised of people from all departments, from all levels, they can convey what they have learned about the SCM system and thus help overcome the initial resistance the system is bound to face.

The implementation of the SCM system demands that the managers and operational staff understand how the new information environment is going to work. They should be given a clear picture about what is to be changed in the current setup and what additional facilities the new technology will give the end user. This is important because the new technology and the additional responsibilities that arise when the new system is in place can overwhelm many people. So it is important to give everybody involved an idea of what to expect before the project starts.

For the right level of participation to occur, a group of representatives selected from various departments of the company will need to involve themselves in several levels. Some members of the project team will work on the project full time—in tandem with the in-house experts, external consultants, and the vendor's team. Others will help coordinate the tasks of the different sections and make available all the resources required to the implementation team. Management's representatives will monitor the progress of the project and make decisions and corrective actions to keep the project on schedule and within budget. Other members will participate part time during workshops and training.

One important thing to keep in mind is that the effective participation of the in-house personnel is not possible without the full commitment of top management. It is the responsibility of top management to see to it that the people who are designated to the implementation team on a full-time basis are not interrupted in any other way or with any other work.

Composition of the implementation team

Who should be assigned to the implementation team? This is a very important question because the success of the implementation and the continued functioning of the system depend on these people and their ability to grasp the new tasks and technologies.

Once the SCM system is implemented, the current processes and procedures will be replaced by new ones. The job descriptions and responsibilities will undergo some changes. The information integration will happen and many a process will be automated. An action taken by an employee can trigger a lot of procedures and affect a lot of other functions—almost instantaneously. The technology will bring with it a series of new concepts and resources that must be mastered and correctly used to get the best out of the SCM system. The format, the speed, and the content of the management information systems will change. The decision-making process will change because the decision makers will be able to get accurate information, in the form they want, when they want it. The SCM packages will institute new development models and practices.

So the company should appoint its best and most efficient employees to the implementation team. The company should invest in these people and should create opportunities for them to excel within the company so that they can grow with it. But these are the people who are actually running the business; these are the people who do not have time for anything else; these are the very same people everybody will turn to in a crisis. But it is these people who should be assigned to the implementation team.

SCM implementation is a very complex and sophisticated project, involving technological as well as cultural changes. It is not the place for people without any initiative, dedication, and enthusiasm. It is not place for people who do not have any team skills or who have communication problems. It is not the place for people whom the boss does not want. In fact, assigning some people just because they are the only ones available is one of the most crucial mistakes that management can make. They can jeopardize the entire project by taking such an action. The SCM implementation project needs people who can grasp new ideas quickly, who have an open mind to new technologies and concepts, and who love challenges. These people should have a never-say-die attitude and should be capable of working as a team. These men and women will be pioneers as they take their organizations through untested environments and uncharted waters, so their ability to think quickly, improvise effortlessly, innovate fast, and act without hesitation is critical to the success of the project.

So when faced with the decision of assigning members to the implementation team, management should be willing to send their best staff members. Invariably, these people are those whose work cannot be interrupted and responsibilities cannot be delegated. But the company has to find a way. If the company decides—early enough—who they are going to send, and if those people are informed, they might be able to train replacements to do their work until they return. But sending the best people is worth the effort.

Organization of the implementation team

Figure 14.1 shows the organizational chart for a typical implementation team for medium to large companies. For a small company there is not much difference in the organization except that the team size will be smaller, and the executive committee and the project management committee might be merged. At the top of the chart is the executive committee headed by somebody from top management. Then there is the project management team, followed by the technical and administrative support personnel. Then we have the work team. Let's look at the functions of each team in some detail.

Figure 14.1   Organization of the SCM implementation project.

Executive committee

The executive committee is made up of the company's top management and is headed by the person who is in charge of the SCM project implementation—a person in whom the company places its highest confidence, someone who is considered a leader and someone who has the necessary authority and carries enough clout within the company. The committee should also include the external consultant's representative. A similar person from the package vendor should also be part of the committee.

The executive committee is responsible for the monitoring and evaluation of the project and its progress. The committee is the body that approves budgets and initiates corrective actions when things are not going according to plan. So the committee should establish a reporting and monitoring mechanism by which it will be kept abreast of progress. The monitoring mechanism should have facilities to alert the committee about impending disasters and delays well in advance so that corrective and preventive measures can be taken. The committee should meet at least once a week with a provision of emergency meetings in case of emergencies.

Project management team

The project management team is comprised of the technical leader (leader of the consultant team) and the executive committee head. The team may also include the senior representative from the vendor's team. These people are responsible for conducting the scheduled work, administering the project, communicating with the in-house team and the consultants, and reporting to the executive committee. The executive committee head (the person who heads the SCM implementation project) should monitor the implementation team's progress, assess the amount and quality of the contribution of the team members—both in-house and consultants—and discuss the issues with the consulting team's head.

This person should also ensure that the company personnel and the consultants are working together as a team and that there is full cooperation between the two groups. The same person is responsible for ensuring that the consultants are transferring their knowledge to the in-house team and all the documentation is done properly. She should make sure that even after the consultants leave, the system will run smoothly.

Work team

The work team is composed of people who will actually perform the tasks set forth in the project plan. These tasks range from migrating the project information to the new system, to user training, to monitoring the start-up of the new system. The people on this team should be the best in the company and should dedicate their full time and attention to the SCM implementation project.

The team's job requires knowledge of the company's work culture and environment, awareness of company policies and regulations, good analysis skills, team spirit, a cooperative attitude, good communication skills, patience, persistence, self-confidence, and above all sound common sense.

The work team normally includes hired consultants and the in-house team. These consultants should have a good understanding of the software that is being implemented. That is why they are hired in the first place. These consultants most certainly must have participated in the implementation of similar projects before.

The company's in-house team is the people with the knowledge of how the company works. They are the people who are going to use and run the system in the future. They and the consultants together decide on how the system should work. The in-house team members will be the first people to receive training on how to operate the software. They must know how the system works in order to evaluate the impact of the software on the company's current business processes. They will also discuss with the consultants and the package vendor the level of customization the product will require in order to function properly in the company. The work team will do the testing of the system once the system is installed. The work team will also participate in the training of the end users of the system. The in-house team will contain people from the company's various functions/departments.

Technical support team

The function of the technical support team is to create an environment that is suitable for the implementation of the software. This team works very closely with the work team and takes care of issues like data migration, data backup and recovery, hardware infrastructure, and performance tuning of the databases.

In short, the technical support staff is responsible for ensuring that the machines will be up and running, the network is functional, and the hardware infrastructure is in good shape for the work team to implement the software package. These are the people who will be doing these activities once the implementation is over and the system is live. So they should interact with the consultants and the package vendor to assess any special arrangements or hardware or maintenance and backup and recovery procedures that may be required for the system.

Administrative support team

The job of the administrative support team is to make the life of all others on the implementation team easier, so that they can concentrate on their tasks and be more productive and efficient. The support teams, responsibilities include making available the workspace, tables, conference rooms, telephones, stationery, filing cabinets (of course, refreshments!), and any other resource required by the project team. Other duties include arranging the meetings and conferences, making photocopies of documents, circulating them to the right people, and any other administrative tasks that could make the life of the work team easier.

We have seen the organization of the SCM implementation project team. Each implementation project is different and will have its own characteristics. So there will be some changes in the exact constitution of the teams, but these components should be there for the proper functioning of the implementation project.

How the implementation team works

So far we have seen how the project implementation team is organized. At the top is the executive committee, and one of the main responsibilities of the executive committee is monitoring and evaluating the progress of the project. It was also specified that the executive committee should develop a management and reporting mechanism so that they know what is happening to the project on a regular basis. In this section we look at how this is done.

How can the company establish an information base to determine whether the work is progressing according to plan? How will the company decide that the present course is the correct one and will lead to the successful completion of the project?

One of the main roles of the members of the executive committee is to check and verify that the work that is being done is satisfactory and that the momentum, morale, and enthusiasm of the work team who are performing the tasks are maintained. During executive committee meetings, the members should receive reports and other information from the project managers as to how the work is progressing and whether everything is going according to schedule. The executive committee should receive data that induces them to maintain confidence in the implementation process.

Before the implementation starts, the external consultants and company representatives prepare a work plan. This plan details each and every activity that needs to be carried out and when they should be carried out. The consultants should lead the process of work plan preparation, because they have experience implementing the same package in similar conditions. The in-house team should point out the issues that are specific to the company and help the consultants create a realistic work plan.

The work plan or the project plan forms the basis for project tracking and monitoring. The project plan contains numerous activities, the person-hours required to complete them, and the resources needed to perform the tasks. The project plan is often built using a project management package (such as MS Project) that permits one to focus on planned activities from various perspectives—the chronological sequence or timetable, specific activities and who is responsible for them, the prerequisites for carrying out a specific task, or a PERT chart of the activities. Preparing the project plan using such a tool helps improve the quality of the plan and makes it easier to make changes and adjustments.

Once the project is under way the plan can be updated on a regular basis and the "planned versus actual" reports can be produced in varying detail and in varying formats including graphical formats. The project management software can generate comparisons between the actual and planned completion dates, expenses, and so on. These software tools allow responsibilities to be assigned to different persons and so it is easy to find out who is lagging behind.

Keep in mind, however, that, irrespective of whether the plan is created manually or using a software package, all the parties involved—the executive committee, the vendor, the consultants, and the in-house team—should be in agreement with the contents of the plan.

How often should the executive committee monitor the project? The answer is "It depends." If the company has really assigned its best personnel to the job, then there will be a natural monitoring of the project's daily activities. The company professional assigned to serve as the project owner or sponsor is in an ideal position to evaluate how things are going. Because company-wide SCM implementation projects last for several weeks, it is quite adequate for the executive committee to meet once a week or once in two weeks (with a provision to hold emergency meetings when necessary).

Another choice is to set up milestones in the project plan and have a meeting when the milestone's planned completion date is over. But there are no hard and fast rules regarding how frequent the executive committee should meet. During the final stages of the project, when the system is being tested the committee might need to meet more frequently to discuss the various issues that could arise.

It is the task of the project management team to report to the executive committee and present the facts and figures. Because these meetings are managerial in nature, the project management team should prepare a presentation that describes the situation at a level of detail appropriate to the audience. Very technical topics should be condensed, and excessive use of jargon should be avoided. It is a good idea for the material used in the presentation to serve also as documentation of the status of the project to that date. This is important, because, in order to track the progress at future meetings, it may become necessary to recall the issues presented in a previous meeting, so as to explain why the evolution of the work has taken a particular route.

Another objective of the executive committee meetings is to address the issues that involve decisions by top management. Such decisions will not be made at every meeting, but when they have to be made they need careful preparation. The project management team should circulate details about the issues well in advance so that the committee members can do their homework and come prepared for the discussions. It is the duty of the project management team to analyze alternative solutions and their advantages, disadvantages, and consequences and circulate them to the committee members well in advance of the meeting.

So in an SCM implementation project, the work plan or the project plan is of paramount importance. Adherence to the plan, along with constant monitoring and the taking of appropriate corrective actions before the project gets out of control, will ensure the success of the project. The key players in project tracking and monitoring are the project management team and the executive committee.

To guarantee that a complex and sophisticated project that requires technological and cultural changes in the company will reach its conclusion successfully, it is not enough to sell it or approve it. The project team needs to resell it constantly, by demonstrating that it is evolving in an appropriate manner toward the stage at which benefits will be generated as initially anticipated.

Pilot project

We have seen that implementing the SCM system in a pilot project is a good idea because it minimizes the risk of failure. This is because the entire implementation team can concentrate on the pilot project. The SCM system can be tested before going in for company-wide deployment. Any issues that were not anticipated during the planning stage that are encountered during the pilot implementation can be considered and the implementation plan can be refined and fine-tuned. During the pilot implementation, the existing data of the pilot project is migrated to the SCM system; team members are given training on the SCM concepts and how to use the SCM system (and tools, if tools are used). The implementation team monitors the various implementation issues such as how people find the system, their feedback, tricky issues in the implementation, the learning period, how long it takes for the users to get comfortable with the system, and whether the user manuals and other implementation documentation are satisfactory or need revisions/modifications.

Based on the experiences of the pilot project implementation, the implementation plan and the implementation guide will be revised and modified. The pilot project will warn the implementation team about what could go wrong, how the potential pitfalls could be avoided, and so on. Also a successful pilot project is a morale booster for the implementation team and a good marketing tool.

SCM tool vendors

Nowadays most SCM systems use some sort of tool (in other words, manual SCM systems are very rare). So the implementation team should include vendor representatives. Vendors are the people who have developed the SCM tools. They are the people who have invested huge amounts of time and effort in research and development to create the packaged solutions. Because the vendors are the people who know the tool best, they definitely have a role to play in the implementation. The vendor should supply the product and its documentation as soon as the contract is signed.

Only after the software is delivered can the company develop the training and testing environment for the implementation team. The vendor is responsible for fixing any problems in the software that the implementation team encounters. So the vendor should have a liaison officer who constantly interacts with the implementation team.

Another role the vendor has to play is that of the trainer—to provide the initial training for the company's key users, people who will play lead roles in the implementation of the system. These key users are the ones who will define, together with the consultants (external experts), how the software is to serve the company. These in-house experts will decide how the functionalities are to be implemented, as well as how to use or adapt the product to suit the company's unique requirements. So it is very critical that these key users be given thorough training on the features of the package. Vendor training should achieve the goal of showing the key users how the package works, what the major components are, how the data and information flow across the system, what is flexible and what is not, what can be configured and what cannot, what can be customized and what should not, the limitations, the strengths and weaknesses, and so on.

The objective of vendor training is to show how the system works, not how it should be implemented. This means that the vendor demonstrates the product as it exists and highlights the available options. The company's employees who are participating in the vendor training should try to understand the characteristics of the package and the impact of the system on the company's business processes. The trainees should use these training sessions to question the vendor on all aspects of the system.

The external consultants (or the package/SCM experts) also have a role to play during this vendor training. They should participate in the training sessions to evaluate how the users react to the reality that is starting to take shape from the detailed presentations and demos. Consultants should also ask questions that the vendors are trying to avoid and the users are unaware of. This is the best way to present the real picture to the users and will also prevent the vendors from making false claims.

The role of the package vendor does not end with the training. The vendor also plays an important project support function and must exercise the quality control with respect to how the product is implemented. It is the vendor who understands the finer details and subtleties of the product and can make valuable suggestions and improvements that can improve the performance of the system. It is also in the best interests of the vendor for this type of participation to continue, because if the implementation fails, most of the blame will fall on the vendor. Also a successful implementation means another satisfied client, improved goodwill, good referrals, and so on. So the vendor will continue to participate in all the phases of the implementation, mostly in an advisory capacity, addressing specific technical questions about the product and technology.

Employees and employee resistance

Implementing an SCM system is a change and it is human nature to resist change. So any SCM implementation will face some amount of resistance. Users will be skeptical about the new system. But for an SCM implementation to succeed, the cooperation of everyone involved is an absolute necessity. As we saw earlier SCM is first an attitude. So if staff are not convinced about the importance of SCM, the benefits of using an SCM tool or system, they will not be fully cooperative, which can result in the failure of the system. It is very important, therefore, that users be won over before implementing the system. Forcing the system on unwilling people will only harden their resolve to revolt.

One main reason for the resistance is ignorance. People always have a lot of misconceptions about SCM—it will increase workload, it will hinder creative work, and so on. But if the SCM implementation team, backed by the management, spends a little time and effort educating users about SCM and how it will help the company and the users, then user resistance can be reduced if not fully eliminated.

Another method of reducing resistance is by creating champions. According to Mosely [1], one of the most efficient ways to transition to new technology is to find a well-respected potential user of the technology. Train the user on the process and the technology, have this user evaluate the technology, and encourage this user to champion the merits of the technology to coworkers and management. The champion becomes the expert user, facilitator, and trainer of the tool. So all the members of the implementation team and the pilot project team are potential champions.

Company-wide implementation

Once the pilot project has been successfully implemented and the implementation strategy and other items such as user manuals and technical guides have been revised and modified, the implementation team can proceed to company-wide implementation, in which the SCM system is implemented in all the projects in the company. This involves (1) training users in SCM and SCM tools and procedures, (2) migrating data to the tool repositories, (3) assigning roles and responsibilities to the project team members wherever necessary, and (4) monitoring the SCM system until it reaches a stable state.

As SCM is implemented in more and more projects, and as people learn of the benefits of an SCM system, the job of the implementation team will become easier. Project team members should be given adequate training and there should be enough documentation (user manuals, FAQs, how-to guides) so that new people joining the project will not have difficulty getting the necessary training and information regarding the SCM tool and SCM concepts.

SCM implementation: The hidden costs

SCM implementation promises great benefits. But what are the costs involved? Exactly how much will a company have to pay to have an SCM system? In most cases the SCM implementation costs exceed the budget. Why is this? Even a well-planned and thought-out budget is often exceeded. In this section we examine the areas that most planners miss accounting for in their budgets—in other words, we discuss the hidden costs of SCM implementation.

Although different companies find different hurdles and traps in the budgeting process, those who have implemented SCM systems agree that some costs are more commonly overlooked or underestimated than others. Armed with insights from across business, SCM implementation veterans agree that one or all of the following four areas are most likely to result in budget overruns: (1) training, (2) integration and testing, (3) data conversion/migration, and (4) external consultants. Each is discussed next.

Training

Training is the unanimous choice of experienced SCM implementers as the most elusive budget item. It is not so much that this cost is completely overlooked as it is consistently underestimated. Training expenses are high because workers almost invariably have to learn a new set of processes, not just a new software interface. Training is the first item that gets cut when budgets have to be squeezed—a major mistake, says most SCM implementers. A successful training experience will account for a minimum of 10% to 15% of the total project budget. Unwise companies that scrimp on training expenses pay the price later. Training costs cannot be avoided, but there are a few ways to keep the price tag under control. One way is train an initial batch of employees who can then train their colleagues in turn. This solves two problems: (1) The huge training bills of consultants are reduced and (2) because the training is done by their own colleagues, resistance to change is reduced and people will be more ready to accept the new system. In fact, it is a good idea to identify these would-be trainers early in the implementation phase and make them part of the implementation group, so that they will have hands-on experience and will understand the "big picture."

Integration and testing

Today's SCM systems are very complex systems. Interfacing with those systems is not an easy task. Testing the links between SCM tools and other corporate software—links that have to be built on a case-by-case basis—is another essential cost that is easily missed. Most companies will have some development environments that will not integrate with the SCM tool and will have to be separately interfaced. In most cases these integrations are costly.

Data conversion/migration

It costs money to move existing project information to the new system. Most data in most legacy systems is rubbish. But most companies seem to deny their data are dirty until they actually have to move it to the new client/server setups. As a result, those companies are more likely to underestimate the cost of data migration. But even clean data may demand some overhaul to match the process modification necessitated—or inspired—by SCM tool implementation.

External consultants

The extravagant cost of external consultants is a well-known fact. Like training expenses, this cost is hard to circumvent. Choosing a lesser known SCM tool to avoid premium-priced consultants does not necessarily help. When users fail to plan for disengagement from the existing system, consulting fees will overshoot the budget. To avoid this, companies should identify objectives for which its consulting partners must aim when training internal staff. It is a good practice to include performance metrics and time schedules for the consultants. For example, a specific number of the company's staff should be trained to a certain specified level of expertise within a specified time.

Postimplementation scenario

Most companies treat SCM implementation as projects, with the assumption that someday the project will end. And they are right; the implementation project will end, but the SCM system cannot end with the implementation. In fact, once the implementation phase ends and staff have started using the SCM system, the real benefits of the SCM will be seen. An SCM system is not a project, it is a way of life. No organization can say "we're finished" and few ever will. There will always be new modules/features and versions to install, new persons to be trained, new technologies to be embraced, refresher courses to be conducted, and so on. Even if an organization could declare final victory on implementation of SCM, more time will be needed to gain real business value from the SCM system. So SCM implementation requires a lifelong commitment by the company management and users of the system.

One problem the SCM implementation can present is what to do with the existing SCM team. This is applicable only in cases where an organization had large SCM teams and decided to introduce an SCM tool. The SCM tool will automate most of the SCM functions and many jobs in the SCM team will become redundant. So the company should have a plan to relocate these people whose jobs are taken over by the SCM tool.

The permanent nature of the SCM system has numerous implications. The following section discusses some of them. SCM implementation is just the beginning. For any organization to succeed and reap the benefits of the SCM system, it has to take actions while keeping in mind the permanent nature of the SCM systems.

Organizational structure

Most organizations create implementation project offices and appoint project managers with the assumption that the project will end and life will go back to normal. But it will not. So what the organizations need is not a project office, but a new organizational structure that reflects the ongoing need for SCM-related activity. "Sponsorship" is one example of the need. Many companies appoint senior executive sponsors for implementation projects. Their expectations are probably that these executives could go back to their responsibilities once the installation is over. But many companies do SCM implementation on an incremental basis. That is, they install the core modules first and then the additional modules until full SCM functionality is achieved. Who is going to oversee those changes and ensure that they fit with the rest of the business? If the executive sponsor is temporary, who will ensure that the system and the business evolve hand in hand? The company should assign a person who is willing to take the ownership of the SCM system on a long-term basis.

Roles and skills

The post-SCM organization will need a different set of roles and skills than an organization with less integrated systems. At a minimum, everyone who uses these systems needs to be trained on how they work, how they relate to the business process, and how a transaction ripples through the entire company whenever they press a key. The training will never end; it is an ongoing process. New people will always be coming in, and new functionality will always be entering the organization.

Many companies use consultants to help with the implementation process. This in itself is not a bad idea, but the problem is *how* most companies use consultants in SCM implementations. They do not transfer knowledge from consultants to internal employees. Because these systems are going to be around for quite some time it is very important for company employees to have good knowledge (as good as the consultants) about how these systems work and how they can be configured to fit the organization. The person in charge of the implementation must make sure that the consultants allow the employees to work side by side with them on the implementation project, and before they leave tap the most knowledgeable consultants on long-term system evolution issues.

In every business function and department that is affected by SCM you will need one or more people who know the system and its relationship to the departmental processes. It is these people who have to save the system in the early days after you install the system. It is these people who have to guide, motivate, and help their colleagues by working with them. They will answer questions, find needed work-arounds, and let you know what is working and what isn't. These people will be the SCM team representatives—the champions—in each department. These people should have a dual reporting relationship with their managers and to the SCM in-charge. It is also useful to convene meetings of these people once in awhile so that they can share knowledge and compare notes.

Knowledge management

It is imperative that the knowledge and experience that is gained during SCM implementation and after are captured on an ongoing basis and made available to all. So when somebody encounters a problem, she can look up the knowledge base to determine if such a problem has occurred before. When new problems are identified and solved, they should be added to the knowledge base. Thus over a period of time your knowledge base will provide answers to most of the problems. In this way, even if a key employee leaves, the knowledge will remain with the company.

SCM tools and technology

Once the SCM tools are introduced, the way in which the companies conduct SCM will change. With the SCM tools come automation and new technologies. The company should make it a point to familiarize users with these technologies and find ways to motivate them to use these technologies. For example, most SCM tools have the facilities to send notifications to the CCB members regarding a change request that was submitted. The CCB member has the facility to see the details of the change request and then query the SCM database to analyze its implications. So the CCB members can send their replies almost immediately. But for this to happen, the CCB members should make use of these technologies. One member abstaining from this process can delay the change request disposition. So the company should have a plan to train and then motivate its employees to get the best out of the new features and facilities that are available to them.

Most systems can be configured to have an escalation mechanism—a mechanism that can escalate the issue to a higher authority if something does not happen within a specified period of time. For example, the system could be configured to send a mail notification to the supervisor of a CCB member if that member has not replied within a specified period. In such cases senior managers should find out why the person is not using the technology and take the necessary steps to get him involved. Many people are dazzled by the technology or are afraid to use it. These fears should be alleviated for the proper functioning of the SCM system and to get the maximum benefit from the system.

As we have seen, the success of an SCM system is not primarily dependent on the sophistication or features of the tools that are installed. It is the attitude and cooperation of the people—the users—that make the SCM systems capable of delivering the quality and productivity improvements that they are capable of.

Conclusion

We have seen how to implement the SCM system in an organization. We have seen how to monitor the implementation project and why it is important to do the monitoring. We saw that one of the most critical factors in the success of an SCM implementation is the participation and cooperation of the users.

We looked at the different methods of making the implementation a success, including vendor participation, user education, and having in-house champions. We discussed the factors that result in cost overruns and how to tackle them. We also saw the permanent nature of the SCM systems and how the organizations should gear up to live with the SCM systems and reap the full benefits from them.

Reference

[1]   Mosley, V., et al., "Software Configuration Management Tools: Getting Bigger, Better, and Bolder," *Crosstalk: The Journal of Defense Software Engineering*, Vol. 9 No. 1, Jan. 1996, pp. 6–10.

Selected bibliography

Dart, S., "Achieving the Best Possible Configuration Management Solution," *Crosstalk: The Journal of Defense Software Engineering*, September 1996.

Dart, S., "To Change or Not to Change," *Application Development Trends*, Vol.4, No. 6, 1997, pp. 55–57.

Kolvik, S. "Introducing Configuration Management in an Organization," *Proc. ICSE '96 SCM-6 Workshops (Selected Papers)*, Berlin, Springer-Verlag, 1996, pp. 220–230.

15

Contents

SCM in very large projects

Introduction

In this chapter we examine some of the peculiarities, problems, and solutions of implementing and practicing software configuration management in very large software projects. By very large software projects I mean a project that has more than 100 team members at a time, a project that requires the effort of more than 1000 human years, a project where a lot of work is subcontracted and there are a large number of subcontractors, a project that involves development of an application for many platforms, a project that is cross-platform, a project that is developed by more than one geographically distributed team, or a project that is a combination of any of the above criteria. These are some indicative figures and criteria, and to qualify as a very large project, the project has to involve a lot of people and must have millions of lines of code.

Here the emphasis is not on the complexity or the criticality of the project, but on the size of the project and project team, the number of groups involved, and so on. The SCM principles used in these projects are the same as those used in small projects or in mission-critical projects, but what makes these projects different is the sheer size and the management and organizational challenges that such a size poses. Some examples of such systems include database management systems (a system like Oracle or DB2), ERP systems (something like SAP R/3 or the BaaN ERP system), and operating systems (Windows, UNIX, MVS), to name a few. Typically these projects will have many modules or subsystems, each of which can function in a semiautonomous fashion. These independent subsystems could be developed by different teams from different companies in different geographical locations.

Management of such complex systems is impossible without a good software configuration management system. This is because in projects of such large size, the chances of all of the classical problems—communications breakdown, shared data problem, simultaneous update problem, and multiple maintenance problem—occurring are very high. Configuration management in these projects is very formal in nature with numerous controls and procedures. It is practically impossible to do the configuration management of these projects manually. So these projects ideally should use a high-end software configuration management tool.

Performance of SCM tools

The SCM tool used in a very large project should be capable of supporting hundreds of developers and testers with tens of millions of lines of code. The system should do this without degradation of performance. So the tool selection process must take these performance factors into account. Questions like how many people will be using the system concurrently, how much data will have to be handled, does the system have to be "up" around the clock (to support people in different time zones), and so on should be considered during selection, and the implication of these factors on the performance of the tool must be analyzed. Only that tool which can take the load without compromising performance should be selected.

Implementation strategy

We saw in the chapter on SCM tools that large projects use SCM tools that fall into a category called *process-oriented tools*. According to Dart [1], these tools include version control capabilities and at least some of the developer-oriented capabilities. These tools have the ability to automate the software flow life cycles, roles, and their responsibilities and to customize the out-of-the-box process model. These tools provide an integrated approach to change management where problem tracking is associated with the code.

So in a very large project where formal procedures are to be implemented and automated, and tools have to carry out more than just version control, these types of tools will be used. Here the key phrases are *process-dependency* and *information automation and integration*. A very large project by its nature requires formalized and automated procedures, so a tool that is capable of taking care of these things is an absolute necessity.

During the implementation of the tool, as we saw earlier, it is better to start with a pilot project. In this case, the pilot project will be a module or subsystem of the project. Because these kinds of projects will be using a lot of automated tools like CASE tools, code generators, test data generators, automatic testing tools, code analyzers, and so on, how the SCM tool will integrate and interact with these tools must be analyzed and studied. If possible it is better to automate the information flow from the other tools used in the project to the SCM tool's repository, so that there is no wasted effort. Suitable interfaces have to be built or bought. But in some cases, it might be wise to enter the information manually from the tools used in the project into the SCM tool's repository because making or buying an interfacing system could be very costly. So here project management will have to do a cost/benefit analysis and decide which strategy to adopt.

During pilot project implementation, all of these issues should be addressed and solutions should be identified. It is better to choose a module or subsystem that is representative and contains all potential elements (tools and other complexities) for the pilot project and face the problems head-on, because doing so will provide much data on how to implement the SCM system and SCM tool in other modules/subsystems. So in the case of very large projects, you should choose the module that is most difficult and most complex as the pilot because of all of the difficulties that could be encountered and solved during the pilot project phase itself.

Also during the pilot project phase, because the SCM implementation team, the SCM experts, and the tool vendor's representatives will be concentrating on one project, the problems could be solved more effectively and efficiently. In very large projects, it is better to have the SCM system in place from the initial phases onward. So if the pilot implementation can be done in a simulated environment where all the tools and other elements representative of the project in question are present, this will give developers the opportunity to understand the problems, solve them, and then to implement the SCM system and the tools, in the project from the initial phase itself. But the simulated environment that is being created for the pilot implementation should be a representative model of the actual project environment.

Distributed, concurrent, and parallel development

Very large projects are characterized by their distributed nature where concurrent and parallel development is commonplace. At any given time many people will be working on the same programs or different variants of it. So the SCM tool that is used in a very large project should be very good at managing variants (branches that will not be merged) and temporary branches (branches that will be merged).

The merging capabilities of these tools also have to be very good. Any tool that is used in a very large project should be capable of supporting distributed development. Now development teams work from different continents, creating different subsystems or modules of a software product. To treat these physically distributed systems as a single logical entity and to manage them in such a fashion that the project managers are not bothered with the underlying complexities is a must for a tool that is used in a very large project.

Change management

In large projects the change management activities cannot be handled by a single change control authority. So there will be multiple CCBs and in many cases multilevel CCBs. Change initiation, change request routing, and change disposition can be automated using SCM tools. But people are needed to make decisions. So the CCB members should be trained to use the technology.

Because there are many CCBs of equal status and priority, there should be a super CCB (SCCB) that is authorized to resolve conflicts between the multiple CCBs. The guidelines for the functioning of the CCBs and how to resolve conflicts should be well documented, and if required they can be automated (a rule-based system) so that the SCM tool can take appropriate actions without human intervention. For example, you need to consider what to do if there is a tie among the members. Should the problem be escalated to the higher level CCB or should the members be informed about the poll result and asked to vote again or to attend a physical CCB meeting? These rules can be coded into the system and many a procedure automated, thus making the best and effective use of the CCB member's time and reducing the time in the disposition of change requests.

Status accounting

Status accounting is the function that documents and reports the information related to configuration items to everyone involved in the project. The status accounting function should also be able to answer ad hoc queries. In a large project, creating and distributing reports, even the routine reports, as hardcopy is expensive as well as an administrative nightmare. So in this kind of a project it is better to publish and post these reports on the corporate intranet and inform staff about the fact that the reports are available via e-mail or any other messaging system that the project is using.

For ad hoc querying, it is better to assign roles—such as developer, tester, and manager—and give selective access to the people who fit these roles. For example, a developer could be given access to query the table that contains information about the configuration items of his module, whereas a manager could be given the access to query any table in the database. This kind of electronic distribution of the status accounting information is necessary for a large project, because the other option—the option of having hardcopies—is a big burden on the SCM budget.

System building

In the case of very large products, system building can take many hours. So the frequency of the builds is important because much time and money is involved with each build. So there should be a build strategy.

There are two types of build: clean and nonclean. A clean build is the process of starting with only the source items and then building the entire system step by step from those source items. A nonclean build uses some derived items as inputs for the build process. For example, in the case of a nonclean build all subsystems that were not changed could be used as is for system building, whereas in the case of a clean build even the subsystems or modules that were not changed would be built again from the source components. In the case of very large projects having a clean build each and every time is neither practical nor needed. The system could be built using derived components or subsystems that were not changed. This will save a lot of time, especially during the integration testing and alpha and beta testing phases.

For the final release, a clean build is best. As we saw earlier we will be using SCM tools in such a large project. The build capabilities of the tool should be adequate enough to produce accurate and reliable builds.

Skill inventory database

We discussed the skill inventory database in Chapter 12. This kind of a database is an absolute must in a large project. The two main reasons are that (1) there will be a huge demand for people to do change evaluation, impact analysis, auditing, and so on, and (2) in a large project the skills and availability of all the people involved with the project are difficult to remember and should therefore be recorded somewhere. So the best, fastest, and easiest method for finding the right people to get the job done is to store the details about the people in a database.

Training

In a very large project, the SCM training of the team members is a very important issue. Because these projects span many years, many different people will be involved with the project. So once the team member training that is done during the implementation phase is over, a system should be in place to train new members who join the project at a later date.

All large projects have induction programs, which the new members have to undertake. These programs usually give a general idea about the project, the major components, the different functions, and so on so that the person will get a bird's-eye view of the project. This is important, because only if one knows the big picture can one understand the consequences of her actions in a module or subsystem. The SCM and SCM tool training should be a part of the induction program, so that all the new members will be trained in that also.

Help desks and other knowledge sharing systems

As we have seen, the team in a very large project is transient in nature. Hence, it is important for all events in a project to be recorded: how a problem was identified, how it was fixed, how a bug escaped the testing phase, what points developers should be aware of when using a tool, and so on. This information should be captured in a knowledge base or help desk and made available to the team members.

This knowledge capturing and sharing function is very important in a very large project because the chances of problems recurring and people reinventing the wheel are enhanced. If all experiences are documented (maybe an expert system could be used), much time could be saved and development productivity improved. Also these help desks are invaluable to the technical support teams and system maintenance personnel.

SCM costs

It is difficult to estimate the cost, effort, time, or size of very large systems with a high degree of accuracy. Even in small- and medium-sized projects, the hidden costs of SCM implementation that were discussed in Chapter 14 apply. In large projects SCM implementation costs will be even more difficult to predict because many factors are difficult to estimate due to project duration. Estimating what the scenario will be 4 years down the road is quite difficult.

Being able to foresee the future with unerring accuracy is not a task that is easily accomplished by people or by machines. Also, the real world does not stand still while large systems are developed; new products and processes are discovered, underlying assumptions are invalidated, new laws are passed, and developers learn new things. So any estimates about SCM implementation and postimplementation will have to be reevaluated frequently in the case of large projects, so that the estimates and budgets can be updated.

Conclusion

In this chapter we looked at the peculiarities of very large projects. Very large projects take many years to complete, employ hundreds of people, and involve millions of lines of code. These projects definitely need a software configuration management system because the lack of it can lead to project failure.

Reference

[1]   Dart, S., "Not All Tools Are Created Equal," *Application Development Trends*, Vol. 3, No. 9, 1996, pp. 45–48.

Contents

Trends in SCM: Future directions

Introduction

The only constant is change. No more so than in the constantly evolving, high-speed world of technical innovation. So the question is this: How will these inevitable changes affect the SCM functions and SCM tools? In this chapter we survey the industry landscape and check out what's on the horizon, keeping in mind that often what appears to loom large in the distance turns out to be a mirage.

That said, SCM industry watchers agree on at least one point: one size does not fit all. Each organization has to choose the tools that are right for its environment and its processes. Also the SCM tools are now no longer concerned with just source code control, but are becoming integrated tools that take care of the entire software development process and life cycle.

Configuration management is the key to managing and controlling the highly complex software projects being developed today. SCM tools have evolved from simple version-control systems targeted at individual developers into systems capable of managing developments by large teams operating at multiple sites around the world. The variety of tools that is being offered in the SCM marketplace means that you can be sure to find one that is a close match to your individual needs.

The SCM tool market is getting more and more competitive as more and more players enter it. Acquisitions and mergers have occurred to create strategic advantages, and SCM tool vendors are loading their products with new features and capabilities. So we can see a fierce fight for market share in the future, which will result in the availability of high-quality products at affordable prices. According to Burrows [1], estimates show that the market for configuration management (CM) tools and services now exceeds $1 billion per year and is still growing rapidly. The market size and growth has led to many of the founding companies in the CM market being acquired by larger companies with no history of involvement in CM.

There are many areas and directions in which the SCM discipline and SCM tools will evolve in the future. We discuss some of these topics in this chapter.

Hardware and software configuration management

The concepts of configuration management originated in the manufacturing industry and then the idea of software configuration management became popular. Now the trend is toward the integration of these two disciplines. The differentiation between hardware and software configuration management is now narrowing. As the integration between hardware and software items becomes more and more seamless and natural, it seems fitting that the configuration management of these systems should be done in the same way, using the same process and using the same tools. In the ECOOP'98 SCM-8 symposium held at Brussels, Belgium, in July 1998, the term *system configuration management* was coined. Now SCM stands for *system configuration management*.

Support for concurrent and parallel development

The days of one-at-a-time modifications to configuration items are a thing of the past. Today's SCM tools have the capability to support parallel branches for concurrent development and variant development. In the case of parallel branches that are used for concurrent development, the sophisticated tools allow more than one user to make modifications to the same file(s) and then the tool merges those parallel versions. The merging capabilities of the SCM tools are increasing and that makes the life of the person doing the merging a lot easier. Now the tools can compare the different parallel versions against a common ancestor and highlight the areas where they are different and where the changes have been made. According to Burrows [1], the capability of modern merge tools is now so strong that users are tempted to accept the tools' automatic resolutions and omit essential testing processes, which is not at all recommended.

Distributed development

Today the development of a software system is done by many teams distributed across different parts of the globe. The capability to manage distributed development is now being offered by many tools. As communications and information technology make rapid strides forward, distributed development is going to be commonplace and the distributed development capabilities of SCM tools are going to get better and better.

Web enabling

As with every other software market, SCM tool vendors are being forced to move from a client/server to a browser/server architecture to web-enable their tools. The popularity of distributed development makes web enabling a must-have feature in SCM tools. Today's developers need to access the corporate databases and repositories when they are on the move and when they are working away from the office. Also the different people working on the same project need to share central databases and repositories. The most cost-effective way to do this is to use the web.

The availability of high-speed Internet access and technologies such as virtual private networks (VPNs) and better encryption methods make the use of the Internet a very cost-effective and secure medium in which to do distributed development. Tomorrow's tools will make use of these technologies. Today the degree of web support provided by the tools is very limited; they are used primarily to access the status accounting information using a web browser. A few tools support check-out/check-in facilities through the web. But the future belongs to the web and all SCM tools will have to incorporate full SCM functionality into their web offerings.

Web site management

Web design and development is a totally different ball game from the normal software development process. Web sites, in order to attract visitors and encourage them to come back, have to change their content and offerings very frequently. An advantage of having a web site is that up-to-the-minute information can be provided to the users. So managing the changes to a web site is more difficult than that of a software product, because of the rate at which the contents of the web site changes. It is not only the contents that change; to make the pages attractive and catchy, the presentation styles, the design elements, the layout, and so on are changed very often.

Another factor that makes web development different from software development is the number of configuration items that must be managed. Even a medium-sized company's web site will have more than 1000 pages, each containing various objects and elements such as downloads, pictures, and movie clips. So we are talking about thousands of objects. Even though some of the modern full-fledged SCM tools can handle a huge number of configuration items, the traditional SCM tools were never designed to manage this huge number of configuration items and, even if they do, it will be at the cost of performance.

Another capability that is required for the management of the Internet sites is the ability to recreate the web page as it was on a particular day or time. Since the rate at which the contents change is extremely rapid (in many cases almost on a daily basis), the information required for the build management tools will be phenomenal. So ensuring repeatable and reliable rebuilds of the thousands of versions of the web site is quite a challenge. So the configuration management of the web sites and Internet sites requires different skills than those used for software management. According to Burrows [1], CM support for web and particularly intranet pages and their embedded objects is creating an important new market for the vendors of CM tools, which in time could exceed the size of the market for managing software development.

Better integration with IDEs and CASE environments

Today's SCM tools do integrate with integrated development environments (IDEs) such as Visual C++, Visual Basic, and PowerBuilder so that the developer need not go outside the IDE for SCM functions. The same is true with CASE tools in which the SCM tools share information from the CASE repository. In the future we will see seamless integration (integration without interfaces and interface packages) of the SCM tools, and IDEs and CASE tools will incorporate SCM functionality. Thus the development environment becomes truly integrated.

The day is not far off when SCM tools will supply information or merge with project management tools, thus enabling seamless information integration and easier and efficient project management. So tomorrow's SCM tools will be part of an all-encompassing development environment in which the SCM tools will seamlessly integrate with IDEs, CASE, project management, and other development tools.

Customization

The era when you had to buy a tool and implement it as it came out of the box is over. SCM tool vendors are now offering the ability to customize their tools. The extent of the customizations varies from tool to tool. According to Dart [2], CM tools are being enhanced with customization facilities so that customers can easily modify certain features of the tools (such as screen layout, colors, and state names and transitions). More complex customizations (such as changing the associated semantics, roles, access rights, and transition conditions of the states) typically require source code changes or additional scripts using triggers and event mechanisms. Vendors are moving toward parameterizing these more complex customizations.

These customization capabilities will help the customer, because he will be able to get tools that perfectly match his requirements. Thus instead of developing a process around the tool, now customers can choose a tool that will integrate seamlessly with their development process.

Better decision-making capabilities

Improving decision support has been another focus of almost all SCM tool vendors. The SCM systems of the future will use data warehouses for storing the information in their repositories and knowledge bases. They will make use of technologies like data mining and OLAP to provide management with better decision-making capabilities.

Increased user awareness and expectations

Tomorrow's SCM user will be more aware of the benefits of SCM and the capabilities of SCM tools. So on one side it will be easier to market the concept of SCM tools to organizations, but on the flip side the customers will be very choosy. Because they know what they want and what is available, vendors will have to be on their toes to keep their products up to date so as to retain the market share they enjoy.

Gone will be the days where the SCM vendor had to educate the customers about SCM and thus create a market. But tomorrow's customer will be asking vendors informed questions and only those products that can cope with the high standards and expectations of the customers will be able to survive. The customers will also want more and more features to be automated which will force the vendor to use the latest technologies.

Reduction in SCM team size

This point has been mentioned before: As more and more tasks become automated, the number of people required to carry out the SCM functions in a project or organization will be drastically reduced. The days of full-fledged SCM teams are long gone and tomorrow's SCM systems will need only a very few people to manage them.

Market snapshot

Almost all of the companies that developed the first SCM tools have been taken over by bigger companies or have merged to gain competitive advantage. Here are some examples:

- Softool along with its CCC product range was bought by Platinum.

- Rational bought Pure Atria and changed the name of Atria to ClearCase.

- Legent was bought by Computer Associates.

- Intersolv and MicroFocus (joint owners of PVCS) have merged to form Merant.

- Visible Systems Corporation acquired Tower Concepts and its configuration management and problem tracking tool, Razor.

- Diamond Optimum Systems (the company, which owned Diamond CM) was acquired by Serena Software and the name of Diamond CM was changed to eChange Man.

SCM tool vendors are definitely extending their reach as they fight to maintain their growth momentum during the transition from client/server through browser/server to the promised land of distributed components. We can expect to see many more acquisitions, increases in user awareness and expectations, and SCM tools becoming richer in features.

Conclusion

In this chapter we saw what is in store for SCM tools in the coming years. As with any predictions, some of the things might not evolve as described here. But one thing is sure: The importance of SCM as a productivity improvement and life-saving mechanism is gaining more and more acceptance. Companies that saw SCM as a necessary evil are now looking at it as a strategic weapon that will improve development effectiveness and productivity.

One main reason for the increased acceptance of SCM is the availability of affordable and easy-to-use tools that make the performance of SCM functions easy. Because SCM tool vendors are trying for market share and the battle for market share is getting hot, and because new companies are joining the fray, in the future customers will get high-quality products with advanced features that use the latest technological developments.

References

[1]   Burrows, C., "Configuration Management: Coming of Age in the Year 2000," *Crosstalk: The Journal of Defense Software Engineering,* Mar. 1999, pp. 12–16.

[2]   Dart, S., "Not All Tools Are Created Equal," *Application Development Trends,* Vol. 3, No. 9, 1996, pp. 45–48.

Selected bibliography

Burrows, C., and I. Wesley, *Ovum Evaluates: Configuration Management,* London: Ovum Limited, 1998.

Denning, D. E., *Information Warfare and Security,* Reading, MA: Addison-Wesley Longman, 1999.

Heiman, R. V., S. Garone, and S. D. Hendrick, "Development Life-Cycle Management: 1999 Worldwide Markets and Trends," Technical Report, Framingham, MA: International Data Corporation, June 1999.

Appendix A

SCM vendors and tools

This appendix provides an alphabetical list of SCM tools, broken down by type, and an alphabetical list of the major SCM vendors and their SCM tool offerings. For most vendors, the following details are provided: the vendor name (in some cases, the developer name), contact information, URL, product name(s), and a brief description of the product(s). The product names are given in bold. Company names are italicized. More information about the tools can be obtained from the vendors' web sites.

The tools are classified into three categories: (1) full-fledged SCM tools, (2) change management and/or version control tools, and (3) public domain tools. The tools that fall in the first category—the full-fledged SCM tools—are the high-end SCM tools that cover all of the SCM functionality and in most cases are process-oriented tools. The tools that are listed in the second category do not cover the full spectrum of functionality, but do cover the major SCM functions such as change management, version control, build management, and so on.

The public domain tools are available free of charge. You can download the tools from the sites specified and use them. The author recommends the use of the freely available tools only if the project is not mission critical and if the project team is competent enough to manage the tool without any technical support. These tools are used mainly in academic projects, in projects where people are more knowledgeable about SCM and can make the tools work with little or no help from the tool providers, and in projects that have budget constraints and need only a basic tool. These tools could also be used by students who want to learn more about SCM and SCM practices without spending money on tools. They are excellent starting points for learning about SCM and SCM tools.

Note: The tool descriptions are taken mainly from the marketing literature of the vendors. These descriptions are not intended as accurate, comprehensive, and objective descriptions about the product. The idea of these descriptions is to introduce the reader to the tool.

SCM tools

Full-fledged SCM tools

AllChange (Intasoft Ltd.)
CCC/Harvest (Platinum Technology)
ClearCase® (Rational Software Corporation)
ClearGuide (Rational Software Corporation)
CMVision (Expertware)
Continuus/CM (Continuus Software Corporation)
Continuus/PT (Continuus Software Corporation)
Continuus/WebSynergy (Continuus Software Corporation)
eChange Man (SERENA Software, Inc.)
Endevor (Computer Associates International, Inc.)
PVCS Dimensions (MERANT)
VisualAge TeamConnection Enterprise Server (IBM Corporation)

Change management and/or version control tools

+1CM (+1 Software Engineering)
AccuRev (Ede Development Enterprises, Inc.)
Agile Product Change Server (Agile Software Corporation)

Alchemist (Sequel UK Ltd.)

Aldon/CMS (Aldon Computer Group)

BitKeeper (BitMover, Inc.)

CA-Librarian (Computer Associates International, Inc.)

CA-PanAPT (Computer Associates International, Inc.)

CA-Panexec (Computer Associates International, Inc.)

CA-Pan/LCM (Computer Associates International, Inc.)

CA-Pan/LCM Configuration Manager (Computer Associates International, Inc.)

CA-Pan/Merge (Computer Associates International, Inc.)

CA-Panvalet (Computer Associates International, Inc.)

CA-VMLib (Computer Associates International, Inc.)

ChangeMaster (Industrial Strength Software Company)

Code Co-op (Reliable Software)

CodeVault (Kestral Computing Pty. Ltd.)

Concorde SiteControl (Crystaliz, Inc.)

CONTROL (Network Concepts, Inc.)

Corporate RCS (Thompson Automation Software)

CS-RCS (Component Software)

EagleSpeed CM (Lockheed Martin Ocean, Radar, and Sensor Systems)

ECMS (Configuration Data Services, Inc.)

GP Version (Quality Software Components)

Harmonizer (Aldon Computer Group)

JavaSafe (JavaSoft)

Lifespan (British Aerospace Land & Sea Systems Limited)

MKS Source Integrity Professional Edition (Mortice Kern Systems [MKS] Inc.)

NeumaCM+ (Neuma Technology Corporation)

Perforce Fast SCM System (Perforce Software, Inc.)

PrimeCode (Data Design Systems, Inc.)

PVCS Configuration Builder (MERANT)

PVCS Professional (MERANT)

PVCS Replicator (MERANT)

PVCS Tracker (MERANT)

PVCS Version Manager (MERANT)

PVCS Version Manager Plus (MERANT)
Quma Version Control System (QVCS) (Quma Software, Inc.)
Rapid Implementation Manager (InRoads Technology, Inc.)
Razor (Tower Concepts)
Red Box Service Management System (Ultracomp)
Revision Control Engine (RCE) (DuraSoft GmbH)
R-Sea-Yes (SEA Software Ever After)
Sablime (Lucent Technologies)
SDM-Implementer (Mortice Kern Systems [MKS] Inc.)
Source Code Manager (SCM) (UniPress Software, Inc.)
SourceOffSite (SourceGear Corporation)
StarTeam (StarBase Corporation)
Sun WorkShop TeamWare (Sun Microsystems, Inc.)
Tesseract Lifecycle Manager (Tesseract Group)
TLIB Version Control (Burton Systems Software)
TurnOver (SoftLanding Systems, Inc.)
Unicenter TNG Change and Configuration Management Option
    (Computer Associates International, Inc.)
VC/m (Version and Configuration Management) (George James
    Software Limited)
ViCiouS Pro (SureHand Software)
Visual Enabler (Softlab GmbH)
Visual SourceSafe (Microsoft Corporation)
Visual SourceSafe for UNIX (Mainsoft Corporation)
VOODOO (UNI Software Plus GmbH)
VOODOO Server (UNI Software Plus GmbH)
Web Integrity (Mortice Kern Systems [MKS] Inc.)

Public domain tools

Aegis (Peter Miller)
Concurrent Versions System (CVS) (Cyclic Software)
DVS (Distributed Versioning System) (Antonio Carzaniga)
jCVS (ICE Engineering, Inc.)
PRCS (Josh MacDonald)
Revision Control System (RCS) (Cyclic Software)
Source Code Control System (SCCS) (Cyclic Software)
tkCVS (Cyclic Software)

SCM tool vendors and their tools

+1 Software Engineering
2510-G Las Posas Road, Suite 438
Camarillo, CA 93010
http://www.plus-one.com/

+1CM

+1CM is a configuration management system supporting identification, variations, baselines, accounting, auditing, and access control.

Agile Software Corporation
One Almaden Blvd.
San Jose, CA 95113-2253
http://www.agilesoft.com/

Agile Product Change Server

Agile Product Change Server, a core component of Agile Anywhere, automates CCB activities. Agile Product Change Server provide the ability to create and approve changes on-line.

Aldon Computer Group
1999 Harrison Street
Suite 1500
Oakland, CA 94612
http://www.aldon.com/

Aldon/CMS

Aldon/CMS is an AS/400 change management system designed to bring control, automation, tools, and information to the software maintenance and development process.

Harmonizer

Harmonizer is an AS/400 source compare and merge tool designed to do all of the following tasks:

> ▶ Automate the process of applying your modifications to new releases of your software package.

▶ Automatically document code changes whenever you move a modified program into production.

▶ Easily find the differences between multiple versions of a program.

▶ Identify and merge the work of two or more programmers who have modified the same program simultaneously.

Harmonizer consists of three modules: Source Compare & Merge, Automated Audit Trail, and Automated Software Upgrades.

Antonio Carzaniga
carzanig@cs.colorado.edu
http://www.cs.colorado.edu/serl/cm/dvs.html

DVS (Distributed Versioning System)

DVS is a simple versioning system based on NUCM 2. DVS adopts a linear versioning schema and a cooperation policy based on check-in/check-out processes with exclusive locks. Single artifacts (i.e., files), as well as collections of artifacts (i.e., directories), can be maintained using DVS. Using NUCM distribution mechanisms, DVS allows every artifact and collection to be stored in a separate NUCM server, making the storage location transparent to the user. This product is available free of cost.

BitMover, Inc.
550 Valley Street
San Francisco, CA 94131
http://www.bitmover.com/

BitKeeper

BitKeeper is a configuration management system that supports distributed development, disconnected operation, compressed repositories, change sets, and named lines of development (branches).

British Aerospace Land & Sea Systems Limited
Software Tools Group
Apex Tower, 7 High Street
New Malden, Surrey KT3 4LH
United Kingdom
http://www.bae.co.uk/

Lifespan

Lifespan is a procedural configuration management tool, which enables an organization to apply its rules and procedures in a top-down fashion (i.e., defined and controlled by management). For organizations with significant CM needs, Lifespan is a highly configurable system, which can be used to model any complex life cycle process. For more modest needs, Lifespan needs no tailoring but, as a minimum, fully implements the CM disciplines of change control, configuration identification, baselining, and status accounting.

Burton Systems Software
P.O. Box 4157
Cary, NC 27519-4157
http://www.burtonsys.com/

TLIB Version Control

TLIB Version Control is a configuration management tool for the PC software development community.

Component Software
http://www.componentsoftware.com/

CS-RCS

Component Software RCS (CS-RCS) manages document revisions. It is used to monitor changes made in files that are accessed by stand-alone or networked workstations. Based on GNU RCS, it is fully integrated with Windows 95 and Windows NT. CS-RCS supports multiplatform workgroups, making it the ideal solution for sites that share common files on UNIX and Windows platforms.

Computer Associates International, Inc.
One Computer Associates Plaza
Islandia, NY 11749
http://www.cai.com/

Endevor

Endevor provides life cycle management, version control, configuration management, release management, change tracking of application changes in many environments such as MVS, UNIX, Windows NT, and so on.

Endevor/DB

Endevor/DB is a management facility that controls and monitors change processing within the MVS CA-IDMS/DC environment. Endevor/DB provides automated facilities for performing change identification and management, and promotion or migration of the data dictionary in the CA-IDMS/DB environment. It also includes security management, information management, and the Endevor/MVS-DB Bridge. When combined, these powerful capabilities improve data dictionary operation and administration.

CA-VMLib

CA-VMLib is a library management and control system for the VM/CMS environment. CA-VMLib provides centralized file management of files accessed by multiple users and tracks changes to those files.

Unicenter TNG Change and Configuration Management Option

The Unicenter TNG Change and Configuration Management Option is a software configuration management system developed specifically for Unicenter clients. Unicenter TNG Change and Configuration Management visually tracks, manages, and automates the workflow of software development projects, supporting the needs of managers and developers.

CA-Panvalet

CA-Panvalet is a product in the area of library management. It centralizes the storage of source, JCL, or object modules of an application. Programmers benefit from member locking, a compare program, and a comprehensive directory. Managers benefit from access controls, extensive reporting, archival procedures, and efficient DASD utilization.

CA-Panexec

CA-Panexec centralizes the storage, management, and control for executable and object members. Other data types may also be stored in a CA-Panexec library.

CA-PanAPT

CA-PanAPT is an automated production turnover system that controls, moves, tracks, and provides an inventory of all entities within an application, throughout the system life cycle.

CA-Pan/Merge

CA-Pan/Merge is a development tool that allows users to easily combine separate sets of program changes into one program. CA-Pan/Merge automatically identifies all change overlays. Any conflicting changes are clearly marked and can easily be resolved on-line using CA-Pan/Merge ISPF panels. Detail and summary reports are available.

CA-Pan/LCM

CA-Pan/LCM provides complete change and configuration management in the PWS environment for the PC-DOS, MS-DOS, OS/2, UNIX, and LAN environments. CA-Pan/LCM provides three major life cycle management environments: development, administration, and report generation. Each environment provides powerful functionality that enables managers, project leaders, programmers, quality assurance personnel, operation support personnel, and auditors to provide the necessary accountability, auditability, and adherence to established standards. CA-Pan/LCM operates in a stand-alone or LAN environment, or cooperatively with CA-Librarian, CA-Panvalet, or PDS files on the mainframe.

CA-Librarian

CA-Librarian manages, secures, and audits your organization's valuable software assets. Its library management facilities provide for secure storage and access to source code. The CA-Librarian Change Control Facility (CCF) complements this source code management by adding automated control features and procedures.

CA-Pan/LCM Configuration Manager

CA-Pan/LCM Configuration Manager provides configuration management capabilities for CA-Librarian, CA-Panvalet, or PDS files. Features such as impact analysis and automated builds help to increase programmer productivity and application quality.

Configuration Data Services, Inc.
19762 MacArthur Boulevard, 3rd Floor
Irvine, CA 92612
http://www.configdata.com/

ECMS

ECMS provides access control in a single database by collecting, control-ling, and storing files on a centralized vault for retrieval and manipulation by multiple users. ECMS functions as a data warehouse providing the capability of recording product definition to ensure complete product integrity and version control while being designed, built, and frozen for replication in the future. ECMS is designed for total program configura-tion management of all product definition used in the design, procure-ment, fabrication, assembly, testing, and delivery phases of a product which must conform to given standards and to contractual and man-agement requirements. ECMS retains the integrity and currency of as-proposed, as-design, as-planned, as-built, and design-to-cost configu-rations. ECMS is specifically designed to provide secure electronic storage and access of product data. All transaction activity is performed with complete audit traceability, while avoiding redundant activities and operator error. ECMS was produced to address the procedural problems and consistency of interorganizational functions, while facilitating an on-line dialog between the various departments concerned for the design and building of product lines.

Continuus Software Corporation
108 Pacifica
Irvine, CA 92618
http://www.continuus.com/

Continuus/CM

Continuus/CM delivers a truly comprehensive set of change manage-ment capabilities. In addition to tracking critical history and status information for all project components and activities, Continuus/CM coordinates and communicates the software development activities of all team members with groupware efficiency. Continuus/CM offers these necessary components:

- Version control;

- Component/object management;

- Distributed and remote development;

- Parallel development;

- Build management; and

- Work area management.

Continuus/PT

Continuus/PT is a full-fledged problem/change tracking tool that integrates with Continuus/CM. Continuus/PT offers complete traceability between change requests and actual changes for software development teams of all sizes.

Continuus/WebSynergy

WebSynergy improves time-to-market and predictability of delivery of web-based applications. The use of WebSynergy dramatically improves the productivity of all contributors by managing the processes and control of all web-based assets, ensuring increased predictability and improved time-to-market in the delivery of web-based applications and information. The change management capabilities of WebSynergy improve web development, web content management, and productivity for content developers, webmasters, testers, approvers, and professional web developers by providing these abilities:

- A common team framework leverages skills of all contributors.

- A shared set of processes/practices improves team coordination.

- Automation of manual tasks eliminates common errors and increases productivity.

- Complete visibility is offered into web development activities.

Continuus/WebSynergy Enterprise Web Asset Management also has these features:

- Increases overall quality of web-based applications.

- Meets the needs of diverse web teams.

▶ Supports the management and development of many different types of web assets.

Crystaliz, Inc.
9 Pond Lane
Suite 4D-B
Concord, MA 01742
http://www.crystaliz.com/

Concorde SiteControl

Concorde SiteControl is a system for product data management, made web-centric and integrated with change management and development activities. Its fundamental innovations and benefits are (1) web-based, cross-linked data, (2) adaptability, and (3) integratability with existing data and with other web-based systems. Concorde SiteControl opens up development to teams distributed worldwide on heterogeneous systems. It provides distributed version control and configuration management. It also provides sophisticated and adaptable product structure management, linking of engineering structure with data and change management, and integration with other product structure plug-ins.

Cyclic Software
SourceGear Corporation
3200 Farber Drive
Champaign, IL 61822
http://www.cyclic.com/

Concurrent Versions System (CVS)

The Concurrent Versions System (CVS) provides network-transparent source control for groups of developers. CVS maintains a history of all changes made to each directory tree it manages. Using this history, CVS can recreate past states of the tree, or show a developer when, why, and by whom a given change was made. CVS supports branches, which help manage long-term changes and bug-fix releases. CVS provides hooks to support process control and change control. CVS provides reliable access to its directory trees from remote hosts, using Internet protocols. Developers at remote sites can perform all the same operations available locally.

Access can be authenticated using the Kerberos network security system. CVS also supports parallel development, allowing more than one developer to work on the same sources at the same time.

Revision Control System (RCS)

RCS is a version control system. It offers a basic level of functionality (for example, it operates on one file at a time). As such, we would generally recommend a more powerful system, such as CVS, even for beginners, but we have listed this program because there seems to be continued interest in RCS (for example, people might be used to RCS or have scripts that rely on the RCS command-line interface). RCS has been widely ported and reimplemented. The free version of RCS is often called GNU RCS to distinguish it from the non-free implementations. RCS can be freely downloaded from *http://download.cyclic.com/pub/rcs/*. Details about RCS can be obtained from *http://www.cyclic.com/cyclic-pages/rcs.html*.

Source Code Control System (SCCS)

SCCS is a version control system. In general terms, it is similar to RCS in terms of functionality (for example, it operates on one file at a time). One popular feature that SCCS and CVS have, that RCS does not, is the ability to print each line of a file along with the version number that made the most recent modification to that line. The original (and still most widely used) version of SCCS is part of UNIX and is not free. But several people have taken a stab at writing a free compatible replacement. More information about SCCS can be obtained at *http://www.cyclic.com/cyclic-pages/sccs.html*.

tkCVS

The tkCVS package is one of the most popular graphical user interfaces for CVS. It is available free of cost. More information about tkCVS can be obtained from *http://www.cyclic.com/tkcvs/index.html*.

Data Design Systems, Inc.
5915 Airport Road, Suite 625
Mississauga, Ontario
Canada L4V 1T1
http://www.datadesign.com/

PrimeCode

PrimeCode is an enterprise SCM tool for managing changes to software applications throughout the entire software life cycle across multiple platforms.

DuraSoft GmbH
Breslauerstr. 14
D-76139 Karlsruhe
Germany
http://wwwipd.ira.uka.de/~RCE/

Revision Control Engine (RCE)

RCE is a product that provides version control. RCE stores and manages an arbitrary number of revisions of files. It automates the storage, retrieval, logging, and identification of revisions of these files, and it provides selection mechanisms for composing configurations. There is no limit to the number of revisions RCE can handle. Furthermore, RCE works with data files of any format, including, but not limited to, ASCII text, source code, object code, word processor data, spreadsheet files, CAD/CAM designs, database formats, and multimedia formats.

Ede Development Enterprises
350 Haverhill Street
North Reading, MA 01864
http://www.ede.com/

AccuRev

AccuRev is a version control system that uses a concept called *Virtual Versions.* Virtual Versions perform all of the tasks previously performed by branching and labeling, but they preserve the past too. Virtual Versions work just like labels. At heart they are just aliases. But unlike labels, they are versioned. If you want to "move" a Virtual Version, you can, but there is a permanent record of the previous version. Because Virtual Versions are first-class objects in the system, you can directly operate on them.

Expertware
Corporate Headquarters
P.O. Box 1847
San Ramón, CA 94583-1529
http://www. cmvision.com/

CMVision

CMVision is a product consisting of an integrated family of modules that automates the many different functions of system configuration management, change management, and problem tracking, including software, hardware, and documentation. CMVision supports all phases of the system life cycle and provides process automation and tracking for all these phases.

George James Software Limited
42 High Street
Shepperton, Middlesex, TW17 9AU
United Kingdom
http://www.gcorgcjamcs.com/

VC/m (Version and Configuration Management)

VC/m is an automated version control and configuration management system for application development on Windows NT, Windows 95, Windows3.X, DOS, UNIX, and open VMS platforms. You can configure it to manage a wide range of scenarios from the small in-house development team to major software package development and distribution.

International Business Machines Corporation
New Orchard Road
Armonk, NY 10504
http://www.ibm.com/

VisualAge TeamConnection Enterprise Server

To coordinate development activities across all phases of a project's life cycle, choose VisualAge TeamConnection Enterprise Server Version 3.0. TeamConnection tightly integrates configuration and library management, version control, process control for change management, build management, and support of electronic delivery. TeamConnection manages complex, heterogeneous development environments with varied tool integration and robust platform support within an open and scalable architecture.

ICE Engineering, Inc.
Rt #1, Box 273J
Lake Linden, MI 49945
http://www.ice.com/java/jcvs/index.shtml

jCVS

jCVS is a Java-based CVS client. CVS is a source code control system based on RCS. The primary benefit of CVS is that it provides a server/client protocol, which allows clients such as jCVS to be written. jCVS allows any Java 1.1 capable machine to be a CVS client, providing for a totally distributed source code management system. This product is available free of cost.

Industrial Strength Software Company
http://www.industrial-strength.com/

ChangeMaster

ChangeMaster is a change management tool. Developers simply check out and check in files. In fact, they don't have to alter the way they make changes, compile, test, and debug their programs. The Check-Out command copies the source and objects to be modified from the production library to a developer's work library. The Check-In command promotes the changes to the testing level library and automatically recreates (recompiles) objects in the test library from the modified source. Object reservation prevents simultaneous modifications to the same object or source member by different programmers working in the same area of a project.

InRoads Technology, Inc.
6144 Calle Real, Suite 201
Santa Barbara, CA 93117
http://www.inroadstech.com/

Rapid Implementation Manager

Rapid Implementation Manager includes two modules—the Implementation Road Maps and the Implementation Explorer. The Implementation Road Maps guides you step by step through the implementation process. The Implementation Explorer acts as the entry point for managing data, creating schedules, and managing the overall project. The Implementation Road Maps shows you exactly when and how to use the Implementation Explorer to best streamline and accelerate the implementation.

Intasoft Ltd.
Tresco House
Westpoint Court
Exeter, EX5 1DJ
United Kingdom
http://www.intasoft.co.uk/intasoft/

AllChange

AllChange is a CM system that provides an active supportive environment for development. It provides information about the makeup of the product or project and actively helps project managers and developers by:

▶ Ensuring that the procedures are carried out according to the specification;

▶ Tracking the progress of change;

▶ Securing components of a product against unauthorized access;

▶ Allowing developers to work together but without getting in each others' way; and

▶ Making information available to those people who require it.

JavaSoft
Sun Microsystems, Inc.
901 San Antonio Road
Palo Alto, CA 94303
http://www.javasoft.com/

JavaSafe

JavaSafe 1.0 provides a source management and revision control system. It gives developers, working alone or in teams, control of their software development projects. JavaSafe 1.0 software builds, maintains, and safeguards directories or "repositories" that provide a centralized, secure environment for web content, source code, or any other type of file that is associated with a project. The JavaSafe 1.0 server manages the repositories and concurrency issues, while the JavaSafe 1.0 client provides file versioning, file check in, and file check out.

Josh MacDonald
jmacd@cs.berkeley.edu
http://www.xcf.berkeley.edu/~jmacd/prcs.html

PRCS

PRCS, the Project Revision Control System, is the front end to a set of tools that (like CVS) provide a way to deal with sets of files and directories as an entity, preserving coherent versions of the entire set. This product is available free of cost.

Kestral Computing Pty. Ltd.
Suite 8a, Level 1
17 Burgundy Street
Heidelberg 3084, Melbourne
Australia
http://www.kestral.com.au/

CodeVault

CodeVault is a version control and change management system.

Lockheed Martin Ocean, Radar, and Sensor Systems
EagleSpeed Software Tools and Processes
P.O. Box 4840
Syracuse, NY 13221-4840
http://www.lmco.com/

EagleSpeed CM

EagleSpeed CM is a configuration management solution that provides an integrated change process and version control.

Lucent Technologies
Software Technology Center
Room 3D-471
600 Mountain Avenue
Murray Hill, NJ 07974-0636
http://www.lucent.com/

Sablime

The Sablime system helps track changes to software, firmware, hardware, and documentation from origination through maintenance, delivery, and support.

Mainsoft Corporation
1270 Oakmead Parkway, Suite 310
Sunnyvale, CA 94086
http://www.mainsoft.com/

Visual SourceSafe for UNIX

Mainsoft took the source code of Microsoft Visual SourceSafe and rehosted it on UNIX with Mainsoft's Windows on UNIX, MainWin. You get native UNIX performance and scalability with the UNIX version with complete Windows functionality.

MERANT
The Lawn
Old Bath Road
Newbury RG14 1QN
United Kingdom
http://www.merant.com/

PVCS Dimensions

PVCS Dimensions is a solution for process-based configuration management. PVCS Dimensions tightly integrates workspace management, version, build and release management, issue and change management, and process management in a single product suite.

PVCS Version Manager and PVCS Version Manager Plus

PVCS Version Manager organizes, manages, and protects software assets, supporting effective SCM across your entire enterprise. PVCS Version Manager Plus adds the power of PVCS VM Server, enabling distributed teams and remote developers to work collaboratively via the web, while sharing protected and centrally managed software archives.

PVCS Configuration Builder

PVCS Configuration Builder automates and accelerates software builds across multiple platforms from a single point of control. Configuration Builder is fully integrated with PVCS Version Manager, shortening build cycles with repeatable, automated, and accurate builds of your software and provides you with a complete audit trail of what is included in each build.

PVCS Professional

PVCS Professional gives teams the power to organize software assets, track and communicate issues, and standardize the software build process for end-to-end software configuration management. PVCS Professional combines PVCS Version Manager, PVCS Tracker, and PVCS Configuration Builder. PVCS Professional Plus adds PVCS VM Server, enabling teams to work collaboratively via the web, anywhere in the world, while sharing protected and centrally managed software archives.

PVCS Replicator

PVCS Replicator enables decentralized and distributed teams to safely engage in efficient parallel and concurrent software development, even within the most rigorously defined life cycles and process-based CM systems. Designed to support multisite development managed with PVCS Dimensions, PVCS Replicator gives organizations the freedom to integrate work undertaken at many different sites into a single cohesive unit. Organizations maximize development resources, reduce development risk, and speed project completion.

PVCS Tracker

PVCS Tracker captures, manages, and communicates the business and technical issues critical to your success. Tracker's unique TrackerLink IDE integration delivers issue and change management that works the way your teams work—within their native development environments, via the web or in Microsoft Windows.

Microsoft Corporation
One Microsoft Way
Redmond, WA 98052-6399
http://www.microsoft.com/

Visual SourceSafe

Visual SourceSafe is a project-oriented version control for web and PC content management that protects your team's most valuable assets, and gives you the tools you need to work efficiently within complex development and authoring environments.

Mortice Kern Systems (MKS), Inc.
Third Floor, Duke's Court
Duke Street, Woking
Surrey GU21 5BH
United Kingdom
http://www.mks.com/

MKS Source Integrity Professional Edition

MKS Source Integrity Professional Edition 3.2 is an SCM solution that allows local and remote team members to contribute to the software development process, manage multiple projects, secure software assets, and meet deadlines. With Source Integrity Professional Edition, all team members have web access to SCM, defect tracking, and process-centric task management. MKS Source Integrity Professional Edition also includes process automation, independent workspaces for parallel development, postrelease maintenance, automated notification, integration into leading IDEs, and advanced security and administration.

Web Integrity

MKS Source Integrity provides robust SCM capabilities to address strategic organizational needs such as project status, postrelease maintenance, and security. Teams can access a stable repository through a web client, command-line, or IDE interface.

SDM-Implementer

SDM-Implementer is a change management package for the IBM AS/400.

Network Concepts, Inc.
9 Mount Pleasant Turnpike
Denville, NJ 07834-3612
http://www. nci-sw.com/

CONTROL

CONTROL Software Management and Library System is a change management and version control system.

Neuma Technology Corporation
1730 St. Laurent Boulevard.
Ottawa, Ontario, K1G 5L1
Canada
http://www.neuma.com/

NeumaCM+

NeumaCM+ combines configuration management with data management and process control. Specific applications cover version control, build and release management, configuration management, change control, and problem and activity tracking. NeumaCM+ can help the development team work to maximum efficiency, ensuring the integrity of the final product.

Perforce Software, Inc.
2420 Santa Clara Avenue, Suite 200
Alameda, CA 94501
http://www.perforce.com/

Perforce Fast SCM System

Perforce Fast SCM System is a configuration management system built on a client/server architecture.

Peter Miller
millerp@canb.auug.org.au
http://www.canb.auug.org.au/~millerp/aegis/aegis.html

Aegis

Aegis is a software configuration management system that provides a framework within which a team of developers can work on many changes to a program independently, and Aegis coordinates integrating these changes back into the master source of the program, with as little disruption as possible. Aegis is written and owned by Peter Miller and is freely distributable under the terms and conditions of the GNU GPL.

Platinum Technology
1815 South Meyers Road
Oakbrook Terrace, IL 60181-5241
http://www.platinum.com/

CCC/Harvest

CCC/Harvest is a change and configuration management solution that synchronizes development activities across heterogeneous platforms during the entire application development life cycle. CCC/Harvest allows users to create a repeatable process through which they manage application development. CCC/Harvest scales up to serve project teams working on your largest enterprise systems and scales down to meet the needs of your smallest groups.

Quality Software Components Ltd.
6 Suttie Way, Bridge of Allan
Stirlingshire, FK9 4NQ
Scotland
http://www.qsc.co.uk/

GP-Version

GP-Version is a version control tool that is built using Delphi and is very ideally suited for managing Delphi projects. GP-Version has two add-ins: GP-Tracker and GP-Builder. The GP-Tracker add-in provides the ability to record and track bugs and change requests on a project-by-project basis. The GP-Builder utility is designed specifically for Delphi 3, and provides the ability to access the command-line compiler graphically. You can create project groups containing all the Delphi projects, and packages used in a particular development project, and configure the compiler options, directories, and conditionals for each item.

Quma Software, Inc.
20 Warren Manor Court
Cockeysville, MD 21030
http://www.qumasoft.com/

Quma Version Control System (QVCS)

QVCS is a version control system.

Rational Software Corporation
18880 Homestead Road
Cupertino, CA 95014
http://www.rational.com/

ClearCase

ClearCase is part of an integrated change management solution from Rational that supports both Windows and UNIX platforms. The ClearCase product family provides a comprehensive solution for software configuration management (ClearCase), distributed development (ClearCase MultiSite), and defect tracking (ClearQuest).

ClearGuide

ClearGuide is the first software process management solution specially designed for the dynamic nature of software development. ClearGuide provides a framework for defining project tasks, prioritizing day-to-day activities, allocating resources, and tracking project progress.

Reliable Software
1011 Boren Avenue, Suite 206
Seattle, WA 98104
http://www.relisoft.com/

Code Co-op

Code Co-op is a server-less version control system for collaborative development. With Code Co-op team members can work together on a software project through the regular exchange of scripts.

SEA Software Ever After
117 Clarinda Road
South Oakleigh
Vic 3167
Australia
http://www.s-e-a.com.au/

R-Sea-Yes

R-Sea-Yes is a source code management and version control system.

Sequel UK Ltd.
Eastlands Court
St. Peters Road
Rugby, CV21 3QP, Warwickshire
United Kingdom
http://www.sequeluk.com/

Alchemist

Alchemist is a powerful, automated software change management system that supports software changes across multiple platforms.

SERENA Software, Inc.
500 Airport Boulevard, 2nd Floor
Burlingame, CA 94010-1904
http://www.serena.com/

eChange Man

eChange Man helps you centrally manage the entire software life cycle on multiple platforms: web, Windows, Windows NT, UNIX, and MPE/iX environments. Its Java client and network-friendly TCP/IP architecture simplify distributed development. eChange Man maintains detailed audit trails, enables cross-platform build management, and integrates with popular IDEs including Microsoft Visual Studio, PowerBuilder, and Oracle Developer.

Softlab GmbH
Zamdorfer Straße 120
81677 Munich
Germany
http://www.softlabna.com/

Visual Enabler

Visual Enabler is an SCM and version control toolset for Visual C++, Visual Basic, and Visual J++ developers who want a team-based development solution.

SoftLanding Systems, Inc.
84 Elm St.
Peterborough, NH 03458
http://www.softlanding.com/

TurnOver

TurnOver is a change management product available for AS/400. TurnOver includes help desk and project management features, change management features, programmer tools, distribution capabilities, and several built-in interfaces.

SourceGear Corporation
3200 Farber Drive
Champaign, IL 61822
http://www.sourceoffsite.com/

SourceOffSite

SourceOffSite is a client/server solution designed to provide quick and reliable access to a SourceSafe database from remote locations.

StarBase Corporation
4 Hutton Centre, Suite 800
Santa Ana, CA 92707
http://www.starbase.com/

StarTeam

StarTeam is an SCM solution with an integrated interface designed to increase development productivity and collaboration.

Sun Microsystems, Inc.
901 San Antonio Road
Palo Alto, CA 94303
http://www.sun.com/

Sun WorkShop TeamWare

Sun WorkShop TeamWare provides a multiplatform software configuration management toolset for development teams that enhances your team's coordination and lets you:

- Easily manage your team's software development activities;
- Increase your team's productivity immediately;
- Improve your product quality;
- Get your product to market faster; and
- Easily distribute and grow your team.

Sun WorkShop TeamWare allows you to conveniently coordinate development across Solaris SPARC and Solaris Intel environments. Sun WorkShop TeamWare is fully compatible with all Sun WorkShop language systems and development tools.

SureHand Software
8816 Manchester, #193
Brentwood, MO 63144
http://www.surehand.com/

ViCiouS Pro

ViCiouS Pro is a version control system for Delphi and C++ Builder.

Tesseract Group
P.O. Box 9
Irene 0062
South Africa
http://www.tesseractgroup.com/

Tesseract Lifecycle Manager

Tesseract Lifecycle Manager is a suite of application for software life cycle management. The suite includes Account Lifecycle Manager, Inventory Lifecycle Manager, Product Lifecycle Manager, and File Lifecycle Manager.

Thompson Automation Software
5616 SW Jefferson
Portland, OR 97221
http://www.tasoft.com/

Corporate RCS

This is a multiplatform revision control system.

Tower Concepts (a subsidiary of *Visible Systems Corporation*)
248 Main Street
Oneida, NY 13421
http://www. tower.com/

Razor

Razor is an integrated tool suite that offers both configuration management and problem tracking. The issues program could be considered the heart of the Razor package. Through the versions program, Razor provides a window interface to all of the standard version control needs: checking files in/out for edit, parallel development, reporting changes, viewing differences, browsing, and so on.

Ultracomp
Ultracomp House
Pinehill Road
Crowthorne, Berks, RG45 7JD
United Kingdom
http://www.ultracomp.co.uk/

Red Box Service Management System

Red Box Service Management System provides a set of application modules addressing the key service support processes of configuration management, change management, and help desk and problem management. Red Box provides a process-oriented approach to these key service management disciplines, based on industry-recognized best practices. Red Box is the only product on the market that was built from the outset to meet the functional requirements of the CCTA's IT Infrastructure Library (ITIL) guidelines.

UNI Software Plus GmbH
Softwarepark Hagenberg
Hauptstraße 99
A-4232 Hagenberg
Germany
http://www.unisoft.co.at/

VOODOO

VOODOO (Versions of Outdated Documents Organized Orthogonally) is a version control solution.

VOODOO Server

VOODOO Server is a version control system for software developers using Metrowerks CodeWarrior under Mac OS.

UniPress Software, Inc.
2025 Lincoln Highway
Edison, NJ 08817
http://www.unipress.com/

Source Code Manager (SCM)

Source Code Manager (SCM) is a configuration management tool for managing the source of projects, especially multiprogrammer projects, tracking revisions to the entire software system and making all releases consistent across the programming team.

Appendix B

SCM standards

Introduction

Configuration management got its start in the U.S. defense industry as a technique to resolve problems of poor quality, wrong parts ordered, and parts not fitting, problems that were leading to inordinate cost overruns. So in 1962, the American Air Force published the first standard on configuration management: AFSCM 375-1. This standard identified configuration management as the key element in the design, development, test, and operation of the item to be delivered, because configuration management procedures facilitated better communication and prevented uncontrolled change.

In 1964, the National Aeronautics and Space Administration (NASA) developed a configuration management standard (NPC 500-1) that was based on AFSCM 375-1, for the design and development of the *Saturn V* spacecraft. This standard played an instrumental role in the *Saturn V* and *Apollo* space programs. During the same time the U.S. Army came out with their version of a configuration management standard (AMCR 11-26) and soon in 1965 the U.S. Navy also followed suit with their standard NAVMATINST 4130.1 (Configuration Management Policy and

Guidance Manual). In 1968 four major standards related to configuration management were published:

1. Department of Defense Directive (DOD D) 5010.19: Configuration Management

2. MIL-STD-480: Configuration Control Engineering Changes, Deviations and Waivers

3. MIL-STD-482: Configuration Status Accounting Data Elements & Related Features

4. MIL-STD-490: Specification Practices

These standards gave a new thrust to the practice of configuration management and were integrated into the defense contracts, so that not only the military used these standards internally, but the defense industry (the government contractors and commercial corporations who supplied materials and equipment to the military) also started subscribing to and implementing these standards.

In 1971, the U.S. Air Force issued MIL-STD-483, Configuration Management Practices for Systems, Equipment, Munitions, & Computer Programs. This was the first standard that recognized configuration management of both hardware and software. Even though the industry, through various associations such as the Electronics Industries Association (EIA), Aerospace Industries Association (AIA), National Security Industrial Association (NSIA), and American Electronics Association (AEA), were reviewing the military standards, it was in 1988 that commercial standards began to appear.

In 1988, the assistant secretary of defense for acquisition, Dr. Costello, wrote a memo indicating that the government should get out of the standards-writing business and entrust the job of developing standards to the organizations who were developing standards on various topics and were adept at it. He also stated that the military would use the standards written by organizations like EIA, IEEE (Institute of Electrical and Electronics Engineers), SAE (Society of Automotive Engineers), ANSI (American National Standards Institute), and ISO (International Organization for Standardization) for procuring materials from the commercial market. These organizations had a good track record at developing standards. For example, EIA had written many standards on electronics, electrical, and communications protocols. The SAE had developed standards on automotive development and related topics. IEEE was one of the pioneers in the development of software standards. Thus commercial standards on configuration management from these organizations began to appear. In the following sections we look at the major configuration management and related standards—both military and commercial.

Military standards

The standards published by the U.S. Department of Defense are used by all NATO countries, and by countries that use military equipment manufactured in the United States. These are the main standards related to configuration management:

- ▶ DOD-STD-2167A: Defense System Software Development

- ▶ DOD-STD-2168: Defense System Software Quality Program

- ▶ MIL-STD-480: Configuration Control Engineering Changes, Deviations and Waivers

- ▶ MIL-STD-481: Configuration Control Engineering Changes (Short Form), Deviations and Waivers

- ▶ MIL-STD-482: Configuration Status Accounting Data Elements & Related Features

- ▶ MIL-STD-483: Configuration Management Practices for Systems, Equipment, Munitions, and Computer Programs

- ▶ MIL-STD-490: Specification Practices

- ▶ MIL-STD-1521B: Technical Reviews and Audits for Systems, Equipment, and Computer Programs

- ▶ MIL-STD-973: Configuration Management

DOD-STD-2167A: Defense system software development

This standard supersedes the DOD-STD-2167, Defense System Software Development, 1985. The purpose of this standard is to establish requirements to be applied during the acquisition, development, or support of software systems. The requirements of this standard apply to the development of computer software configuration items (CSCIs).

Even though this standard was developed for the DOD environment, it can be tailored to handle rapidly evolving software technology and to accommodate a wide variety of state-of-the-practice software engineering techniques. The standard allows the user to incorporate the SCM plan into the software development plan (SDP) or to treat it as a separate document. The benefit of handling the SCM plan as part of the SDP is that, for projects where SCM is either tightly tied to the development life cycle or where the SCM function is relatively small, it allows the SCM plan to be placed in the SDP where it is more appropriate.

DOD-STD-2168: Defense system software quality program

This standard contains requirements for the development, documentation, and implementation of a software quality program. This program includes planning for and conducting evaluations of the quality of software, associated documentation, and related activities, and planning for and conducting the follow-up activities necessary to ensure timely and effective resolution of problems. This standard, together with other military specifications and standards governing software development, configuration management, specification practices, project reviews and audits, and subcontractor management, provides a means for achieving, determining, and maintaining quality in software and associated documentation.

MIL-STD-480: Configuration control engineering changes, deviations and waivers

This standard establishes the requirements, formats, and procedures to be utilized in the preparation of configuration control documentation. Included are these requirements:

▶ Maintaining configuration control of configuration items (CIs), both hardware and software;

▶ Preparing and submitting engineering change proposals (ECPs), requests for deviations/waivers (RFDs/RFWs), notices of revision (NORs), and specification change notices (SCNs); and

- Evaluating, coordinating, and approving or disapproving ECPs and RFDs/RFWs applicable to the DOD, commercial, or nondevelopmental items (NDIs).

The purpose of this standard is to establish configuration control requirements and procedures applicable to the acquisition and modification of items procured by the DOD.

This standard is to be used by contractors and government activities to:

1. Establish and maintain effective configuration control of the approved configuration identification.

2. Propose engineering changes to configuration items, both hardware and software which are designed, developed, or modified for DOD activities.

3. Request deviations or waivers pertaining to such items.

4. Prepare NORs and SCNs.

5. Control the form, fit, and function of privately developed items used in configuration items, including NDI items.

MIL-STD-481: Configuration control engineering changes (short form), deviations and waivers

This standard establishes requirements, formats, and procedures for the preparation, submission, and approval or disapproval of abbreviated engineering change proposals (ECPs). Where complete descriptions of ECPs are required, MIL-STD-480 should be specified in contracts. The purpose of this standard is to establish configuration control requirements and procedures applicable to the acquisition and modification of items procured by the Department of Defense (DOD). It is intended that this standard be applied to contracts or orders for procurement of the following:

- Multiapplication or standard items that were not developed as subdivisions of a specific system;

- Items fabricated in accordance with a mandatory detail design that was not developed by the fabricator; and

▸ Privately developed items (e.g., commercial off-the-shelf items), when the procuring activity has determined that the application of change control to such items is necessary and that the short-form ECP is applicable.

MIL-STD-482: Configuration status accounting data elements and related features

To ensure the use of uniform, clearly defined status accounting management information throughout DOD and the DOD–defense industry interface, this standard prescribes status accounting standard data elements, interim (nonstandard) data elements, and their related data items, codes, use identifiers, and data chains (referred to as "related features"). The data elements and related features are to be used as the content of those configuration status accounting records prepared by or for the department or agencies of DOD in accordance with the provisions of DOD Directive 5010.19 and DOD Instruction 5010.21.

MIL-STD-483: Configuration management practices for systems, equipment, munitions, and computer programs

This military standard sets forth configuration management practices that are to be tailored to specific programs and implemented by the contract work statement. The standard also establishes configuration management requirements that are not covered in MIL-STD-480, MIL-STD-481, MIL-STD-482, and MIL-STD-490.

MIL-STD-490: Specification practices

This military standard sets forth practices for the preparation, interpretation, change, and revision of program-specific specifications prepared by or for the departments and agencies of the Department of Defense. This military standard was prepared to establish uniform specification practices in response to the need for a document comparable to DOD-STD-100 covering engineering drawing practices and in recognition of the configuration identification concepts of the DOD configuration management program established by DOD Directive 5010.19 and DOD Instruction 5010.21.

MIL-STD-1521B: Technical reviews and audits for systems, equipment, and computer programs

This supersedes MIL-STD-1521 (Technical Reviews & Audits for Systems, Equipment, & Computer Software). This standard prescribes the requirements for the conduct of technical reviews and audits on systems, equipment, and computer software. The program manager shall select the following technical reviews and audits at the appropriate phase of program development:

- System Requirements Review (SRR)
- System Design Review (SDR)
- Software Specification Review (SSR)
- Preliminary Design Review (PDR)
- Critical Design Review (CDR)
- Test Readiness Review (TRR)
- Functional Configuration Audit (FCA)
- Physical Configuration Audit (PCA)
- Formal Qualification Review (FQR)
- Production Readiness Review (PRR)

Technical reviews and audits defined in this standard are to be conducted in accordance with this standard to the extent specified in the contract clauses, statement of work, and the contract data requirements list.

MIL-STD-973: Configuration management

This standard defines configuration management requirements, which are to be selectively applied, as required, throughout the life cycle of any configuration item (1) developed wholly or partially with government funds, including nondevelopmental items when the development of technical data is required to support off-the-shelf equipment or software; or (2) designated for configuration management for reasons of integration, logistics support, or interface control. This standard applies to DOD activities and contractors who are tasked with the application of configuration management.

International/commercial standards

There are a host of standards by many organizations like the EIA, Electric Power Research Institute (EPRI), European Computer Manufacturers Institute (ECMI), Federal Aviation Authority (FAA), Institute of Nuclear Power Operations (INPO), European Space Agency (ESA), Nuclear Information & Records Management Association (NIRMA), National Aeronautics and Space Administration (NASA), and North Atlantic Treaty Organization (NATO). But the usage of these standards is limited to the members of those organizations. The most popular international standards on configuration management are those by ANSI/IEEE and ISO:

- IEEE Std-828-1998: IEEE Standard for Software Configuration Management Plans
- ANSI/IEEE Std-1042-1987: IEEE Guide to Software Configuration Management
- ANSI/IEEE Std-730-1998: IEEE Standard for Software Quality Assurance Plans
- ANSI/IEEE Std-730.1-1995: IEEE Guide for Software Quality Assurance Planning
- IEEE Std-610.12-1990: IEEE Standard Glossary of Software Engineering Terminology
- ANSI/IEEE Std-1028-1988: Standard for Software Reviews and Audits
- ISO 9000-3: Guidelines for the Application of ISO 9001 to the Development and Maintenance of Software
- ISO 10007: Quality Management—Guidelines for Configuration Management

IEEE Std-828-1998: IEEE standard for software configuration management plans

This standard is concerned with the activity of planning for software configuration management. SCM activities, whether planned or not, are performed on all software development projects; planning makes these activities more effective. Good planning results in a document that captures the planning information, makes the information the property of the project, communicates to all who are affected, and provides a basis for ongoing planning. This standard establishes the minimum required contents of an SCM plan.

ANSI/IEEE Std-1042-1987: IEEE guide to software configuration management

This is the most comprehensive international standard available on SCM. This standard describes the application of configuration management disciplines to the management of software engineering projects. SCM consists of two major aspects—planning and implementation.

For those planning SCM activities, this standard provides insights into the various factors that must be considered. Users implementing SCM disciplines will find suggestions and detailed examples of SCM plans in this standard. This standard introduces the essential concepts of SCM, particularly those of special significance (for example, libraries and tools) to software engineering. It then presents the planning for SCM in terms of documenting a plan following the outline of the ANSI/IEEE Std-828, so that a user who is unfamiliar with the disciplines of SCM can gain valuable insights into the issues. For those preparing SCM plans, the second part of the guide provides sample plans for consideration.

ANSI/IEEE Std-730-1998: IEEE standard for software quality assurance plans

The purpose of this standard is to provide uniform, minimum acceptable requirements for preparation and content of software quality assurance plans (SQAPs). This standard applies to the development and maintenance of critical software. For noncritical software, or for software already developed, a subset of the requirements of this standard may be applied.

ANSI/IEEE Std-730.1-1995: IEEE guide for software quality assurance planning

This guide explains and clarifies the contents of each section of an SQAP that satisfies the requirements of IEEE Std-730-1989. The guide supersedes IEEE Std-983-1986 and does not constitute further requirements than those stated in IEEE Std-730-1989. An organization can claim compliance with IEEE Std-730-1989 without following this guide completely.

This guide presents the consensus of those in the software development and maintenance community with expertise or experience in generating, implementing, evaluating, and modifying SQAPs. The SQAP should describe the plans and activities for the software quality assurance (SQA) staff. The SQA staff observes the development process and reports deficiencies observed in the procedures and the resulting products.

IEEE Std-610.12-1990: IEEE standard glossary of software engineering terminology

This glossary defines terms in the field of software engineering. Topics covered include addressing; assembling, compiling, linking, loading; computer performance evaluation; configuration management; data types; errors, faults, and failures; evaluation techniques; instruction types; language types; libraries; microprogramming; operating systems; quality attributes; software documentation; software and system testing; software architecture; software development process; software development techniques; and software tools.

ANSI/IEEE Std-1028-1988: Standard for software reviews and audits

The purpose of this standard is to provide definitions and uniform requirements for review and audit processes. It does not establish the need to conduct specific reviews or audits; that need is defined by local policy. Where specific reviews and audits are required, standard procedures for their execution must be defined. This standard provides such definitions for review and audit purposes that are applicable to products and processes throughout the software life cycle. Each organization should specify where and when this standard applies and any intended deviations form this standard.

ISO 9000-3: Guidelines for the application of ISO 9001 to the development and maintenance of software

The ISO 9000 series of standards was not designed primarily for software but for manufacturing processes. ISO 9001 is the model for quality assurance in design/development, production, installation, and servicing (in other words, manufacturing processes, which have design aspects). Standard ISO 9000-3 contains guidelines for the application of ISO 9001 to the development, supply, and maintenance of software. The coverage of software configuration management in this standard is very minimal but for configuration management functions and procedures this standards refers to ISO 10007.

ISO 10007: Quality management—guidelines for configuration management

This international standard gives guidance on the use of configuration management in industry and its interface with other management systems and procedures. It first provides a management overview, then describes the process, organization, and detailed procedures. It is applicable to the support of projects from concept through to design, development, procurement, production, installation, operation and maintenance, and disposal of products.

The application of configuration management may be tailored to suit individual projects, taking into account the size, complexity, and nature of the work. The standard offers excellent definition of the configuration management terms and its Annex A provides an excellent template for creating a configuration management plan. Annex C provides an excellent correlation between the different project life cycle phases and the various configuration management activities.

Conclusion

The ANSI/IEEE standards are the most widely used SCM standards, and the coverage of software configuration management and its functions is quite elaborate, comprehensive, and thorough. ISO 9000-3 and ISO 10007 provide another set of very good configuration management standards.

The DOD standards are mainly used in defense industry projects and even though they could be tailored for any project, their use is generally limited to the defense industry and military organizations within and outside the United States.

The SCM standards are the starting point for the practice of configuration management and related functions in any project or organization. It is the first place that one should look for guidance when starting a configuration management program. Unless your organization does not deal with the defense industry, then it would be better to base your SCM system on one of the commercial standards like ANSI/IEEE or ISO. This is because these standards are written for the entire industry (whereas the DOD standards were written for their specific segments of industry) and hence they are more flexible and can be customized more easily to suit your needs. Also these standards have greater potential for timely updates than the DOD standards; because these standards are used by the general industry, they must maintain relevance to the current software engineering principles and practices or face obsolescence.

The configuration management standards have played a very crucial role in shaping the way in which the configuration management is being practiced today. To achieve certification by international bodies like International Organization for Standardization (ISO 9000 quality standards) and Software Engineering Institute (capability maturity model, CMM), the existence of formal configuration management and procedures is a must.

Selected bibliography

Ben-Menachem, M., *Software Configuration Management Guidebook*, New York: McGraw-Hill, 1994.

Berlack, R. H., *Software Configuration Management*, New York: John Wiley & Sons, 1992.

Caputo, K., *CMM Implementation Guide*, Reading, MA: Addison-Wesley, 1998.

Ince, D., *ISO 9001 and Software Quality Assurance*, London: McGraw-Hill International, 1994.

Peach, R. W. (Ed.), *The ISO 9000 Handbook*, New York: McGraw-Hill, 1997.

Pressman, R. S., *Software Engineering: A Practitioner's Approach*, New York: McGraw-Hill, 1997.

Sommerville, I., *Software Engineering*, Reading, MA: Addison-Wesley, 1996.

Whitgift, D., *Methods and Tools for Software Configuration Management*, Chichester, England: John Wiley & Sons, 1991.

Appendix C

SCM resources on the Internet

Organizations and institutes

American National Standards Institute
(http://www.ansi.org)

The American National Standards Institute (ANSI) has served in its capacity as administrator and coordinator of the U.S. private sector voluntary standardization system for 80 years. Founded in 1918 by five engineering societies and three government agencies, the institute remains a private, nonprofit membership organization supported by a diverse constituency of private and public sector organizations. ANSI does not itself develop American national standards (ANSs); rather it facilitates development by establishing consensus among qualified groups. The institute ensures that its guiding principles—consensus, due process, and openness—are followed by the more than 175 distinct entities currently accredited under one of the federation's three methods of accreditation (organization, committee, or canvass).

Association for Computing Machinery
(http://www.acm.org)

The Association for Computing Machinery (ACM) is the world's oldest and largest educational and scientific computing society. Since 1947 ACM has provided a vital forum for the exchange of information, ideas, and discoveries. Today, ACM serves a membership of more than 80,000 computing professionals in more than 100 countries in all areas of industry, academia, and government.

Association for Configuration and Data Management
(http://www.acdm.org/)

The Association for Configuration and Data Management (ACDM) is a professional organization for configuration and data management professionals. The mission of ACDM is to be the premier professional organization that shares and refines the disciplines that accomplish configuration management (CM) and data management (DM) necessary for the delivery and support of products and services in a competitive and regulated business environment.

CM Certification Team
(http://spiderweb.btg.com/Spider2?CMCert)

The Certification Team (CMCert) is a body formed by volunteer CM professionals from all parts of the world to develop a standardized certification program for the worldwide configuration management community. This site is used by the team to distribute and comment on the work products it produces, and to communicate the status of the project to the CM community.

Configuration Management, Inc.
(http://www.softwareconfiguration.com)

Configuration Management, Inc. (CMI) was founded to assist computer professionals in managing changes to software, firmware, hardware, and documentation. CMI's mission is to support its customer base with a professional team of software configuration management specialists and to develop career paths for configuration management specialists. CMI provides its customers with a wide range of CM services including determination of the correct CM tools and processes for a project, initial implementation of tools and processes, ongoing support, and user administrator training.

Configuration Management Specialist Group of British Computer Society (http://www.cmsg.org.uk/)

The Configuration Management Specialist Group (CMSG) was set up in 1995 to provide a forum for developing and promoting CM as a discrete management process. The group facilitates the free and open exchange of CM ideas, experiences, and best practices at regular workshops and special events. There are also subgroups to research, develop, and provide valuable advice on CM processes, CM tools, and professional development and training.

European Society for Configuration Management (http://www.bluefox.co.uk/escm/index.html)

The European Society for Configuration Management (ESCM) is the only European professional body solely dedicated to the advancement of configuration management. A nonprofit organization, its charter is to develop the professional activities of configuration management across all business processes. The mission of ESCM is to establish the foremost institutional environment dedicated to the establishment of professional competency and recognition of the CM activity. Through its membership, it seeks to develop, promote, and influence best practice CM across all business platforms.

The society exists to foster professionalism in the field of CM, promote theory, techniques, and practice; establish and maintain a CM body of knowledge; disseminate information to the CM professional, establish educational standards for the profession, and advance professional recognition.

Institute of Configuration Management—The Home of CMII (http://www.icmhq.com/index.html)

The Institute of Configuration Management is headquartered in Scottsdale, Arizona. The institute is one of the world's leading training facilities in configuration management. The institute's mission is to strive to improve and advance the state of the art of CM and the interfaces between CM and all other disciplines throughout the business enterprise.

The institute is known for its CMII model, which is the basis for the courses that it offers in configuration management and its certification program. Courses I through VI, which are required to achieve CMII certification, are repeated each year in 18 cities across the United States, Canada, the United Kingdom, and Germany.

CM is the process of managing products, facilities, and processes by managing their requirements, including changes, and ensuring conformance in each case. The best CM process is one that can best (1) accommodate change; (2) accommodate the reuse of standards and best practices; (3) ensure that all requirements remain clear, concise, and valid; (4) communicate (1), (2), and (3) promptly and precisely; and (5) ensure conformance in each case. CMII is CM plus continuous improvement in all five.

Institute of Electrical and Electronics Engineers, Inc. (http://www.ieee.org)

The IEEE promotes the engineering process of creating, developing, integrating, sharing, and applying knowledge about information technologies and sciences for the benefit of humanity and the profession. Through its members, the IEEE is a catalyst for technological innovation and a leading authority in technical areas ranging from computer engineering, biomedical technology, and telecommunications to electric power and aerospace and consumer electronics.

The IEEE is a not-for-profit association and has more than 330,000 individual members in 150 countries. Through its technical publishing, conferences, and consensus-based standards activities, the IEEE produces 30% of the world's published literature in electrical engineering, computers, and control technology, annually holds more than 300 major conferences, and has more than 800 active standards with 700 under development.

International Organization for Standardization (http://www.iso.ch/)

The International Organization for Standardization (ISO) is a worldwide federation of national standards bodies from some 130 countries, one from each country. ISO is a nongovernmental organization established in

1947. The mission of ISO is to promote the development of standardization and related activities in the world with a view to facilitating the international exchange of goods and services, and to developing cooperation in the spheres of intellectual, scientific, technological, and economic activity. ISO's work results in international agreements, which are published as international standards.

International Society for Configuration Management (http://www.iscmus.com/)

The International Society for Configuration Management (ISCM) was established in 1995. Their charter is to provide a global organization for CM professionals to exchange ideas and create standards and publications. The society provides a certification program for a Certified International Configuration Manager (CICM). There are two levels of certification—Level I (Fundamental CM) and Level II (Software Specific CM).

NASA Web (http://www.nasa.gov/hqpao/welcome.html)

The home page of NASA (NASA On-line) is the result of NASA's effort to spread the unique knowledge that flows from its aeronautics and space research using the Internet.

National Aeronautics and Space Administration (NASA) (http://www.nasa.gov)

This is the home page of NASA.

Software Configuration Management Group (http://www.supelec.fr/see/cercle_configuration/ cercle_configuration_us.html)

The Software Configuration Management Group (SCMG) belongs to the software engineering committee of the French Society of Electrical and Electronics engineers (SEE). SEE is a noncommercial association of engineers whose vocation is to disseminate technical experience within the French industry by means of conferences, meetings, workshops, symposia, courses, and training.

The SCMG group intends to facilitate technology transfer among and between users, systems developers, and researchers in the field of software configuration management. The group will provide the novice and experienced person with practical information and materials for organizing or improving software configuration management activities and work.

Software Engineering Institute's SCM Home Page (http://www.sei.cmu.edu/legacy/scm/scmHomePage.html)

The Software Engineering Institute (SEI) is a federally funded research and development center established in 1984 by the U.S. Department of Defense with a broad charter to address the transition of software engineering technology. The SEI is an integral component of Carnegie Mellon University and is sponsored by the Office of the Under Secretary of Defense for Acquisition and Technology.

The software configuration management home page of SEI contains the details of the configuration management research done by the SEI between 1988 and 1994 and provides pointers to other useful sources of information on SCM.

Software Technology Support Center (http://www.stsc.hill.af.mil/home.asp)

In 1987, the U.S. Air Force selected Ogden Air Logistics Center (OO-ALC), Hill Air Force Base, Utah, to establish and operate its Software Technology Support Center (STSC). It was chartered to be the command focus for proactive application of software technology in weapon, command and control, intelligence, and mission-critical systems. The STSC provides hands-on assistance in adopting effective technologies for software-intensive systems.

The CM Research Foundation (http://www.cmref.org)

The CM Research Foundation exists to provide the best possible research forum for those working toward the advancement of configuration management across all disciplines. Established in 1996, the foundation is managed by the Configuration Research Group at Leeds University Business School.

The Configuration Management Information Center
(http://www.pdmic.com/cmic/)

This site is jointly hosted by Product Data Management Information Center and CMstat Corporation, a CM tool vendor. The site contains useful information about CM.

Resource pages

Brad Appleton's Software Configuration Management Links
(http://www.enteract.com/~bradapp/links/
scm-links.html#SCM)

A very good site that contains more than 260 CM-related links. The sections include CM resources; CM projects, groups, and conference; CM guides and tutorials; CM research papers and experience reports; commercial CM vendors, free CM tools, and free tracking tools.

CM Bibliography
(http://www.cmsg.org.uk/cm_bibliography.html)

Gives a list of configuration management references and standards.

CMII Key Articles Index Page
(http://www.icmhq.com/key/keyarticles.html)

A site that contains links to various CMII and other related articles.

CM Terminology
(http://www.cmsg.org.uk/cm_terminology.html)

A list of CM-related abbreviations and a CM glossary.

CM Tools & Vendors
(http://www.cmsg.org.uk/cm_tools.html)

Gives a list of most of the CM tools and vendors.

Configuration Management Yellow Pages (Software Engineering Research Laboratory of the University of Colorado) (http://www.cs.colorado.edu/users/andre/ configuration_management.html)

One of the most comprehensive and regularly updated configuration management resource pages on the Internet. The site contains information about the following: configuration management conferences, workshops, symposia, meetings, job-related information, details about other CM web sites, an very comprehensive list of commercial, public domain, and free configuration management tools and tool vendors, details about CM research, a excellent collection of links to papers on configuration management, information about CM consultants and trainers, and details about commercial, free, and public domain problem tracking systems. The site is maintained by André van der Hoek, and sponsored by the Software Engineering Research Laboratory of the University of Colorado.

Pascal Molli's CM Bubbles (http://www.loria.fr/~molli/cm-index.html)

This page contains numerous CM-related links in the following categories: books and reports, research projects, companies, free CM tools, commercial CM tools, related CM tools, free problem management tools, commercial problem management tools, general URLs on CM/PM, CM user group, CM related events, and CM vacancies.

SCM Links by Mária Bieliková (http://www.dcs.elf.stuba.sk/~bielik/scm/links.htm)

This page contains links to various SCM-related sites. The sections include research and universities, reviews, references, tutorials, free and commercial SCM tools, and SCM experts.

Steve Easterbrook's CM Resource Guide On-Line (http://www.cmiiug.com/Sites.htm)

An excellent source of CM-related information. The contents include CM postings, CM software vendors and integrators, software tools for configuration management, PDM add-ons, requirements traceability tools, documentation control classification/coding systems/imaging services, evaluation of PDM and software CM tools, CM and PDM (and related) conferences, CM and related Internet mail lists and news groups, CM/PDM consultants, CM education, CMII lead assessor training, CM-related education, CM and related books and manuals, CM and related articles, papers, reports, and conference proceedings, CM-specific journals and newsletters, CM-related journals, magazines, and newsletters, CM and related professional organizations, users groups, and research groups, and CM and related standards, guidelines, and position papers.

Yahoo! Configuration Management Links (http://dir.yahoo.com/Computers_and_Internet/Software/Programming_Tools/Software_Engineering/Configuration_Management/)

A comprehensive list of configuration management links by Yahoo!

Commercial research organizations

Butler Group (http://www.butlergroup.com)

Butler Group offers a range of services for both the users of IT and vendors of IT equipment, products, and services. Butler Group produces research reports, management guides, journals, technology audits, and white papers on many information technology-related areas including configuration management.

International Data Corporation (IDC) (http://www.idc.com)

International Data Corporation delivers accurate, relevant, and high-impact data and insight on information technology to help organizations make sound business and technology decisions. IDC forecasts worldwide IT markets and adoption and technology trends, and analyzes IT products and vendors, using a combination of rigorous primary research and in-depth competitive analysis.

Ovum Ltd.
(http://www.ovum.com)

Ovum Limited is a London-based research organization that publishes technical reports, analysis documents, trend predictions, evaluations, and so on in many areas such as configuration management, CASE tools, client/server development tools, and data mining. Ovum's report on CM tools—*Ovum Evaluates: Configuration Management*—is a leading publication about SCM tools. This report contains product/tool evaluations, market forecasts, vendor analysis, and so on.

Digital/On-line libraries

ACM Digital Library
(http://www.acm.org/dl/)

The ACM Digital Library features electronic publication of ACM magazines, journals, and proceedings, with a 6-year on-line archive and a bibliographical reference database going back to 1985 for most ACM publications. The Digital Library bibliographic database is a service ACM will offer to the public at no charge.

IEEE/IEE Electronic Library Home Page
(http://www.ieee.org/products/online/iel/)

The IEEE/IEE Electronic Library provides libraries and research facilities with a single source to almost a third of the world's current electrical engineering and computer science literature, granting access to publications from the IEEE and the Institution of Electrical Engineers (IEE). The digital library consists of more than 500,000 articles from over 12,000 publications, including journals, conference proceedings, and IEEE standards, more than two million full-page PDF images, including all original charts, graphs, diagrams, photographs, and illustrative material, full-text archives to IEEE and IEE publications from 1988 to the present, and unlimited access to a subset of the INSPEC bibliographic and abstract database.

Magazines and periodicals

ACM Computing Reviews
(http://www.acm.org/reviews/)

Computing Reviews aims to furnish computer-oriented persons in mathematics, engineering, the natural and social sciences, the humanities, and other fields with critical information about current publications in any area of the computing sciences, and to further, thereby, the development of the computing sciences as a discipline, as an art, and as a tool for revolutionizing our technology and our patterns of thinking.

ACM Computing Surveys
(http://www.acm.org/surveys/)

Computing Surveys is a journal published by the Association for Computing Machinery. The publication contains surveys, tutorials, and special reports on all areas of computing research. Volumes are published yearly in four issues appearing in March, June, September, and December.

ACM Transactions on Software Engineering and
Methodology
(http://www.acm.org/tosem/)

ACM's *Transactions on Software Engineering and Methodology* (TOSEM) publishes original and significant results in all areas of software engineering research. In general, the systems to which the results apply should be sufficiently complex and long-lived to justify investment in languages, methods, and tools that support specification, design, implementation, validation, documentation, maintenance, reengineering, and other related activities. Published articles address important research topics; results are reproducible, extensible, scaleable, and have practical relevance. Experience reports on the use of advanced software engineering techniques are in principle excluded unless they provide thoughtful insights about the development world or the application of a technology; that result in the identification of new important challenges for software engineering research.

Application Development Trends
(http://www.adtmag.com/)

Application Development Trends magazine delivers strategic and tactical information to IS application development managers in large enterprises.

CM Today
(http://www.cmtoday.com/)

CM Today is an excellent source for daily configuration management news. The idea for cmtoday.com came from the recognition of the total lack of any kind of single source for CM news. *CM Today* contains nuggets of CM-related news found around the web—brief descriptions combined with a link to the source. *CM Today* is published by Ede Development Enterprises (EDE), a CM tool vendor.

Communications of the ACM
(http://www.acm.org/cacm/)

The *Communications of the ACM* is a leading publication that brings articles, news items, and features about the new technologies and emerging technological trends. The readership represents approximately 85,000 professionals from every known computing discipline: 80% are computing practitioners working in industry; 20% work in government and academia. The majority of readers have been involved in computing for over 12 years, and 65% have advanced degrees.

CrossTalk Home
(http://www.stsc.hill.af.mil/CrossTalk/index.asp)

CrossTalk: The Journal of Defense Software Engineering is an approved Department of Defense journal. *CrossTalk*'s mission is to encourage the engineering development of software in order to improve the reliability, maintainability, and responsiveness of the war fighting capability and to instruct, inform, and educate readers on up-to-date policy decisions and new software engineering technologies.

IEEE Annals of the History of Computing
(http://www.computer.org/annals/)

From the analytical engine to the supercomputer, from Pascal to von Neumann, from punched cards to CD-ROMs, the *Annals of the History of Computing* covers the breadth of computer history. Featuring scholarly articles by leading computer scientists and historians, as well as firsthand accounts by computer pioneers, the *Annals* is the primary publication for recording, analyzing, and debating the history of computing. The *Annals* also serves as a focal point for people interested in uncovering and preserving the records of this exciting field. The quarterly publication is an active center for the collection and dissemination of information on historical projects and organizations, oral history activities, and international conferences.

IEEE Computer (http://www.computer.org/computer/)

IEEE Computer serves the needs of computing professionals who need more technical substance than they can get in trade magazines, yet who are too busy to study research journals. From software to hardware, from the workplace to the lab, *IEEE Computer* clearly defines the major trends in computer science and engineering without compromising technical quality. *IEEE Computer* has earned the loyalty and respect of computer scientists and engineers worldwide for more than 30 years. Its reputation for delivering current, reliable content is unequaled. *Computer* is sent each month to all members of the IEEE Computer Society.

IEEE Computing in Science & Engineering
(http://www.computer.org/cse/)

Physics, medicine, astronomy—these and other hard sciences share a common need for efficient algorithms, system software, and computer architecture to address large computational problems. And yet, useful advances in computational techniques that could benefit many researchers are rarely shared. To meet that need, *IEEE Computing in Science & Engineering* presents scientific and computational contributions to the practice of science and engineering in a clear and accessible format. *Computing in Science & Engineering* is copublished by the IEEE Computer Society and the American Institute of Physics in technical co-sponsorship with the IEEE Antennas and Propagation Society and the IEEE Signal Processing Society.

IEEE IT Professional
(http://www.computer.org/itpro/)

IEEE IT Professional is written for the developers and managers of enterprise information systems. It explains technology to help in building and managing your information systems today and provides advance notice of trends that may shape your business in the next few years.

IEEE Software
(http://www.computer.org/software/)

IEEE Software covers useful advances in software technology, design, development, and implementation techniques.

IEEE Spectrum
(http://www.spectrum.ieee.org/)

Spectrum magazine serves engineering, engineering management, and scientific professionals identified in the high-technology sectors of industry, business, government, and education. Targeted audience includes electronics engineers; computer engineers and scientists; software engineers; systems designers; design, research, and development engineers and scientists; and engineering managers and corporate executives.

IEEE Transactions on Computers
(http://www.computer.org/tc)

IEEE Transactions on Computers contains state-of-the-art research papers on the theory, design, and applications of computer systems.

IEEE Transactions on Software Engineering
(http://www.computer.org/tse)

IEEE Transactions on Software Engineering covers specification, design, development, maintenance, and documentation of software systems.

Journal of the ACM
(http://www.acm.org/jacm/)

The *Journal of the ACM* (JACM) provides coverage of the most significant work going on in computer science, broadly construed. It is a peer-reviewed journal, published six times a year by Association for Computing Machinery.

General

Alex Lobba's Software Team Development Page
(http://www.silcom.com/~alobba/)

Web pages from Alex Lobba to help software development teams select and implement the team development product that best matches their needs, environment, and culture. Site contains an overview to team development, product reviews, a free guide on how to select the right team development product, links to other CM sites, and so on.

Association for Configuration and Data Management (ACDM) Configuration Management Resource Guide— Acronyms
(http://www.acdm.org/acron.html)

This page contains more than 250 CM-related acronyms and their expansions.

Association for Configuration and Data Management (ACDM) Configuration Management Resource Index
(http://www.acdm.org/resource.html)

This page contains CM- and DM-related links.

Australian Army Configuration Management Manual
(http://www.defence.gov.au/ARMY/CMMANUAL/index.html)

The configuration management manual of the Australian army. Contains three parts and sections on CM abbreviations and definition of CM terms. The three sections contain 12 chapters dealing with subjects like configuration management policy, configuration management organization, CM procedures, army configuration management, CM plans, CM documentation, software configuration management, and SCM procedures.

Brad Appleton's SCM Definitions Page
(http://www.enteract.com/~bradapp/acme/scm-defs.html)

This page contains more than 20 definitions of configuration management. The definitions include those by Bersoff, Henderson and Siegel, IEEE, Berlack, U.S. Department of Defense, British Standard Institute, Babich, Narayanaswamy and Scacchi, Tichy, Whitgift, Humphrey, Compton and Conner, SEI, Dart, MacKay, Eaton, McConnell, and Rawlings.

CM Home Page of Information Technology Center (ITC) of the Natural Resources Conservation Service (United States Department of Agriculture)
(http://cody.itc.nrcs.usda.gov/cfgmgt/)

The NRCS Information Technology Center (ITC) is located in Fort Collins, Colorado. The mission of the ITC is to provide the information technology infrastructure and application information systems to support the delivery of NRCS programs and services. The site contains various links to configuration management tools and other related areas.

comp.software.config-mgmt FAQ: Configuration Management Tools Summary
(http://www.cis.ohio-state.edu/hypertext/faq/usenet/ sw-config-mgmt/cm-tools/faq.html)

This is the Software Configuration Management Tools section of the Frequently Asked Questions (FAQ) file for the newsgroup comp.software.config-mgmt.

comp.software.config-mgmt FAQ: General Questions
(http://www.cis.ohio-state.edu/hypertext/faq/usenet/ sw-config-mgmt/faq/faq.html)

This is the Software Configuration Management General Questions section of the Frequently Asked Questions (FAQ) file for the newsgroup comp.software.config-mgmt.

comp.software.config-mgmt FAQ: Problem Management Tools Summary (http://www.cis.ohio-state.edu/hypertext/faq/usenet/sw-config-mgmt/prob-mgt-tools/faq.html)

This is the Problem Management Tools section of the Frequently Asked Questions (FAQ) file for the newsgroup comp.software.config-mgmt.

Configuration Management Tools (http://www.loria.fr/~molli/cm/cm-FAQ/tools_top.html)

This site contains a list of configuration management tools with a short description about each tool. Also provides a list of CM tools with WWW sites and links to those sites.

CrossTalk Articles on Configuration Management (http://stsc.hill.af.mil/CM/cmxtlk.asp)

Contains the list of SCM-related articles that have appeared in the *CrossTalk* magazine from 1994 onward.

Database and Selectors Cel (DaSC) SCM Home Page (http://wwwsel.iit.nrc.ca/projects/scm/)

This page contains details about SCM research by DaSC, a list of the various white papers and research papers, and also links to other SCM-related sites.

Department of Defense Single Stock Point (DODSSP) for Military Specifications, Standards and Related Publications (http://dodssp.daps.mil/)

The Department of Defense Single Stock Point was created to centralize the control, distribution, and access to the extensive collection of military specifications, standards, and related standardization documents either prepared by or adopted by the DoD.

The DODSSP mission and responsibility was assumed by the Defense Automated Printing Service (DAPS) Philadelphia Office in October 1990. The responsibilities of the DODSSP include electronic document storage, indexing, cataloging, maintenance, publish-on-demand, distribution, and sale of military specifications, standards, and related standardization documents and publications comprising the DODSSP Collection.

The DODSSP also maintains the Acquisition Streamlining and Standardization Information System (ASSIST) management/research database. The document categories in the DODSSP collection include military/performance/detail specifications, military standards, DoD-adopted nongovernment/industry specifications and standards, federal specifications and standards, and military handbooks.

Hal Render's Bibliography on Software Configuration Management
(http://liinwww.ira.uka.de/bibliography/SE/scm.html)

An excellent site that contains information about SCM books with a small description about the content of each book.

Honeywell Inc.—Industrial Automation & Control (IAC) Configuration Management Page
(http://www.iac.honeywell.com/Pub/Tech/CM/index.html)

Honeywell Inc. IAC manages and updates the Frequently Asked Questions lists for the newsgroup comp.software.config-mgmt. This page contains links to the FAQs, which is divided into three parts: General CM Questions, Configuration Management Tools, and Problem Management Tools.

IIT Software Engineering Group's SCM Resource Page
(http://wwwsel.iit.nrc.ca/favs/CMfavs.html)

Maintained by the IIT Software Engineering Group of National Research Council, Canada, this site contains various CM-related links. The categories include CM-related resource pages, archives and FAQs , associations, conferences and courses, SCM products (commercial, research, and free), and other software engineering resources.

Ken Rigby's Configuration Management Glossary
(http://www.airtime.co.uk/users/wysywig/gloss.htm)

This is an excellent glossary of CM-related terms.

Ken Rigby's Configuration Management Plan Model Text
(http://www.airtime.co.uk/users/wysywig/cmp.htm)

This site by Ken Rigby contains an example model text that provides a framework that can be adapted to specific projects. The table of contents of the text includes scope, referenced documents, organization, configuration identification, configuration control, configuration management status accounting, subcontractor/vendor control, program phasing, management of configuration management, configuration audits, software specific configuration management, and notes.

List of 20 Most Popular CM Standards by Software
Engineering Process Technology (SEPT)
(http://www.12207.com/test.htm)

This site contains the list and ordering information about the most popular CM standards. Also available are links to other SCM-related sites, details about SCM books, and a list of acronyms.

Military Standards Collection
(http://www-library.itsi.disa.mil/)

This site is the military standards document library maintained by Defense Information Systems Agency (DISA).

NASA Software Configuration Management Guidebook
(http://satc.gsfc.nasa.gov/GuideBooks/cmpub.html)

This page contains the NASA *Software Configuration Management Guidebook* (SMAP-GB-A201). This guidebook defines SCM and describes its constituent functions, processes, and procedures. The guidebook also describes a generic set of organizational elements and responsibilities for operation of SCM. It defines the role of SCM, its interfaces, and its functions throughout the software development life cycle. This guidebook also provides a basis for tailoring SCM for different projects with different life cycles and project specific requirements.

NASA's Software Assurance Technology Center (http://satc.gsfc.nasa.gov/)

The Software Assurance Technology Center (SATC) was established in 1992 in the Systems Reliability and Safety Office at NASA Goddard Space Flight Center (GSFC). The SATC was founded to become a NASA center of excellence in software assurance, dedicated to making measurable improvement in the quality and reliability of software developed for GSFC and NASA. The SATC has programs in the primary technical areas such as software metrics research and development, configuration management, assurance tools and techniques, and continuous risk management.

Papers and Presentations Related to Software Configuration Management (http://home.okstate.edu/homepages.nsf/toc/level2.SCMref.html)

This site contains links to SCM-related sites and PowerPoint presentations on topics such as SCM process, SCM plan, sample SCM desktop procedures, SCM policy, and SCM tool selection procedures.

SE Web—Public Domain CM Tools (http://see.cs.flinders.edu.au/seweb/scm/pd-tools.html)

Contains a listing and description of the public domain SCM tools.

SE Web—SCM Papers (http://see.cs.flinders.edu.au/seweb/scm/SCM-Papers.html)

This page provides some brief papers and articles available on the web.

SE Web—Software Configuration Management Introduction (http://see.cs.flinders.edu.au/seweb/scm/SCM-Intro.html)

This page contains many useful links to SCM-related articles on the Internet. Also available is a three-part lecture on configuration management and version control. The SE web site is maintained by Chris Marlin of the Flinders University of South Australia.

**SEI—Summary of Available CM Related Documents
(http://www.sei.cmu.edu/legacy/scm/scmDocSummary.html)**

This page contains a list of all CM-related documents, technical reports, and slide shows/presentations prepared by the Software Engineering Institute of Carnegie Mellon University.

**Software Configuration Management Index
(http://www.faqs.org/faqs/sw-config-mgmt/)**

Home page of Software Configuration Management (sw-config-mgmt) Usenet newsgroup.

**Software Configuration Management Without Tears
(http://www.netcom.com/~sjasthi/scm.html)**

This site, maintained by Shashi Jasthi, contains the philosophy of an incremental approach to SCM implementation.

**Sources for Standards Documents
(http://www-library.itsi.disa.mil/org/std_src.html)**

This page maintained by the Defense Information Systems Agency (DISA) contains links to the sources of various government and commercial standards. The sources include IEEE, CCITT, CORBA, EIA, IAB, IETF, ISO, ITU-T, OMG, TIA, FIPS, etc.

**SPAWAR Systems Center San Diego Software Engineering
Process Office (SEPO) documentation
(http://sepo.nosc.mil/Docs.html)**

This site contains a lot of useful information on various topics: requirements management, software configuration management, organization process focus, quantitative process management, defect prevention, software project planning, organization process definition, software quality management, technology change management, software project tracking and oversight, training program, process change management, software subcontract management, integrated software management, software quality assurance, software product engineering, intergroup coordination, and peer reviews. All documents are available for download as MS Word files.

Appendix D

SCM bibliography

Abu-Shakra, M., and G. L. Fisher, "Multi-grain Version Control in the Historian System," *System Configuration Management: ECOOP'98 SCM-8 Symp. Proc.*, B. Magnusson, Ed., Berlin: Springer-Verlag, 1998, pp. 46–56.

Proc. 3rd Int. Workshop on Software Configuration Management, New York: Association for Computing Machinery, 1991.

Second Int. Workshop: Software Configuration Management Proc., New York: Association for Computing Machinery, 1989.

Adams, C., "Why Can't I Buy an SCM Tool?" *Software Configuration Management: ICSE SCM 4 and SCM 5 Workshops (Selected Papers)*, J. Estublier, Ed., Berlin: Springer-Verlag, 1995, pp. 278–281.

Adams, P., and Solomon, M., "An Overview of the CAPITAL Software Development Environment," *Software Configuration Management: ICSE SCM 4 and SCM 5 Workshops (Selected Papers)*, J. Estublier, Ed., Berlin: Springer-Verlag, 1995, pp. 1–34.

Alder, P. S., and A. Shenhar, "Adapting Your Technological Base: The Organizational Challenge," *Sloan Management Review*, Fall 1990, pp. 25–37.

Alder, R. S., "Today's Software Complexity Demands Good CM," *Crosstalk: The Journal of Defense Software Engineering*, Feb. 1998, p. 2.

Allen, L., et al., "ClearClase MultiSite: Supporting Geographically Distributed Software Development," *Software Configuration Management: ICSE SCM 4 and SCM 5 Workshops (Selected Papers)*, J. Estublier, Ed., Berlin: Springer-Verlag, 1995, pp. 194–214.

Ambriola, V., and L. Bendix, "Object-Oriented Configuration Control," *Second Int. Workshop: Software Configuration Management Proc.*, Princeton, NJ, October 1989, New York: Association for Computing Machinery, 1989, pp. 135–136.

Andriole, S. J., *Managing Systems Requirements: Methods, Tools, and Cases*, New York: McGraw-Hill, 1996.

ANSI/IEEE Std-1028-1988, *Standard for Software Reviews and Audits*, 1988.

ANSI/IEEE Std-1042-1987, *IEEE Guide to Software Configuration Management*, 1987.

ANSI/IEEE Std-730. 1-1995, *IEEE Guide for Software Quality Assurance Planning*, 1995.

ANSI/IEEE Std-730-1998, *IEEE Standard for Software Quality Assurance Plans*, 1998.

Aquilino, D., et al., "Supporting Reuse and Configuration: A Port Based SCM Model," *Proc. 3rd Int. Workshop on Software Configuration Management*, Trondheim, Norway, June 1991, New York: Association for Computing Machinery, 1991, pp. 62–67.

Asklund, U., and B. Magnusson, "A Case-study of Configuration Management with ClearCase in an Industrial Environment," *Software Configuration Management: ICSE'97 SCM-7 Workshop Proc.*, R. Conradi, Ed., Boston, MA, May 1997, Berlin: Springer-Verlag, 1997, pp. 201–221.

Atkins, D. L., "Version Sensitive Editing Change History as a Programming Tool," *System Configuration Management: ECOOP'98 SCM-8 Symp. Proc.*, B. Magnusson, Ed., Berlin: Springer-Verlag, 1998, pp. 146–157.

Auer, A., and J. Taramaa, "Experience Report on the Maturity of Configuration Management of Embedded Software," *Software Configuration Management: ICSE '96 SCM-6 Workshop (Selected Papers)*, I. Sommerville, Ed., Berlin, Germany, March 1996, Berlin: Springer-Verlag, 1996, pp. 187–197.

Ayer, S., and F. S. Patrinostro, *Documenting the Software Development Process: A Handbook of Structured Techniques*, New York: McGraw-Hill, 1992.

Ayer, S., and F. S. Patrinostro, *Software Configuration Management: Identification, Accounting, Control, and Management*, New York: McGraw-Hill, 1992.

Baalbergen, E. H., K. Verstoep, and A. S. Tanenbaum, "On the Design of the Amoeba Configuration Manager," *Second Int. Workshop: Software Configuration Management Proc.*, Princeton, NJ, October 1989, New York: Association for Computing Machinery, 1989, pp. 15–22.

Babich, W. A., *Software Configuration Management: Coordination for Team Productivity*, Boston, MA: Addison Wesley, 1986.

Bays, M. E., *Software Release Methodology*, NJ: Prentice-Hall PTR, 1999.

Belanger, D., D. Korn, and H. Rao, "Infrastructure for Wide-area Software Development," *Software Configuration Management: ICSE '96 SCM-6 Workshop (Selected Papers)*, I. Sommerville, Ed., Berlin, Germany, March 1996, Berlin: Springer-Verlag, 1996, pp. 154–165.

Bendix, L., "Fully Supported Recursive Workspaces," *Software Configuration Management: ICSE '96 SCM-6 Workshop (Selected Papers)*, I. Sommerville, Ed., Berlin, Germany, March 1996, Berlin: Springer-Verlag, 1996, pp. 256–261.

Bendix, L., et al., "CoEd—A Tool for Versioning of Hierarchical Documents," *System Configuration Management: ECOOP '98 SCM-8 Symp. Proc.*, B. Magnusson, Ed., Berlin: Springer-Verlag, 1998, pp. 174–187.

Ben-Menachem, M., *Software Configuration Guidebook*, London: McGraw-Hill International, 1994.

Berlack, H. R., "Evaluation and Selection of Automated Configuration Management Tools," *Crosstalk: The Journal of Defense Software Engineering*, Nov. 1995.

Berlack, H. R., *Software Configuration Management*, New York: John Wiley & Sons, 1992.

Berrada, K., F. Lopez, and R. Minot, "VMCM, A PCTE Based Version and Configuration Management System," *Proc. 3rd Int. Workshop on Software Configuration Management*, Trondheim, Norway, June 1991, New York: Association for Computing Machinery, 1991, pp. 43–52.

Bersoff, E. H., V. D. Henderson, and S. G. Siegel, *Software Configuration Management, An Investment in Product Integrity*, Englewood Cliffs, NJ: Prentice-Hall, 1980.

Bielikova, M., and P. Navrat, "Modeling Versioned Hypertext Documents," *System Configuration Management: ECOOP'98 SCM-8 Symp. Proc.*, B. Magnusson, Ed., Berlin: Springer-Verlag, 1998, p. 188–197.

Black, R., *Managing the Testing Process*, Redmond, WA: Microsoft Press, 1999.

Blanchard, B. S., *System Engineering Management*, New York: John Wiley & Sons, 1991.

Bochenski, B., "Managing It All: Good Management Boosts C/S Success," *Software Magazine Client/Server Computing Special Edition*, Nov. 1993, pp. 98.

Boehm, B. W., "A Spiral Model for Software Development and Enhancement," *IEEE Computer*, Vol. 21, No. 5, 1988, pp. 61–72.

Boehm, B. W., and P. N. Papaccio, "Understanding and Controlling Software Costs," *IEEE Trans. on Software Engineering*, Vol. 14, No. 10, 1988, pp. 1462–1477.

Bohem, B. W., *Software Engineering Economics*, Englewood Cliffs, NJ: Prentice-Hall, 1981.

Bouldin, B. M., *Agents of Change: Managing the Introduction of Automated Tools*, Englewood Cliffs, NJ: Yourdon Press, 1989.

Bounds, N. M., and S. Dart, "CM Plans: The Beginning to Your CM Solution," Technical Report, Software Engineering Institute, Carnegie-Mellon University, 1998.

Brereton, P., and P. Singleton, "Deductive Software Building," *Software Configuration Management: ICSE SCM 4 and SCM 5 Workshops (Selected Papers)*, J. Estublier, Ed., Berlin: Springer-Verlag, 1995, pp. 81–87.

Brooks F. P., "No Silver Bullet: Essence and Accidents of Software Engineering," *IEEE Computer*, Vol. 20, No. 4, 1987, pp. 10–19.

Brooks, F. P., *The Mythical Man-Month*, New York: Addison-Wesley Longman, 1995.

Brown, A., et al., "The State of Automated Configuration Management," Technical Report, Software Engineering Institute, Carnegie-Mellon University, 1991.

Brown, W. J., *Antipatterns and Patterns in Software Configuration Management*, New York: John Wiley & Sons, 1999.

Buckle, J. K., *Software Configuration Management*, Basingstoke, UK: Macmillan, 1982.

Buckley, F. J., *Implementing Configuration Management: Hardware, Software, and Firmware*, Los Alamitos, CA: IEEE Computer Society Press, 1996.

Buffenbarger, J., "Syntactic Software Merging," *Software Configuration Management: ICSE SCM 4 and SCM 5 Workshops (Selected Papers)*, J. Estublier, Ed., Berlin: Springer-Verlag, 1995, pp. 153–172.

Buffenbarger, J., and K. Gruell, "What Have You Done for Me Lately? (Branches, Merges and Change Logs)," *Software Configuration Management: ICSE'97 SCM-7 Workshop Proc.*, R. Conradi, Ed., Boston, MA, May 1997, Berlin: Springer-Verlag, 1997, pp. 18–24.

Burrows, C., "Configuration Management: Coming of Age in the Year 2000," *Crosstalk: The Journal of Defense Software Engineering*, Mar. 1999, pp. 12–16.

Burrows, C., and I. Wesley, *Ovum Evaluates: Configuration Management*, London: Ovum Limited, 1998.

Burrows, C., S. Dart, and G. W. George, *Ovum Evaluates: Software Configuration Management*, London: Ovum Limited, 1996.

Burton, T., "Software Configuration Management Helps Solve Year 2000 Change Integration Obstacles," *Crosstalk: The Journal of Defense Software Engineering*, Jan. 1998, pp. 7–8.

Cagan, M., and D. W. Weber, "Task-Based Software Configuration Management: Support for 'Change Sets' in Continuus/CM," Technical Report, Continuus Software Corporation, 1996.

Cagan, M., "Untangling Configuration Management," *Software Configuration Management: ICSE SCM 4 and SCM 5 Workshops (Selected Papers)*, J. Estublier, Ed., Berlin: Springer-Verlag, 1995, pp. 35–52.

Caputo, K., *CMM Implementation Guide*, Reading, MA: Addison-Wesley, 1998.

Cave, W. C., and G. W. Maymon, *Software Lifecycle Management: The Incremental Method*, Basingstoke, UK: Macmillan, 1984.

Choi, S. C., and W. S. Scacchi, "Assuring the Correctness of Configured Software Descriptions," *Second Int. Workshop: Software Configuration Management Proc.*, Princeton, NJ, October 1989, New York: Association for Computing Machinery, 1989, pp. 66–75.

Chris, A., "Why Can't I Buy an SCM Tool?" *Software Configuration Management: ICSE SCM 4 and SCM 5 Workshops (Selected Papers)*, J. Estublier, Ed., Berlin: Springer-Verlag, 1995, pp. 278–281.

Christensen, A., and T. Egge, "Store—A System for handling Third-Party Applications in a Heterogeneous Computer Environment," *Software Configuration Management: ICSE SCM 4 and SCM 5 Workshops (Selected Papers)*, J. Estublier, Ed., Berlin: Springer-Verlag, 1995, pp. 263–276.

Christensen, H. B., "Experiences with Architectural Software Configuration Management in Ragnarok," *System Configuration Management: ECOOP'98 SCM-8 Symp. Proc.*, B. Magnusson, Ed., Berlin: Springer-Verlag, 1998, pp. 67–74.

Ci, J. X., et al., "ScmEngine: A Distributed Software Configuration Management Environment on X. 500," *Software Configuration Management: ICSE'97 SCM-7 Workshop Proc.*, R. Conradi, Ed., Boston, MA, May 1997, Berlin: Springer-Verlag, 1997, pp. 108–127.

Clemm, G. M., "Replacing Version-Control with Job-Control," *Second Int. Workshop: Software Configuration Management Proc.*, Princeton, NJ, October 1989, New York: Association for Computing Machinery, 1989, pp. 162–169.

Clemm, G. M., "The Odin System," *Software Configuration Management: ICSE SCM 4 and SCM 5 Workshops (Selected Papers)*, J. Estublier, Ed., Berlin: Springer-Verlag, 1995, pp. 241–262.

Compton, S. B., and G. R. Conner, *Configuration Management for Software*, New York: Van Nostrand Reinhold, 1994.

Conradi, R., (Ed.), *Software Configuration Management: ICSE'97 SCM-7 Workshop Proc.*, Berlin: Springer-Verlag, 1997.

Conradi, R., and C. R. Malm, "Cooperating Transactions against the EPOS Database," *Proc. 3rd Int. Workshop on Software Configuration Management*, Trondheim, Norway, June 1991, New York: Association for Computing Machinery, 1991, pp. 98–101.

Conradi, R., and B. Westfechtel, "Configuring Versioned Software Products," *Software Configuration Management: ICSE'96 SCM-6 Workshop (Selected Papers)*, I. Sommerville, Ed., Berlin, Germany, March 1996, Berlin: Springer-Verlag, 1996, pp. 88–109.

Conradi, R., and B. Westfechtel, "Towards a Uniform Version Model for Software Configuration Management," *Software Configuration Management: ICSE'97 SCM-7 Workshop Proc.*, R. Conradi, Ed., Boston, MA, May 1997, Berlin: Springer-Verlag, 1997, pp. 1–17.

Continuus Software Corporation, "Change Management for Software Development," Continuus Software Corporation, 1998.

Continuus Software Corporation, "Distributed Code Management for Team Engineering," Continuus Software Corporation, 1998.

Continuus Software Corporation, "Problem Tracking and Task Management for Team Engineering," Continuus Software Corporation, 1998.

Continuus Software Corporation, "Software Configuration Management for Team Engineering," Continuus Software Corporation, 1998.

Continuus Software Corporation, "Task-Based Configuration Management: A New Generation Of Software Configuration Management," Continuus Software Corporation, 1997.

Crnkovic, I., "Experience of Using a Simple SCM Tool in a Complex Development Environment," *Software Configuration Management: ICSE '96 SCM-6 Workshop (Selected Papers),* I. Sommerville, Ed., Berlin, Germany, March 1996, Berlin: Springer-Verlag, 1996, pp. 262–263.

Crnkovic, I., "Experience with Change-Oriented SCM Tool," *Software Configuration Management: ICSE '97 SCM-7 Workshop Proc.,* R. Conradi, Ed., Boston, MA, May 1997, Berlin: Springer-Verlag, 1997, pp. 222–234.

Crnkovic, I., and P. Willfor, "Change Measurements in an SCM Process," *System Configuration Management: ECOOP '98 SCM-8 Symp. Proc.,* B. Magnusson, Ed., Berlin: Springer-Verlag, 1998, pp. 26–32.

Daniels, M. A., *Principles of Configuration Management,* Annandale, VA: Advanced Application Consultants, 1985.

Dart, S., "Adopting an Automated Configuration Management Solution," Technical Paper, STC'94 (Software Technology Center), Utah, April 12, 1994.

Dart, S., "Achieving the Best Possible Configuration Management Solution," *Crosstalk: The Journal of Defense Software Engineering,* Sep. 1996.

Dart, S., "Best Practice for a CM Solution," *Software Configuration Management: ICSE '96 SCM-6 Workshop (Selected Papers),* I. Sommerville, Ed., Berlin, Germany, March 1996, Berlin: Springer-Verlag, 1996, pp. 239–255.

Dart, S., "Concepts in Configuration Management Systems," *Proc. 3rd Int. Workshop on Software Configuration Management,* Trondheim, Norway, June 1991, New York: Association for Computing Machinery, 1991, pp. 1–18.

Dart, S., "Concepts in Configuration Management Systems," Technical Report, Software Engineering Institute, Carnegie-Mellon University, 1994.

Dart, S., "Configuration Management Bibliography," Technical Report, Software Engineering Institute, Carnegie Mellon University, 1992.

Dart, S., "Containing the Web Crisis Using Configuration Management," *Web Engineering Workshop at the Conference on Software Engineering (ICSE'99)*, Los Angeles, CA, May 16–17, 1999.

Dart, S., "Content Change Management: Problems for Web Systems," *Int. Symp. on System Configuration Management SCM9*, Toulouse France, Sep. 5–7, 1999.

Dart, S., "Not All Tools Are Created Equal," *Application Development Trends*, Vol. 3, No. 9, 1996, pp. 45–48.

Dart, S., "Parallels in Computer-Aided Design Framework and Software Development Environment Efforts," Technical Report, Software Engineering Institute, Carnegie-Mellon University, 1994.

Dart, S., "Past, Present and Future of CM Systems," Technical Report, Software Engineering Institute, Carnegie-Mellon University, 1992.

Dart, S., "Spectrum of Functionality in Configuration Management Systems," Technical Report, Software Engineering Institute, Carnegie-Mellon University, 1990.

Dart, S., "The Agony and Ecstasy of Configuration Management (Abstract)," *System Configuration Management: ECOOP'98 SCM-8 Symp. Proc.*, B. Magnusson, Ed., Berlin: Springer-Verlag, 1998, pp. 204–205.

Dart, S., "To Change or Not to Change," *Application Development Trends*, Vol. 4, No. 6, 1997, pp. 55–57.

Dart, S., "Tool Configuration Assistant," *Second Int. Workshop: Software Configuration Management Proc.*, Princeton, NJ, October 1989, New York: Association for Computing Machinery, 1989, pp. 110–113.

Dart, S., "WebCrisis.Com: Inability to Maintain," *Software Magazine*, Sep. 1999.

Dart, S., and J. Krasnov, *"Experiences in Risk Mitigation with Configuration Management," 4th SEI Risk Conference*, Nov. 1995.

Davis, A., and P. Sitaram, "A Concurrent Process Model for Software Development," *Software Engineering Notes*, Vol. 19, No. 2, pp. 38–51.

Davis, A. M., *201 Principles of Software Development*, New York: McGraw-Hill, 1995.

Dehforooz, A., and F. J. Hudson, *Software Engineering Fundamentals*, New York: Oxford University Press, 1996.

DeMillo, R. A., et al., *Software Testing and Evaluation*, Iowa: Benjamin Cummings, 1987.

Deustsch, M. S., *Software Verification and Validation: Realistic Project Approaches*, Englewood Cliffs, NJ: Prentice-Hall, 1982.

Dinsart, A., et al., "Object Derivation and Validation from a Data Base Definition," *Second Int. Workshop: Software Configuration Management Proc.*, Princeton, NJ, October 1989, New York: Association for Computing Machinery, 1989, pp. 170–178.

Dix, A., T. Rodden, and I. Sommerville, "Modeling the Sharing of Versions," *Software Configuration Management: ICSE'96 SCM-6 Workshop (Selected Papers)*, I. Sommerville, Ed., Berlin, Germany, March 1996, Berlin: Springer-Verlag, 1996, pp. 282–290.

DOD-STD-2167A, *Defense System Software Development*, 1988.

DOD-STD-2168, *Defense System Software Quality Program*, 1988.

Donaldson, S. E., and S. G. Siegel, *Cultivating Successful Software Development: A Practitioner's View*, Upper Saddle River, NJ: Prentice-Hall PTR, 1997.

Dyer, M., *The Cleanroom Approach to Quality Software Development*, New York: John Wiley & Sons, 1992.

Eggerman, W. V., *Configuration Management Handbook*, Blue Ridge Summit, PA: Tab Books, 1990.

Eidnes, H., D. O. Hallsteinsen, and D. H. Wanvik, "Separate Compilation in CHIPSY," *Second Int. Workshop: Software Configuration Management Proc.*, Princeton, NJ, October 1989, New York: Association for Computing Machinery, 1989, pp. 42–45.

Eilfield, P., "Configuration Management as 'Gluware' for Development of Client/Server Applications on Heterogeneous and Distributed Environments," *Software Configuration Management: ICSE'96 SCM-6 Workshop (Selected Papers)*, I. Sommerville, Ed., Berlin, Germany, March 1996, Berlin: Springer-Verlag, 1996, pp. 264–271.

Estublier,J. (Ed.), *Software Configuration Management: ICSE SCM 4 and SCM 5 Workshops (Selected Papers)*, Berlin: Springer-Verlag, 1995.

Estublier, J., "Workspace Management in Software Engineering Environments," *Software Configuration Management: ICSE '96 SCM-6 Workshop (Selected Papers)*, I. Sommerville, Ed., Berlin, Germany, March 1996, Berlin: Springer-Verlag, 1996, pp. 127–138.

Estublier, J., and R. Casallas, "Three Dimensional Versioning," *Software Configuration Management: ICSE SCM 4 and SCM 5 Workshops (Selected Papers)*, J. Estublier, Ed., Berlin: Springer-Verlag, 1995, pp. 118–135.

Estublier, J., S. Dami, and M. Amiour, "High Level Process Modeling for SCM Systems," *Software Configuration Management: ICSE '97 SCM-7 Workshop Proc.*, R. Conradi, Ed., Boston, MA, May 1997, Berlin: Springer-Verlag, 1997, pp. 81–97.

Estublier, J., J. Favre, and P. Morat, "Toward SCM/PDM Integration?" *System Configuration Management: ECOOP'98 SCM-8 Symp. Proc.*, B. Magnusson, Ed., Berlin: Springer-Verlag, 1998, pp. 75–94.

Evans, M. W., *Productive Software Test Management*, Chichester, England: John Wiley & Sons, 1984.

Falkerngerg, B., "Configuration Management for a Large (SW) Development," *Second Int. Workshop: Software Configuration Management Proc.*, Princeton, NJ, October 1989, New York: Association for Computing Machinery, 1989, pp. 34–37.

Feiler P. H., "Software Configuration Management: Advances in Software Development Environments," Technical Report, Software Engineering Institute, Carnegie-Mellon University, 1990.

Feiler, P. H., "Managing Development of Very Large Systems: Implications for Integrated Environment Architectures," Technical Paper, Software Engineering Institute, Carnegie-Mellon University, 1988.

Feiler, P. H., "Software Configuration Management: Advances in Software Development Environments," Technical Paper, Software Engineering Institute, Carnegie-Mellon University, 1990.

Feiler, P. H., "Configuration Management Models in Commercial Environments," Technical Report, Software Engineering Institute, Carnegie-Mellon University, 1991.

Feiler, P. H., and G. F. Downey, "Tool Version Management Technology: A Case Study," Technical Report, Software Engineering Institute, Carnegie-Mellon University, 1990.

Feiler P. H., and G. F. Downey, "Transaction-Oriented Configuration Management: A Case Study," Technical Report, Software Engineering Institute, Carnegie-Mellon University, 1990.

Frohlich, P., and W. Nejdl, "WebRC: Configuration Management for a Cooperation Tool," *Software Configuration Management: ICSE'97 SCM-7 Workshop Proc.,* R. Conradi, Ed., Boston, MA, May 1997, Berlin: Springer-Verlag, 1997, pp. 175–185.

Gallagher, K., "Conditions to Assure Semantically Consistent Software Merges in Linear Time," *Proc. 3rd Int. Workshop on Software Configuration Management,* Trondheim, Norway, June 1991, New York: Association for Computing Machinery, 1991, pp. 80–83.

Gardy, R. B., *Successful Software Process Improvements,* Upper Saddle River, NJ: Prentice-Hall PTR, 1997.

Gentleman, W. M., S. A. MacKay, and D. A. Stewart, "Commercial Real-Time Software Needs Different Configuration Management," *Second Int. Workshop: Software Configuration Management Proc.,* Princeton, NJ, October 1989, New York: Association for Computing Machinery, 1989, pp. 152–161.

Gilb, T., *Principles of Software Engineering Management,* New York: Addison-Wesley, 1988.

Gill, T., "Stop-Gap Configuration Management," *Crosstalk: The Journal of Defense Software Engineering,* Feb. 1998, pp. 3–5.

Glass, R. L., *Software Runaways,* Upper Saddle River, NJ: Prentice-Hall, 1998.

Godart, C., et al., "About Some Relationships between Configuration Management, Software Process and Cooperative Work: COO Environment," *Software Configuration Management: ICSE SCM 4 and SCM 5 Workshops (Selected Papers),* J. Estublier, Ed., Berlin: Springer-Verlag, 1995, pp. 173–178.

Gulla, P., and J. Gorman, "Experiences with the Use of a Configuration Language," *Software Configuration Management: ICSE'96 SCM-6 Workshop (Selected Papers)*, I. Sommerville, Ed., Berlin, Germany, March 1996, Berlin: Springer-Verlag, 1996, pp. 198–219.

Gustavsson, A., "Maintaining the Evolution of Software Objects in an Integrated Environment," *Second Int. Workshop: Software Configuration Management Proc.*, Princeton, NJ, October 1989, New York: Association for Computing Machinery, 1989, pp. 114–117.

Hall, R. S., D. Heimbigner, and A. L. Wolf, "Requirements for Software Deployment Languages and Schema," *System Configuration Management: ECOOP'98 SCM-8 Symp. Proc.*, B. Magnusson, Ed., Berlin: Springer-Verlag, 1998, pp. 198–203.

Haque, S., "Introducing Process into Configuration Management," *Crosstalk: The Journal of Defense Software Engineering*, June 1996.

Haque, T., "Process-Based Configuration Management: The Way to Go to Avoid Costly Product Recalls," *Crosstalk: The Journal of Defense Software Engineering*, April 1997.

Haque, T., "The F-16 Software Test Station Program: A Success Story in Process Configuration Management," *Crosstalk: The Journal of Defense Software Engineering*, Nov. 1997.

Hedin, G., L. Ohlsson, and J. McKenna, "Product Configuration Using Object-Oriented Grammars," *System Configuration Management: ECOOP'98 SCM-8 Symp. Proc.*, B. Magnusson, Ed., Berlin: Springer-Verlag, 1998, pp. 107–126.

Heiman, R. V., and E. Quinn, "Software Configuration Management Meets the Internet," Technical Report, Framingham, MA: International Data Corporation, Nov. 1997.

Heiman, R. V., S. Garone, and S. D. Hendrick, "Development Life-Cycle Management: 1999 Worldwide Markets and Trends," Technical Report, Framingham, MA: International Data Corporation, June 1999.

Heiman, R. V., S. Garone, and S. D. Hendrick, "Development Life-Cycle Management: 1998 Worldwide Markets and Trends," Technical Report, Framingham, MA: International Data Corporation, May 1998.

Heiman, R. V., et al., "Programmer Development Tools: 1997 Worldwide Markets and Trends," Technical Report, Framingham, MA: International Data Corporation, July 1997.

Heiman, R. V., "The Growing Market for Software Configuration Management Tools," Technical Report, Framingham, MA: International Data Corporation, Sep. 1997.

Heimbigner, D., and A. L. Wolf, "Post-Deployment Configuration Management," *Software Configuration Management: ICSE'96 SCM-6 Workshop (Selected Papers)*, I. Sommerville, Ed., Berlin, Germany, March 1996, Berlin: Springer-Verlag, 1996, pp. 272–276.

Hoek, A., et al., "Software Deployment: Extending Configuration Management Support into the Field," *Crosstalk: The Journal of Defense Software Engineering*, Feb. 1998, pp. 9–13.

Hoek, A., D. Heimbigner, D., and A. L. Wolf, "Does Configuration Management Research Have a Future?" *Software Configuration Management: ICSE SCM 4 and SCM 5 Workshops (Selected Papers)*, J. Estublier, Ed., Berlin: Springer-Verlag, 1995, pp. 305–309.

Hoek, A., D. Heimbigner, and A. L. Wolf, "System Modeling Resurrected," *System Configuration Management: ECOOP'98 SCM-8 Symp. Proc.*, B. Magnusson, Ed., Berlin: Springer-Verlag, 1998, pp. 140–145.

Holdsworth, J., *Software Process Design: Out of the Tar Pit*, London: McGraw-Hill International, 1994.

Humphrey, W. S., *Managing the Software Process*, New York: Addison-Wesley, 1989.

Hunt, J. J., et al., "Distributed Configuration Management via Java and the World Wide Web," *Software Configuration Management: ICSE'97 SCM-7 Workshop Proc.*, R. Conradi, Ed., Boston, MA, May 1997, Berlin: Springer-Verlag, 1997, pp. 161–174.

Hunt, J. J., K. Vo, and W. F. Tichy, "An Empirical Study of Delta Algorithms," *Software Configuration Management: ICSE'96 SCM-6 Workshop (Selected Papers)*, I. Sommerville, Ed., Berlin, Germany, March 1996, Berlin: Springer-Verlag, 1996, pp. 49–66.

IEEE Std-610.12-1990, *IEEE Standard Glossary of Software Engineering Terminology*, 1990.

IEEE Std-828-1998, *IEEE Standard for Software Configuration Management Plans*, 1998.

IEEE, *IEEE Software Engineering Standards Collection: 1999 Edition*, New Jersey: IEEE, 1999.

Ince, D., *An Introduction to Software Quality Assurance and its Implementation*, London: McGraw-Hill International, 1994.

Ince, D., *ISO 9001 and Software Quality Assurance*, London: McGraw-Hill International, 1994.

Ingram, P., C. Burrows, and I. Wesley, *Configuration Management Tools: A Detailed Evaluation*, London: Ovum Limited, 1993.

Intersolv, "Cost Justifying Software Configuration Management," PVCS Series for Configuration Management White Paper, Intersolv, 1998.

Intersolv, "Software Configuration Management for Client/Server Development Environments: An Architecture Guide," White Paper, Intersolv, 1998.

Intersolv, "Software Configuration Management: A Primer for Development Teams and Managers," White Paper, Intersolv, 1997.

ISO 10007, *Quality Management—Guidelines for Configuration Management*, 1995.

ISO 9000-3, *Guidelines for the Application of ISO 9001:1994 to the Development, Supply, Installation and Maintenance of Computer Software*, 1997.

ISO 9001, *Quality Systems—Model for Quality Assurance in Design, Development, Production, Installation and Servicing*, 1994.

Jacobson, I., M. Griss, and P. Jonsson, *Software Reuse: Architecture, Process, and Organization for Business Success*, New York: ACM Press, 1997.

Jenner, M. G., *Software Quality Measurement and ISO 9001: How to Make Them Work for You*, New York: John Wiley & Sons, 1995.

Jones, C., *Software Quality: Analysis and Guidelines for Success*, London: International Thompson Press, 1997.

Jones, C. T., *Estimating Software Costs*, New York: McGraw-Hill, 1998.

Jones, G. W., *Software Engineering*, New York: John Wiley & Sons, 1990.

Jordan, M., "Experiences in Configuration Management for Modula-2," *Second Int. Workshop: Software Configuration Management Proc.*, Princeton, NJ, October 1989, New York: Association for Computing Machinery, 1989, pp. 126–128.

Kaiser, G. W., "Modeling Configuration as Transactions," *Second Int. Workshop: Software Configuration Management Proc.*, Princeton, NJ, October 1989, New York: Association for Computing Machinery, 1989, pp. 133–134.

Kasse, T., "Software Configuration Management for Project Leaders," Technical Paper, Institute for Software Process Improvement, Belgium, 1998.

Kelly, M. V., *Configuration Management: The Changing Image*, New York: McGraw-Hill, 1995.

Keyes, J., *Software Engineering Productivity Handbook*, New York: McGraw-Hill, 1993.

Kilpi, T., "Product Management Requirements for SCM Discipline," *Software Configuration Management: ICSE'97 SCM-7 Workshop Proc.*, R. Conradi, Ed., Boston, MA, May 1997, Berlin: Springer-Verlag, 1997, pp. 186–200.

Kinball, J., and A. Larson, "Epochs, Configuration Schema, and Version Cursors in the KBSA Framework CCM Model," *Proc. 3rd Int. Workshop on Software Configuration Management*, Trondheim, Norway, June 1991, New York: Association for Computing Machinery, 1991, pp. 33–42.

Kingsbury, J., "Adopting SCM Technology," *Crosstalk: The Journal of Defense Software Engineering*, Mar. 1996.

Kirzner, R., "Managing Content: The Key to Success in Web Business," Technical Report, Framingham, MA: International Data Corporation, June 1999.

Kolvik, S., "Introducing Configuration Management in an Organization," *Software Configuration Management: ICSE'96 SCM-6 Workshop (Selected Papers)*, I. Sommerville, Ed., Berlin, Germany, March 1996, Berlin: Springer-Verlag, 1996, pp. 220–230.

Korel, B., et al., "Version Management in Distributed Network Environment," *Proc. 3rd Int. Workshop on Software Configuration Management,* Trondheim, Norway, June 1991, New York: Association for Computing Machinery, 1991, pp. 161–166.

Kramer, S. A., "History Management System," *Proc. 3rd Int. Workshop on Software Configuration Management,* Trondheim, Norway, June 1991, New York: Association for Computing Machinery, 1991, pp. 140–143.

Lacroix, M., and P. Lavency, "The Change Request Process," *Second Int. Workshop: Software Configuration Management Proc.,* Princeton, NJ, October 1989, New York: Association for Computing Machinery, 1989, pp. 122–125.

Lacroix, S. M. J., D. Roelants, and J. E. Waroquier, "Flexible Support for Cooperation in Software Development," *Proc. 3rd Int. Workshop on Software Configuration Management,* Trondheim, Norway, June 1991, New York: Association for Computing Machinery, 1991, pp. 102–108.

Lago, P., and R. Conradi, "Transaction Planning to Support Coordination," *Software Configuration Management: ICSE SCM 4 and SCM 5 Workshops (Selected Papers),* J. Estublier, Ed., Berlin: Springer-Verlag, 1995, pp. 145–151.

Lange, R., and R. W. Schwanke, "Software Architecture Analysis: A Case Study," *Proc. 3rd Int. Workshop on Software Configuration Management,* Trondheim, Norway, June 1991, New York: Association for Computing Machinery, 1991, pp. 19–28.

Larson, J., and H. M. Roald, "Introducing ClearCase as a Process Improvement Experiment," *System Configuration Management: ECOOP'98 SCM-8 Symp. Proc.,* B. Magnusson, Ed., Berlin: Springer-Verlag, 1998, pp. 1–12.

Leblang, D. B., "Managing the Software Development Process with Clear-Guide," *Software Configuration Management: ICSE'97 SCM-7 Workshop Proc.,* R. Conradi, Ed., Boston, MA, May 1997, Berlin: Springer-Verlag, 1997, pp. 66–80.

Leblang, D. B., and P. H. Levine, "Software Configuration Management: Why Is It Needed and What Should It Do?" *Software Configuration Management: ICSE SCM 4 and SCM 5 Workshops (Selected Papers),* J. Estublier, Ed., Berlin: Springer-Verlag, 1995, pp. 53–60.

Lee, T., P. Thomas, and V. Lowen, "An Odyssey Towards Best SCM Practices: The Big Picture," *Software Configuration Management: ICSE'96 SCM-6 Workshop (Selected Papers)*, I. Sommerville, Ed., Berlin, Germany, March 1996, Berlin: Springer-Verlag, 1996, pp. 231–238.

Lehman, M. M., "Software Engineering, the Software Process and Their Support," *Software Engineering Journal*, Vol. 6, No. 5, 1991, pp. 243–258.

Lehman, M. M., and L. Belady, "A Model of Large Program Development," *IBM Systems Journal*, Vol. 15. No. 3, 1976, pp. 225–252.

Lehman, M. M., and L. Belady, *Program Evolution: Processes of Software Change*, London: Academic Press, 1985.

Lie, A., et al., "Change Oriented Versioning in a Software Engineering Database," *Second Int. Workshop: Software Configuration Management Proc.*, Princeton, NJ, October 1989, New York: Association for Computing Machinery, 1989, pp. 56–65.

Lientz, B. P., and E. B. Swanson, *Software Maintenance Management*, Reading, MA: Addison-Wesley, 1980.

Lin, Y., and S. P. Reiss, "Configuration Management in Terms of Modules," *Software Configuration Management: ICSE SCM 4 and SCM 5 Workshops (Selected Papers)*, J. Estublier, Ed., Berlin: Springer-Verlag, 1995, pp. 101–117.

Lindsay, P., and O. Traynor, "Supporting Fine-grained Traceability in Software Development Environments," *System Configuration Management: ECOOP'98 SCM-8 Symp. Proc.*, B. Magnusson, Ed., Berlin: Springer-Verlag, 1998, pp. 133–139.

Lubkin, D., "Heterogeneous Configuration Management with DSEE," *Proc. 3rd Int. Workshop on Software Configuration Management*, Trondheim, Norway, June 1991, New York: Association for Computing Machinery, 1991, pp. 153–160.

Lundholm, P., "Design Management in Base/OPEN," *Second Int. Workshop: Software Configuration Management Proc.*, Princeton, NJ, October 1989, New York: Association for Computing Machinery, 1989, pp. 38–41.

Lyn, F., *Change Control During Computer Systems Development*, Englewood Cliffs, NJ: Prentice-Hall, 1991.

Lyon, D. D., *Practical CM*, Pittsfield, MA: Raven Publishing, 1994.

MacKay, S. A., "Changesets Revisited and CM of Complex Documents," *Software Configuration Management: ICSE'96 SCM-6 Workshop (Selected Papers)*, I. Sommerville, Ed., Berlin, Germany, March 1996, Berlin: Springer-Verlag, 1996, pp. 277–281.

MacKay, S. A., "The State-of-the-Art in Concurrent Distributed Configuration Management," *Software Configuration Management: ICSE SCM 4 and SCM 5 Workshops (Selected Papers)*, J. Estublier, Ed., Berlin: Springer-Verlag, 1995, pp. 180–193.

Mack-Crane, B., and A. Pal, "Conflict Management in a Source Version Management System," *Second Int. Workshop: Software Configuration Management Proc.*, Princeton, NJ, October 1989, New York: Association for Computing Machinery, 1989, pp. 149–151.

B. Magnusson, Ed., *System Configuration Management: ECOOP'98 SCM-8 Symp. Proc.*, Berlin: Springer-Verlag, 1998.

Magnusson, B., and U. Asklund, "Fine Grained Version Control of Configurations in COOP/Orm," *Software Configuration Management: ICSE'96 SCM-6 Workshop (Selected Papers)*, I. Sommerville, Ed., Berlin, Germany, March 1996, Berlin: Springer-Verlag, 1996, pp. 31–48.

Marshall A. J., "Demystifying Software Configuration Management," *Crosstalk: The Journal of Defense Software Engineering*, May 1995.

Marshall A. J., "Software Configuration Management: Function or Discipline?" *Crosstalk: The Journal of Defense Software Engineering*, Oct. 1995.

Martin, J., and C. McClure, *Software Maintenance: The Problem and Its Solutions*, Englewood Cliffs, NJ: Prentice-Hall, 1983.

Martin, J., *Rapid Application Development*, Englewood Cliffs, NJ: Prentice-Hall, 1991.

McClure, C., *Software Reuse Techniques: Adding Reuse to the System Development Process*, Upper Saddle River, NJ: Prentice-Hall, 1997.

McClure, S., "Web Development Life-Cycle Management Software," Technical Report, Framingham, MA: International Data Corporation, June 1999.

McConnel, S., *Software Project Survival Guide*, Redmond, WA: Microsoft Press, 1998.

McDermid, J. A., (Ed.), *Software Engineer's Reference Book*, Boca Raton, FL: CRC Press, 1994

McDonald, J., P. N. Hilfinger, and L. Semenzato, "PRCS: The Project Revision Control System," *System Configuration Management: ECOOP'98 SCM-8 Symp. Proc.*, B. Magnusson, Ed., Berlin: Springer-Verlag, 1998, pp. 33–45.

Meiser, K., "Software Configuration Management Terminology," *Crosstalk: The Journal of Defense Software Engineering*, Jan. 1995.

Micallef, J., and G. M. Clemm, "The Asgard System: Activity-based Configuration Management," *Software Configuration Management: ICSE'96 SCM-6 Workshop (Selected Papers)*, I. Sommerville, Ed., Berlin, Germany, March 1996, Berlin: Springer-Verlag, 1996, pp. 175–186.

Mikkelsen, T., and S. Pherigo, *Practical Software Configuration Management: The Latenight Developer's Handbook*, Upper Saddle River, NJ: Prentice-Hall PTR, 1997.

Milewski, B., "Distributed Source Control System," *Software Configuration Management: ICSE'97 SCM-7 Workshop Proc.*, R. Conradi, Ed., Boston, MA, May 1997, Berlin: Springer-Verlag, 1997, pp. 98–107.

Miller, D. B., R. G. Stockton, and C. W. Krueger, "An Inverted Approach to Configuration Management," *Second Int. Workshop: Software Configuration Management Proc.*, Princeton, NJ, October 1989, New York: Association for Computing Machinery, 1989, pp. 1–4.

Miller, T. C., "A Schema for Configuration Management," *Second Int. Workshop: Software Configuration Management Proc.*, Princeton, NJ, October 1989, New York: Association for Computing Machinery, 1989, pp. 26–29.

MIL-STD-1521B, *Technical Reviews and Audits for Systems, Equipment and Computer Programs*, 1985.

MIL-STD-480B, *Configuration Control Engineering Changes, Deviations and Waivers*, 1988.

MIL-STD-481B, *Configuration Control Engineering Changes (Short Form), Deviations and Waivers*, 1988.

MIL-STD-482A, *Configuration Status Accounting Data Elements & Related Features*, 1974.

MIL-STD-483A, *Configuration Management Practices for Systems, Equipment, Munitions and Computer Programs*, 1985.

MIL-STD-490A, *Specification Practices*, 1985.

MIL-STD-973, *Configuration Management*, 1995.

Molli, P., "COO-Transaction: Supporting Cooperative Work," *Software Configuration Management: ICSE'97 SCM-7 Workshop Proc.*, R. Conradi, Ed., Boston, MA, May 1997, Berlin: Springer-Verlag, 1997, pp. 128–141.

Moore, J. W., *Software Engineering Standards: A User's Road Map*, New Jersey: IEEE, 1997.

Mosley, V., et al., "Software Configuration Management Tools: Getting Bigger, Better, and Bolder," *Crosstalk: The Journal of Defense Software Engineering*, Jan. 1996, pp. 6–10.

Munch, B. P., "HiCoV—Managing the Version Space," *Software Configuration Management: ICSE'96 SCM-6 Workshop (Selected Papers)*, I. Sommerville, Ed., Berlin, Germany, March 1996, Berlin: Springer-Verlag, 1996, pp. 110–126.

Musa, J. D., "Software Engineering: The Future of a Profession," *IEEE Software*, Vol. 22, No. 1, 1985, pp. 55–62.

Narayanaswamy, K., "A Text-Based Representation for Program Variants," *Second Int. Workshop: Software Configuration Management Proc.*, Princeton, NJ, October 1989, New York: Association for Computing Machinery, 1989, pp. 30–33.

NASA, "NASA Software Configuration Management Guidebook," Technical Report SMAP-GB-A201, NASA, 1995.

Newbery, F. J., "Edge Concentration: A Method for Clustering Directed Graphs," *Second Int. Workshop: Software Configuration Management Proc.*, Princeton, NJ, October 1989, New York: Association for Computing Machinery, 1989, pp. 76–85.

Nicklin, P. J., "Managing Multi-Variant Software Configuration," *Proc. 3rd Int. Workshop on Software Configuration Management*, Trondheim,

Norway, June 1991, New York: Association for Computing Machinery, 1991, pp. 53–57.

Nierstrasz, "Component-Oriented Software Development," *Communications of the ACM*, Vol. 35, No. 9, 1992, pp. 160–165.

Noll, J., and W. Scacchi, "Supporting Distributed Configuration Management in Virtual Enterprises," *Software Configuration Management: ICSE '97 SCM-7 Workshop Proc.*, R. Conradi, Ed., Boston, MA, May 1997, Berlin: Springer-Verlag, 1997, pp. 142–160.

Ochuodho, S. J., and A. W. Brown, "A Process-Oriented Version and Configuration Management Model for Communications Software," *Proc. 3rd Int. Workshop on Software Configuration Management*, Trondheim, Norway, June 1991, New York: Association for Computing Machinery, 1991, pp. 109–120.

Pakstas, A., "Aladdin/Lamp: Configuration Management Tools for Distributed Computer Control Systems," *Second Int. Workshop: Software Configuration Management Proc.*, Princeton, NJ, October 1989 New York: Association for Computing Machinery, 1989, pp. 141–144.

Parker, K., "Customization of a Commercial CM System to Provide Better Management Mechanisms," *Software Configuration Management: ICSE SCM 4 and SCM 5 Workshops (Selected Papers)*, J. Estublier, Ed., Berlin: Springer-Verlag, 1995, pp. 289–292.

Peach, R. W. (Ed.), *The ISO 9000 Handbook*, New York: McGraw-Hill, 1997.

Perry, D. E., "Dimensions of Consistency in Source Versions and System Compositions," *Proc. 3rd Int. Workshop on Software Configuration Management*, Trondheim, Norway, June 1991, New York: Association for Computing Machinery, 1991, pp. 29–32.

Perry, D. E., "System Compositions and Shared Dependencies," *Software Configuration Management: ICSE '96 SCM-6 Workshop (Selected Papers)*, I. Sommerville, Ed., Berlin, Germany, March 1996, Berlin: Springer-Verlag, 1996, pp. 139–153.

Persson, A., "Experiences of Customization and Introduction of a CM Model," *Software Configuration Management: ICSE SCM 4 and SCM 5 Workshops (Selected Papers)*, J. Estublier, Ed., Berlin: Springer-Verlag, 1995, pp. 293–303.

Pfleeger, S. L., *Software Engineering: Theory and Practice*, Upper Saddle River, NJ: Prentice-Hall, 1998.

Platinum, "Configuration Management and Software Testing," White Paper, Platinum Technology, 1999.

Platinum, "Controlling Application Development Costs Using Software Configuration Management (CM)," White Paper, Platinum Technology, 1999.

Platinum, "How to Evaluate a CM Tool for Client/Server Environments?" White Paper, Platinum Technology, 1999.

Platinum, "Strategic Thinking About Software Change Management," White Paper, Platinum Technology, 1999.

Platinum, "The Expanding Role of Software Change and Configuration Management (CM)," White Paper, Platinum Technology, 1999.

Platinum, "What Is CM?" White Paper, Platinum Technology, 1999.

Ploedereder, E., and A. Fergany, "The Data Model of the Configuration Management Assistant (CMA)," *Second Int. Workshop: Software Configuration Management Proc.*, Princeton, NJ, October 1989, New York: Association for Computing Machinery, 1989, pp. 5–14.

Powers, J., *Configuration Management Procedures*, Santa Ana, CA: Global Engineering Documents, 1984.

Pressman, R. S., *Software Engineering: A Practitioner's Approach*, New York: McGraw-Hill, 1997.

Pressman. R. S., *A Manager's Guide to Software Engineering*, New York: McGraw-Hill, 1993.

Rahikkala, T., J. Taramma, and A. Valimaki, "Industrial Experiences from SCM Current State Analysis," *System Configuration Management: ECOOP'98 SCM-8 Symp. Proc.*, B. Magnusson, Ed., Berlin: Springer-Verlag, 1998, pp. 13–25.

Rawlings, J. H., *SCM for Network Development Environments*, New York: McGraw-Hill, 1994.

Ray, R. J., "Experiences with a Script-based Software Configuration Management System," *Software Configuration Management: ICSE SCM 4 and SCM 5 Workshops (Selected Papers)*, J. Estublier, Ed., Berlin: Springer-Verlag, 1995, pp. 282–287.

Reichberger, C., "Orthogonal Version Management," *Second Int. Workshop: Software Configuration Management Proc.*, Princeton, NJ, October 1989, New York: Association for Computing Machinery, 1989, pp. 137–140.

Reichenberger, C., "Delta Storage for Arbitrary Non-Text Files," *Proc. 3rd Int. Workshop on Software Configuration Management*, Trondheim, Norway, June 1991, New York: Association for Computing Machinery, 1991, pp. 144–152.

Reichenberger, C., "VOODOO—A Tool for Orthogonal Version Management," *Software Configuration Management: ICSE SCM 4 and SCM 5 Workshops (Selected Papers)*, J. Estublier, Ed., Berlin: Springer-Verlag, 1995, pp. 61–79.

Render, H., and R. Campbell, "An Object-Oriented Model of Software Configuration Management," *Proc. 3rd Int. Workshop on Software Configuration Management*, Trondheim, Norway, June 1991, New York: Association for Computing Machinery, 1991, pp. 127–139.

Reps, T., and T. Bricker, "Illustrating Interference in Interfering Versions of Programs," *Second Int. Workshop: Software Configuration Management Proc.*, Princeton, NJ, October 1989, New York: Association for Computing Machinery, 1989, pp. 46–55.

Reuter, J., et al., "Distributed Version Control via the WWW," *Software Configuration Management: ICSE'96 SCM-6 Workshop (Selected Papers)*, I. Sommerville, Ed., Berlin, Germany, March 1996, Berlin: Springer-Verlag, 1996, pp. 166–174.

Rich, A., and M. Solomon, "A Logic-Based Approach to System Modeling," *Proc. 3rd Int. Workshop on Software Configuration Management*, Trondheim, Norway, June 1991, New York: Association for Computing Machinery, 1991, pp. 84–93.

Rigg, W., C. Burrows, and P. Ingram, *Ovum Evaluates: Configuration Management Tools*, London: Ovum Limited, 1995.

Rosenblum, D. S., and B. Krishnamurthy, "An Event-based Model of Software Configuration Management," *Proc. 3rd Int. Workshop on Software Configuration Management*, Trondheim, Norway, June 1991, New York: Association for Computing Machinery, 1991, pp. 94–97.

Royce, W. ,"*Managing the Development of Large Software Systems: Concepts and Techniques*," WESCON, IEEE, 1970.

Royce, W., *Software Project Management: A Unified Framework*, Reading, MA: Addison Wesley Longman, 1998.

Rustin, R., (Ed.), *Debugging Techniques in Large Systems*, Englewood Cliffs, NJ: Prentice-Hall, 1971.

Samaras, T. T., and F. Czerwinski, *Fundamentals of Configuration Management*, Chichester, England: John Wiley & Sons, 1971.

Samaras, T. T., *Configuration Management Deskbook: Vol. 1*, Annandale, VA: Advanced Application Consultants, 1988.

Samaras, T. T., *Configuration Management Deskbook: Vol. 2, Instruction Supplement*, Annandale, VA: Advanced Application Consultants, 1988.

Schach, S. R., *Software Engineering*, Boston, MA: Richard D. Irwin, 1990.

Schmerl, B. R., and C. D. Maralin, "Designing Configuration Management Facilities for Dynamically Bound Systems," *Software Configuration Management: ICSE SCM 4 and SCM 5 Workshops (Selected Papers)*, J. Estublier, Ed., Berlin: Springer-Verlag, 1995, pp. 88–100.

Schmerl, B. R., and C. D. Maralin, "Versioning and Consistency for Dynamically Composed Configurations," *Software Configuration Management: ICSE'97 SCM-7 Workshop Proc.*, R. Conradi, Ed., Boston, MA, May 1997, Berlin: Springer-Verlag, 1997, pp. 49–65.

Schroeder, U., "Incremental Variant Control," *Second Int. Workshop: Software Configuration Management Proc.*, Princeton, NJ, October 1989, New York: Association for Computing Machinery, 1989, pp. 144–148.

Schulmeyer, G. G., and J. I. McManus, *Handbook of Software Quality Assurance*, London: International Thompson Press, 1996.

Schwanke, R. W., and M. A. Platoff, "Cross References are Features," *Second Int. Workshop: Software Configuration Management Proc.*, Princeton, NJ,

October 1989, New York: Association for Computing Machinery, 1989, pp. 86–95.

SEI, "A Quick Guide to Information about Software Environments, Configuration Management, and CASE," Technical Report, Software Engineering Institute, Carnegie-Mellon University, 1995.

SEI, Carnegie-Mellon University, *The Capability Maturity Model: Guidelines for Improving the Software Process*, Reading, MA: Addison Wesley Longman, 1994.

Seiwald, C., "Inter-file Branching—A Practical Method for Representing Variants," *Software Configuration Management: ICSE'96 SCM-6 Workshop (Selected Papers)*, I. Sommerville, Ed., Berlin, Germany, March 1996, Berlin: Springer-Verlag, 1996, pp. 67–75.

Sheedy, C., "Sorceress: A Database Approach to Software Configuration Management," *Proc. 3rd Int. Workshop on Software Configuration Management*, Trondheim, Norway, June 1991, New York: Association for Computing Machinery, 1991, pp. 121–126.

Simmonds, I., "'Duplicates': A Convention for Defining Configurations in PCTE-Based Environments," *Proc. 3rd Int. Workshop on Software Configuration Management*, Trondheim, Norway, June 1991, New York: Association for Computing Machinery, 1991, pp. 58–61.

Simmonds, I., "Configuration Management in the PACT Software Engineering Environment," *Second Int. Workshop: Software Configuration Management Proc.*, Princeton, NJ, October 1989, New York: Association for Computing Machinery, 1989, pp. 118–121.

Sodhi, J., and P. Sodhi, *Software Reuse: Domain Analysis and Design Process*, New York: McGraw-Hill, 1999.

Sommerville, I., (Ed.), *Software Configuration Management: ICSE'96 SCM 6 Workshop (Selected Papers)*, Berlin, Germany, March 1996, Berlin: Springer-Verlag, 1996.

Sommerville, I., *Software Engineering*, Reading, MA: Addison-Wesley, 1996.

Sorensen, R., "CCB—An Acronym for "Chocolate Chip Brownies?" *Crosstalk: The Journal of Defense Software Engineering*, Mar. 1999, pp. 3–6.

Starbuck, R. A., "Using CM to Recapture Baselines for Y2K Compliance Efforts," *Crosstalk: The Journal of Defense Software Engineering*, Mar. 1999, pp. 7–11.

Starbuck, R. A., "Software Configuration Management by MIL-STD-498," *Crosstalk: The Journal of Defense Software Engineering*, June 1996.

Starbuck, R. A., "Software Configuration Management: Don't Buy a Tool First," *Crosstalk: The Journal of Defense Software Engineering*, Nov. 1997.

Thomas, I., "Version and Configuration Management on a Software Engineering Database," *Second Int. Workshop: Software Configuration Management Proc.*, Princeton, NJ, October 1989, New York: Association for Computing Machinery, 1989, pp. 23–25.

Thomson, R., and I. Sommerville, "Configuration Management Using SySL," *Second Int. Workshop: Software Configuration Management Proc.*, Princeton, NJ, October 1989, New York: Association for Computing Machinery, 1989, pp. 106–109.

Tibrook, D., "An Architecture for a Construction System," *Software Configuration Management: ICSE'96 SCM-6 Workshop (Selected Papers)*, I. Sommerville, Ed., Berlin, Germany, March 1996, Berlin: Springer-Verlag, 1996, pp. 76–87.

Tichy, W. F., *Configuration Management*, New York: John Wiley & Sons, 1994.

Tryggeseth, E., B. Gulla, and R. Conradi, "Modeling Systems with Variability Using the PROTEUS Configuration Language," *Software Configuration Management: ICSE SCM 4 and SCM 5 Workshops (Selected Papers)*, J. Estublier, Ed., Berlin: Springer-Verlag, 1995, pp. 216–240.

Vacca, J., *Implementing a Successful Configuration Change Management Program*, Information Systems Management Group, 1993.

Van De Vanter, M. L., "Coordinated Editing of Versioned Packages in the JP Programming Environment," *System Configuration Management: ECOOP'98 SCM-8 Symp. Proc.*, B. Magnusson, Ed., Berlin: Springer-Verlag, 1998, pp. 158–173.

Ventimiglia, B., "Effective Software Configuration Management," *Crosstalk: The Journal of Defense Software Engineering*, Feb. 1998, pp. 6–8.

Viskari, J., "A Rationale for Automated Configuration Status Accounting," *Software Configuration Management: ICSE SCM 4 and SCM 5 Workshops (Selected Papers)*, J. Estublier, Ed., Berlin: Springer-Verlag, 1995, pp. 138–144.

Wallnau, K. C., "Issues and Techniques of CASE Integration with Configuration Management," Technical Report, Software Engineering Institute, Carnegie-Mellon University, 1992.

Watts, F. B., *Engineering Documentation Control Handbook: Configuration Management for Industry*, Park Ridge, NJ: Noyes Data Corporation/Noyes Publications, 1993.

Weatherall, B., "A Day in the Life of a PVCS Road Warrior: Want to Get PVCS Organized Quickly in a Mixed-Platform Environment?" Technical Paper, Synergex International Corporation, 1997.

Weber, D. W., "Change Sets Versus Change Packages: Comparing Implementations of Change-Based SCM," *Software Configuration Management: ICSE'97 SCM-7 Workshop Proc.*, R. Conradi, Ed., Boston, MA, May 1997, Berlin: Springer-Verlag, 1997, pp., pp. 25–35.

Weber, D. W., *"Change-based SCM Is Where We're Going,"* Continuus Software Corporation, 1997.

Wein, M., et al., "Evolution Is Essential for Software Tool Development," Position Paper, Institution of Information Technology, National Research Council Canada, 1995.

Westfechtel, B., "Revision Control in an Integrated Software Development Environment," *Second Int. Workshop: Software Configuration Management Proc.*, Princeton, NJ, October 1989, New York: Association for Computing Machinery, 1989, pp. 96–105.

Westfechtel, B., "Structure-Oriented Merging of Revisions of Software Documents," *Proc. 3rd Int. Workshop on Software Configuration Management*, Trondheim, Norway, June 1991, New York: Association for Computing Machinery, 1991, pp. 68–79.

Westfechtel, B., and R. Conradi, "Software Configuration Management and Engineering Data Management: Differences and Similarities," *System Configuration Management: ECOOP'98 SCM-8 Symp. Proc.*, B. Magnusson, Ed., Berlin: Springer-Verlag, 1998, pp. 95–106.

Whitgift, D., *Methods and Tools for Software Configuration Management*, Chichester, England: John Wiley & Sons, 1991.

Wingerd, L., and C., Seiwald, "Constructing a Large Product with Jam," *Software Configuration Management: ICSE'97 SCM-7 Workshop Proc.*, R. Conradi, Ed., Boston, MA, May 1997, Berlin: Springer-Verlag, 1997, pp. 36–48.

Wingerd, L., and C. Seiwald, "High-level Best Practices in Software Configuration Management," *System Configuration Management: ECOOP'98 SCM-8 Symp. Proc.*, B. Magnusson, Ed., Berlin: Springer-Verlag, 1998, pp. 57–66.

Yourdon, E., *Death March: The Complete Software Developer's Guide to Surviving "Mission Impossible" Projects*, Upper Saddle River, NJ: Prentice-Hall PTR, 1997.

Zahran S., *Software Process Improvement: Practical Guidelines for Business Success*, Harlow, England: Addison Wesley Longman, 1998.

Zave, P., "The Operational versus Conventional Approach to Software Development," *Communications of the ACM*, Vol. 27, No. 2, 1992, pp. 104–118.

Zeller, A., "Smooth Operations with Square Operations—The Version Set Model in ICE," *Software Configuration Management: ICSE'96 SCM-6 Workshop (Selected Papers)*, I. Sommerville, Ed., Berlin, Germany, March 1996, Berlin: Springer-Verlag, 1996, pp. 8–31.

Zeller, A., "Versioning System Models through Description Logic," *System Configuration Management: ECOOP'98 SCM-8 Symp. Proc.*, B. Magnusson, Ed., Berlin: Springer-Verlag, 1998, pp. 127–132.

SCM glossary and acronyms

Abend   Abbreviation for abnormal end, i.e., termination of a process before completion.

Acceptance testing   Testing conducted to determine whether or not a system or product is acceptable to the customer, user, or client.

Adaptive maintenance   Software maintenance performed to make a computer program work in an environment that is different from the one for which it was originally designed.

Allocated baseline   Allocated baseline is the initial approved specifications governing the development of configuration items that are part of a higher level configuration item.

Allocated configuration identification   The current approved specifications governing the development of configuration items that are part of a higher level configuration item.

Allocation   The process of distributing requirements, resources, or other entities among the components of a system or program.

AEA   American Electronics Association.

AIA   Aerospace Industries Association.

ANSI   American National Standards Institute.

Application software   Software designed to fulfill specific needs of a user/client.

Audit   An independent examination or review conducted to assess whether a product or process or set of products or processes is in compliance with specifications, standards, contractual agreements, or some other criteria.

Baseline   A specification or product that has been formerly reviewed and agreed on, and serves as a basis for further development, which can be changed only through change management procedures. Baselines can be defined at various parts of the development life cycle.

Baseline management   The application of technical and administrative direction to designate the documents and changes to those documents that formerly identify and establish baselines at specific times during the life cycle of a configuration item. In other words, the set of activities performed for establishing and maintaining the different baselines in a project.

Bug   An error, defect, fault, or problem.

Build   The process (or the final result of the process) of generating an executable, testable, system from source code.

CA   Configuration audit.

CASE   Computer-aided software engineering. CASE is the use of computers to aid in the software engineering process. This can include the application of software tools to software design, requirements analysis, code generation, testing, documentation, and other software engineering activities.

CCA   Configuration control authority. Another name for CCB.

CCB   Change control board. A group of people responsible for evaluating and approving/disapproving changes to configuration items. Also known as configuration control board.

Certification   A written guarantee that a system or component complies with its specified requirements and is acceptable for operational use.

Change control   *See* Configuration control.

CI   Configuration item. An aggregation of hardware or software or both that is designated for configuration management and treated as a single entity in the configuration management process.

CM   Configuration management.

CMM   Capability maturity model.

Configuration   The functional and/or physical characteristics of hardware or software item as set forth in the technical documentation and achieved in a product.

Configuration audit   Auditing that is carried out to ensure that the software system is functioning correctly and ensuring that the configuration has been tested to demonstrate that it meets its functional requirements and that it contains all deliverable entities.

Configuration control   Configuration control is the element of configuration management consisting of the evaluation, coordination, approval or disapproval, and implementation of changes to configuration items after formal establishment of their configuration identification.

Configuration identification   An element of SCM, consisting of selecting the configuration items for a system and recording their functional and physical characteristics in technical documentation.

Configuration status accounting   An element of SCM consisting of the recording and reporting of information needed to manage a configuration effectively.

Corrective maintenance   Maintenance that is performed to correct faults in software.

COTS software   Commercial off-the-shelf software.

CPC   Computer program component.

CPCI   Computer program configuration item.

CR   Change request. A request to make a change or modification.

Change request form   A form (paper or electronic) that is used to initiate a change. It contains the details of the change such as the name of the change originator, item to be changed, and details of changes.

Crash   The sudden and complete failure of a computer system or component.

Criticality   The degree of impact that a requirement, module, error, fault, or failure has on the development or operation of a system. Synonymous with severity.

CSC   Computer software component. A functionally or logically distinct part of a computer software configuration item.

CSCI   Computer software configuration item. A software item that is identified for configuration management.

Datagram   *See* Packet.

Debug   To detect, locate, and correct faults in a computer program.

Delta   A version storage technique in which only the differences between versions are stored as opposed to storing each version in its entirety. Forward deltas store the original version in its entirety and later versions as deltas. Reverse deltas store the most recent version in its full form and previous versions as deltas.

Design phase   The period of time in the software development life cycle during which the designs for architecture, software components, interfaces, and data are created, documented, and verified to satisfy requirements.

Design standard   A standard that describes the characteristics of a design or design description of data or program components.

Detailed design   The process of refining and expanding the preliminary design of a system or component to the extent that the design is sufficiently complete to be implemented.

Development testing   Testing conducted during the development of a system or component. This kind of testing is usually done in the development environment by the developer.

Developmental configuration The software and associated technical documentation that define the evolving configuration of a computer software configuration item during development.

ECMI European Computer Manufacturers Institute.

ECP Engineering change proposal. A proposed engineering change and the documentation by which the change is described and suggested.

EIA Electronics Industries Association.

EIA Electronic Industries of America.

Engineering change An alteration in the configuration of a configuration item after formal establishment of its configuration identification.

EPRI Electric Power Research Institute.

ERP Enterprise resource planning.

ESA European Space Agency.

Evaluation The process of determining whether an item or activity meets specified criteria.

FAA Federal Aviation Administration.

Failure The inability of a component or system to perform its required functions within specified performance requirements.

FCA Functional configuration audit. FCA is an audit conducted to verify that the development of a configuration item has been completed satisfactorily, that the item has achieved the performance and functional characteristics specified in the functional and allocated configuration identification, and that its operational and support documents are complete and satisfactory.

Firmware The combination of hardware device and computer instructions and/or computer data that reside as read-only software on the hardware device.

Form, fit, and function The configuration comprising of the physical and functional characteristics of an item as an entity, but not including any characteristics of the elements making up the item.

Formal specification   A specification written and approved in accordance with established standards and guidelines.

Formal testing   Testing conducted in accordance with test plans and procedures that have been reviewed and approved by a customer, user, or designated approving authority.

FR   Fault report. Same as problem report; *see* PR.

Functional baseline   The initial approved technical documentation for a configuration item. Also known as requirements baseline.

Functional specification   A document that specifies the functions that a system or component must perform.

Functional testing   The testing process that ignores the internal mechanism of a system or component and focuses solely on the outputs generated in response to selected inputs and execution conditions. Also known as black-box testing.

FQR   Formal qualification review. The test or inspection by which a group of configuration items comprising a system is verified to have met specific contractual performance requirements.

Hardware   Devices or machines that are capable of accepting and storing computer data, executing a systematic sequence of operations on computer data, or producing control outputs. Such devices can perform substantial interpretation, computation, communication, control, or other logical functions.

HWCI   Hardware configuration item.

IDE   Integrated development environment. An environment in which the user can design, develop, debug, test, and run an application. Some popular IDEs are Visual C++, PowerBuilder, and Delphi.

IEEE   Institute of Electrical and Electronics Engineers.

Incremental development   A software development methodology in which requirements definition, design, implementation, and testing occur in an overlapping and interactive manner, resulting in incremental completion of the overall software product.

Informal testing Testing conducted in accordance with test plans and procedures that have not been reviewed and approved by a customer, user, or designated approving authority.

INPO Institute of Nuclear Power Operations.

Inspection A static analysis technique that relies on visual examination of development products to detect errors and faults.

Integration testing The testing process where the software components, hardware components, or both are combined and tested to evaluate the interaction between them and how they perform in combination.

Integrity The degree to which a system or component prevents unauthorized access to or modifications of computer programs or data.

Interface A shared boundary across which information is passed.

Interface control The process of identifying all functional and physical characteristics relevant to the interfacing of two or more configuration items provided by one or more organizations and ensuring that the proposed changes to these characteristics are evaluated and approved prior to implementation.

IP Internet Protocol. IP specifies the format of packets (also called datagrams) and the addressing scheme. Most networks IP with a higher level protocol called Transmission Control Protocol (TCP), which establishes a virtual connection between a destination and a source. IP by itself is like the postal system. It allows one to address a package and drop it in the system, but there is no direct link between the sender and the recipient. TCP/IP, on the other hand, establishes a connection between two hosts so that they can send messages back and forth for a period of time.

ISO International Organization for Standardization.

IV&V Independent verification and validation. Verification and validation that is performed by an organization that is technically, managerially, and financially independent of the development organization.

JCL Job Control Language. A language used to identify a sequence of jobs, describe their requirements to an operating system, and control their execution.

Maintenance   The process of modifying a software system or component after delivery to correct faults, improve performance or some other attribute, or adapt to a changed environment.

Metrics   Measures used to indicate progress or achievement.

MMI   Man/machine interface.

NASA   National Aeronautics and Space Administration.

NATO   North Atlantic Treaty Organization.

NIRMA   Nuclear Information and Records Management Association.

NOR   Notice of revision. A form used in configuration management to propose revisions to a drawing or list, and, after approval, to notify users that the drawing or list has been or will be revised accordingly.

NSIA   National Security Industrial Association.

Object-oriented design   A software development technique in which a system or component is built using objects and connections between those objects.

Operational testing   The testing that is conducted to evaluate the performance of a system or component in its operational environment.

Packet   A piece of message transmitted over a packet-switching network. One of the key features of a packet is that it contains the destination address in addition to the data. In IP networks, packets are called datagrams.

Packet switching   Refers to protocols in which messages are divided into packets before they are sent. Each packet is then transmitted individually and can even follow different routes to its destination. Once all the packets forming a message arrive at a destination, they are recompiled into the original message.

Parser   A software tool that parses computer programs or other text, often as the first step in assembly, compilation, interpretation, or analysis. In configuration management the parsers are used for automatically finding the dependencies between configuration items.

Patch   A modification made to a source program as a last-minute fix.

PCA   Physical configuration audit. An audit conducted to verify that a configuration item, as built, conforms to the technical documentation that defines it.

Perfective maintenance   Software maintenance performed to improve the performance, maintainability, or other attributes of a computer program.

Performance specification   A document that specifies the performance characteristics that a system or component must possess.

Performance testing   Testing conducted to evaluate the compliance of a system or component with specified performance requirements.

PR   Problem report. A report of a problem found in the software system or documentation that needs to be corrected.

Preliminary design   The process of analyzing design alternatives and defining the architecture, components, interfaces, and timing and sizing estimates for a system or component.

Preventive maintenance   Maintenance performed for the purpose of preventing problems before they occur.

Product baseline   The product baseline is the initial approved technical documentation (including source code, object code and other deliverables) defining a configuration item during the production, operation, maintenance, and logistic support of its life cycle.

Product support   The act of providing information, assistance, and training to install and make the software operational in its intended environment.

QA   Quality assurance. A planned and systematic pattern of all actions necessary to provide adequate confidence that an item or product conforms to established technical requirements.

QC   Quality control. A set of activities designed to evaluate the quality of a developed product. In the case of QC the focus is to find the defect, whereas in QA the focus is to prevent the defect from occurring.

Query language   A language used to access information stored in a database.

Rapid prototyping   A type of prototyping in which emphasis is placed on developing prototypes early in the development process to permit early feedback and analysis in support of the development process.

Regression testing   The process of testing a software system again usually using the original test plan and test data with the objective of ensuring that the modifications that were carried out have not caused unintended effects and that the system or component still complies with its specified requirements.

Release   A configuration management action whereby a particular version of software is made available for a specific purpose.

RFD   Requests for deviations. A formal request to deviate from a specified procedure.

RFW   Requests for waiver. A request to waive or omit some parts or parts of a standard procedure.

Requirements analysis   The process of studying user needs to arrive at a definition of system, hardware, or software requirements.

Requirements phase   The period of time in the software development life cycle during which the requirements of a software product are defined and documented.

Requirements specification   A document that specifies the requirements for a system or component. Also known as requirements definition document (RDD).

Response time   The elapsed time between the end of an inquiry or command to an interactive computer system and the beginning of the system's response.

Retirement   Permanent removal of a system or component from its operational environment.

Retirement phase   The period of time in the software development life cycle during which support for a software product is terminated.

Reusability   The degree to which a software component can be used in more than one computer program or system.

SAE   Society of Automotive Engineers.

SCM   Software configuration management. The set of methodologies, procedures, and techniques used to manage and control change in the software development process and to ensure that the products that are developed satisfy the requirements. IEEE defines SCM as a discipline applying technical and administrative direction and surveillance to identify and document the functional and physical characteristics of a configuration item, control changes to those characteristics, record and report change processing and implementation status, and verify compliance with specified requirements.

SCMP   Software configuration management plan. The SCM plan documents what SCM activities are to be done, how they are to be done, who is responsible for doing specific activities, when they are to happen, and what resources are required.

SCM tool   Software that is used to automate the SCM functions of change management, problem tracking, version management, build management, status accounting, and so on that would otherwise have to be performed manually.

SCN   Specification change notice. SCN is a document used in configuration management to propose, transmit, and record changes to a specification.

SDLC   Software development life cycle. The period of time that begins when a software product is conceived and ends when the software is no longer available for use. The SDLC typically includes different phases: analysis, design, development, testing, release, and maintenance.

Software   Computer programs, procedures, and associated documentation and data pertaining to the operation of a computer system.

Software development process   The software development process is that set of actions required for efficiently transforming the user's need into an effective software solution.

Software engineering   The application of a systematic, disciplined, and quantifiable approach to the development, operation, and maintenance of software. The practice of software engineering is a discipline with a well-defined process (or system) that produces a product (the software, documentation, etc.) and has a set of (automated) tools for improving the productivity and quality of work.

Software program   A combination of computer instructions and data definitions that enable computer hardware to perform computational or control functions.

Software tool   A computer program used in the development, testing, analysis, or maintenance of a program or its documentation.

Source code   Computer instructions and data definitions expressed in a form suitable for input to an assembler, compiler, or other translator.

Spiral model   A model of the software development process in which the constituent activities, typically requirements analysis, preliminary and detailed design, coding, integration, and testing are performed interactively until the software is complete.

SPR   Software problem report. Same as problem report; *see* PR.

SQA   Software quality assurance. The discipline of applying quality assurance principles to the software development process.

SQAP   Software quality assurance plan. Document that records the procedures and guidelines for practicing software quality assurance.

System testing   Testing conducted on the complete system to evaluate whether it meets the specified requirements.

U.S. DOD   United States Department of Defense.

Unit testing   The testing of individual units in a software system.

Usability   The ease with which a user can learn to operate, prepare inputs, and interpret outputs of a system or component.

Variant   Versions that are functionally equivalent but designed for different hardware and software environments.

Version   Version is an initial release or rerelease of a configuration item. It is an instance of the system that differs in some way from the other instances. New versions of the system may have additional functionality or different functionality. Their performance characteristics may be different or they may be the result of fixing a bug that was found by the user/customer.

VPN   Virtual private network. A VPN connects the geographically dispersed facilities (networks) of an enterprise over a public network like the Internet. It essentially provides secure global communications across the enterprise without the need for private leased lines. The VPN can be implemented with dedicated hardware or with software, or it can be integrated into a firewall. A VPN is a cheaper alternative to leased lines. VPN over the Internet can be implemented using IP-layer encryption.

Waterfall model   A model of the software development process in which the different phases, requirements, analysis, design, coding, testing, and implementation are performed in that order, without any overlap or interaction.

WWW   World Wide Web.

Sources

Defense System Software Development Standards (DOD-STD-2167A).

Configuration Management Standards (MIL-STD-973).

Configuration Management Practices for Systems, Equipment, Munitions and Computer Programs (MIL-STD-483).

Freedman, A., *The Computer Glossary: The Complete Illustrated Dictionary*, 8th ed., New York: Amacom, 1998.

IEEE Standard for Software Configuration Management Plans (IEEE Std-828-1998), Piscataway, NJ: IEEE, 1998.

IEEE Standard Glossary of Software Engineering Terminology (IEEE Std-610.12-1990), Piscataway, NJ: IEEE, 1990.

Margolis, P. E., *Computer and Internet Dictionary*, 3rd ed., New York: Random House, 1999.

About the author

Alexis Leon is the cofounder and managing director of L & L Consultancy Services Pvt. Ltd., a company specializing in software engineering, Web design and development, groupware and workflow automation, software procedures, management and industrial engineering, Internet/intranet development, and client/server application development.

He graduated from Kerala University with first rank and distinction in industrial engineering in 1989. In 1991, he earned his master's degree (M.Tech.) in industrial engineering with distinction also from the University of Kerala.

He has written more than 20 books on topics including CICS, DB2, Oracle, PowerBuilder, Developer/2000, mainframes, Year 2000 solutions, Internet, information technology, SQL, and ERP. His two books on business computing are prescribed textbooks for the Diploma in Advanced Computing (DAC), a course conducted by the Center for Development of Advanced Computing (C-DAC), Department of Electronics, government of India. His books on ERP, Internet, Oracle, and information technology are prescribed textbooks in many universities and training institutes in India.

Before starting his own company, he worked with Pond's India Ltd. as an industrial engineer and with Tata Consultancy Services as a software consultant. You can contact him via e-mail at alexis@lnl.net or through his home page at http://www.lnl.net/alexis.

Index

A

Action taken report (ATR), 130
AFSCM 375–1, 3, 287
American National Standards
     Institute (ANSI), 4, 155, 160
Analysis
  capabilities of SCM, 191
  causal, 50, 122, 125–26, 181
  change, 112
  cost/benefit, 24, 243
  impact, 6, 24, 28, 118, 167,
     181, 196
  problem, 125, 167
  requirements, 19, 22–23, 53,
     55, 95, 97, 206
  risk, 16
  systems, 19, 23–25, 55
  team, 122
Anomaly, 120, 122, 146
  See also Defect
Ancestor, 64, 197, 251
ANSI. *See* American National
     Standards Institute
ANSI/IEEE Std–1042–1987, 155,
     160–61, 170

ANSI/IEEE Std-828-1998, 155,
     158–59, 160–62
Assigners, 179–80
ATR. *See* Action taken report
Auditing
  defined, 8, 73, 145, 200
  external, 146, 169
  functional configuration, 8–9,
     31, 88, 96, 146, 147
  functions of, 8–9, 145–46
  NCR and, 149, 169
  physical configuration, 9, 31,
     88, 96, 146, 147–48
  purpose of, 145
  SCM plan and, 159, 168–69
  SCM system and, 6, 8–9, 148
  SCM team and, 148–49
  SCM tools and, 149, 200
  subcontractor, 169
  team, 147, 149
  trails, 141, 199
  what should be, 9
  when performed, 9, 104, 146
  who should do, 9, 146

Recent Titles in the Artech House Computing Library

Advanced ANSI SQL Data Modeling and Structure Processing, Michael M. David

Business Process Implementation for IT Professionals and Managers, Robert B. Walford

Data Modeling and Design for Today's Architectures, Angelo Bobak

Data Quality for the Information Age, Thomas C. Redman

Data Warehousing and Data Mining for Telecommunications, Rob Mattison

Distributed and Multi-Database Systems, Angelo R. Bobak

Electronic Payment Systems, Donal O'Mahony, Michael Peirce, and Hitesh Tewari

Future Codes: Essays in Advanced Computer Technology and the Law, Curtis E. A. Karnow

Global Distributed Applications With Windows® DNA, Enrique Madrona

A Guide to Programming Languages: Overview and Comparison, Ruknet Cezzar

A Guide to Software Configuration Management, Alexis Leon

Guide to Software Engineering Standards and Specifications, Stan Magee and Leonard L. Tripp

Guide to Standards and Specifications for Designing Web Software, Stan Magee and Leonard L. Tripp

How to Run Successful High-Tech Project-Based Organizations, Fergus O'Connell

Information Hiding Techniques for Steganography and Digitial Watermarking, Stefan Katzenbeisser and Fabien A. P. Petitcolas, editors

Internet Commerce Development, Craig Standing

Internet Digital Libraries: The International Dimension, Jack Kessler

Internet and Intranet Security, Rolf Oppliger

Managing Computer Networks: A Case-Based Reasoning Approach, Lundy Lewis

Metadata Management for Information Control and Business Success, Guy Tozer

Multimedia Database Management Systems, Guojun Lu

Practical Guide to Software Quality Management, John W. Horch

Practical Process Simulation Using Object-Oriented Techniques and C++, José Garrido

Risk Management Processes for Software Engineering Models, Marian Myerson

Secure Electronic Transactions: Introduction and Technical Reference, Larry Loeb

Software Process Improvement With CMM, Joseph Raynus

Software Verification and Validation: A Practitioner's Guide, Steven R. Rakitin

Solving the Year 2000 Crisis, Patrick McDermott

User-Centered Information Design for Improved Software Usability, Pradeep Henry

For further information on these and other Artech House titles, including previously considered out-of-print books now available through our In-Print-Forever® (IPF®) program, contact:

Artech House
685 Canton Street
Norwood, MA 02062
Phone: 781-769-9750
Fax: 781-769-6334
e-mail: artech@artechhouse.com

Artech House
46 Gillingham Street
London SW1V 1AH UK
Phone: +44 (0)20 7596-8750
Fax: +44 (0)20 7630-0166
e-mail: artech-uk@artechhouse.com

Find us on the World Wide Web at:
www.artechhouse.com